ANOTHER DAY IN THE DEATH OF AMERICA

Gary Younge is an award-winning journalist for the *Guardian* and *The Nation* magazine in the US. He was posted to the US for the *Guardian* for twelve years before returning to London in 2015. In 2009 he won the James Cameron Award for the 'combined moral vision and professional integrity' of his coverage of the Obama campaign. In 2015 he won the David Nyhan Prize for Political journalism from Harvard's Shorenstein Center. 'It's the powerless on whose behalf he writes,' said the centre's acting director. Formerly the Belle Zeller Visiting Professor of Public Police and Social Administration at Brooklyn College, CUNY, he is also the Alfred Knobler Fellow for The Nation Institute.

Praise for *Another Day in the Death of America*

'Formidably intelligent and tenacious. A tour de force of regulated passion.'

Martin Amis

'This is Gary Younge's masterwork. You will never read news reports about gun violence the same way again. Brilliantly reported, quietly indignant and utterly gripping. A book to be read through tears.'

Naomi Klein

'This book is a righteous challenge to the big insanities of American society; gun ubiquity, racism, poverty and the supine and bland media which taboos genuine discourse on them. It's all the more daring and subversive for its controlled and mannered tone, as it breaks the unwritten law: thou shall not humanize the victims of this ongoing carnage.'

Irvine Welsh

'Younge's steady, near-clinical detachment has helped make his twelve years of writing for the *Guardian* some of the best reportage from America in decades.'

Simon Winchester, *New Statesman*

'Gary Younge's book deserves widespread attention: the deaths he chronicles say more about the way America is heading than the familiar images of a smiling land.'

Robert Chesshyre, *Literary Review*

'It is exactingly argued, fluidly written and extremely upsetting. This is your country on guns . . . A book like this has potential pitfalls, highhandedness not least among them. But Mr Younge makes for a personable, unusual narrator. As a Briton, he brings a fresh perspective to this topic.'

Jennifer Senior, *New York Times*

'A work of careful research and measured rage.'

Dan Brotzel, *Irish News*

'Despite the composure of his writing, there is passion in Younge's condemnation of a system that renders the poor and the dark in America invisible. In illuminating the stories of some of these people and of their communities, Younge has provided us with a beautifully told and empathic account that wrenches at the heart even as it continues to engage the brain.'

Gillian Slovo, *Observer*

'This might not be a book to make you eagerly turn pages, only because you might need to put it down to catch your breath and marshal your feelings, as one heartrending story follows another . . . Only in his afterword does Younge reveal some of the emotion fuelling his meticulous investigative journalism.'

Margaret Busby, *Sunday Times*

'In focussing so narrowly on a single day's worth of material, Mr Younge makes abundantly clear the ubiquity and broad acceptance of the deaths of children by the American population: as he shows, in case after case, these children's deaths are not widely reported, leave almost no trace on the popular consciousness. If a child anywhere in the United Kingdom is killed with a gun, one hears about it on the news, and of course that is as it should be. In America, if every such murder were reported nationwide, there would be no time for news of anything else. Simply by reporting on these lives at some length, then, and bringing them to public attention, Mr Younge is doing respectful and very valuable work.'

Panoptic

'An evocative, powerful, well-written book that puts a human face – young human faces – to the shocking toll of largely unreported gun fatalities. It made me angry, sad, despairing and, on occasion, tearful . . . I'd like to think Younge's book will snap America into some kind of action but sadly, it won't.'

Piers Morgan, *Mail on Sunday*

'*Another Day in the Death of America* is as one would imagine it: sad and bleak, an altogether terrible tale . . . His success is that for the hours you are absorbed in it, you start to see how life on the streets can be normal.'

Eric Weinberger, *Spectator*

'Younge writes that this is not a book about race or gun control. This is true in that he avoids polemic and sticks closely to his case studies, though he barely needs to spell out their implications . . . The book functions as an argument for how the socio-economic realities and geography of institutional racism combined with the flood of easily available guns dictate that "there are places in almost every American city where . . . the deaths of young people by gunfire do not contradict a city's general understanding of how the world should work but rather confirm it." . . . Younge holds few illusions that there won't be many more.'

Neil Munshi, *Financial Times*

'A magnificent piece of reportage . . . It's apparent from the start that Younge has used his not inconsiderable investigative journalistic talents to go about finding the material he needs . . . At times, one is reminded of the work of that other great chronicler of American life, Studs Terkel, and of Polish journalist Ryszard Kapuściński, whose dispatches from the world's trouble-spots transformed the humble job of reporting into literary art.'

David Pratt, *Sunday Herald*

'Immensely moving chapters devoted to each victim skilfully trace the narrative of these lost lives and the confluence of circumstances which led to such horrific endings, capturing the agony of their wasted potential. This is an unflinching examination of "structural inequality" which gets to the heart of communities "ripped apart by violence and poverty", offering insight into grief and suffering.'

Anita Sethi, *i* newspaper

'The book is at its most powerful and moving when it describes the effects of violence, on, for instance, the mother of a murdered nine-year-old who, a year on, stays awake to avoid her nightmares, then finds it hard to get out of bed in the morning and drag herself to work. Though his style is unhistrionic and his arguments measured, Younge is no outside observer, but someone with, as he puts it, "skin in the game. Black skin in a game where the odds are stacked against it."'

Hari Kunzru, *Guardian*

'A harrowing account of children's lives cut short by the ubiquity of violence in the United States. Drawn from suburbs and cities of every demographic, these sensitively researched portraits of virtually unknown victims and their grieving families expose the structural ties of race, class, and the lack of gun control. Younge's book completes the picture of what violence looks like in contemporary America.'

Claudia Rankine

Also by Gary Younge

The Speech: The Story Behind Dr Martin Luther King Jr's Dream
Who Are We – And Should It Matter in the 21st Century?
Stranger in a Strange Land: Encounters in the Disunited States
No Place Like Home: A Black Briton's Journey Through the American South

GARY YOUNGE

ANOTHER DAY IN THE DEATH OF AMERICA

First published in 2016
by Guardian Books, Kings Place, 90 York Way, London N1 9GU
and Faber & Faber Ltd, Bloomsbury House,
74–77 Great Russell Street, London WC1B 3DA
This paperback edition published in 2017

Map by Bill Donohoe

A CIP record for this book is available from the British Library

ISBN: 978-1-78335-1022

Typeset by Guardian Faber
Printed and bound by CPI Group (UK) Ltd, Croydon, CR0 4YY

2 4 6 8 10 9 7 5 3 1

To Jaiden, Kenneth, Stanley, Pedro, Tyler, Edwin,
Samuel, Tyshon, Gary and Gustin
for who you were
and who you might have been

You already know enough. So do I. It is not knowledge we lack. What is missing is the courage to understand what we know and to draw conclusions.

Sven Lindqvist, *Exterminate All the Brutes*

Contents

Introduction 1
Author's Note 9

1 Jaiden Dixon, Grove City, Ohio 11
2 Kenneth Mills-Tucker, Indianapolis, Indiana 43
3 Stanley Taylor, Charlotte, North Carolina 65
4 Pedro Cortez, San Jose, California 97
5 Tyler Dunn, Marlette, Michigan 107
6 Edwin Rajo, Houston, Texas 141
7 Samuel Brightmon, Dallas, Texas 167
8 Tyshon Anderson, Chicago, Illinois 205
9 Gary Anderson, Newark, New Jersey 233
10 Gustin Hinnant, Goldsboro, North Carolina 251

Afterword 279
Acknowledgements 283
Notes 285
Bibliography 304

Introduction

The most common adjective employed by weather reporters on Saturday, 23 November 2013, was 'treacherous'. But in reality there was not a hint of betrayal about it. The day was every bit as foul as one would expect the week before Thanksgiving. A 'Nordic outbreak' of snow, rain and high winds barrelled through the desert states and northern plains towards the Midwest. Wet roads and fierce gusts in northeast Texas forced Willie Nelson's tour bus into a bridge pillar not far from Sulphur Springs in the early hours, injuring three band members and resulting in the tour's suspension. With warnings of a 500-mile tornado corridor stretching north and east from Mississippi, the weather alone killed more than a dozen people.[1] And as the low front shifted eastwards, so did the threat to the busiest travel period of the year, bringing chaos so predictable and familiar that it has provided the plot line for many a seasonal movie.

There was precious little in the news to distract anyone from these inclement conditions. A poll that day showed President Barack Obama suffering his lowest approval ratings for several years. That night he announced a tentative deal with Iran over its nuclear programme. Republican Senate minority whip John Cornyn believed that the agreement, hammered out with six allies as well as Iran, was part of a broader conspiracy to divert the public gaze from the hapless roll-out of the new health care website. 'Amazing what WH [White House] will do to distract attention from O-care,' he tweeted.[2] Not surprisingly, another of the day's polls revealed that two-thirds of Americans thought the country was heading in the wrong direction. That night, Fox News was the most popular cable news channel; *The Hunger Games: Catching Fire* was the highest-grossing movie, and the college football game between Baylor and Oklahoma State was the most-watched programme on television.

It was just another day in America. And as befits an unremarkable Saturday in America, ten children and teens were killed by gunfire. Like the weather that day, none of them would make big news beyond their immediate locale because, like the weather, their deaths did not intrude on the accepted order of things but conformed to it. So in terms of what one might expect of a Saturday in America, there wasn't a hint of 'betrayal' about this either; it's precisely the tally the nation has come to expect. Every day, on average, 7 children and teens are killed by guns; in 2013 it was 6.75 to be precise.[3] Firearms are the leading cause of death among black children under the age of nineteen and the second-leading cause of death for all children of the same age group, after car accidents.[4] Each individual death is experienced as a family tragedy that ripples through a community but the sum total barely earns a national shrug.

Those shot on any given day in different places and very different circumstances lack the critical mass and tragic drama to draw the attention of the nation's media in the way a mass shooting in a cinema or church might. Far from being considered newsworthy, these everyday fatalities are simply a banal fact of death. They are white noise set sufficiently low to allow the country to go about its business undisturbed: a confluence of culture, politics and economics that guarantees that each morning several children will wake up but not go to bed while the rest of the country sleeps soundly.

It is that certainty on which this book is premised. The proposition is straightforward. To pick a day, find the cases of as many young people who were shot dead that day as I could, and report on them. I chose a Saturday because although the daily average is 6.75 that figure is spread unevenly. It is over the weekend, when school is out and parties are on, that the young are most likely to be shot. But the date itself – 23 November – was otherwise arbitrary. That's the point. It could have been any day. (Were I searching for the highest number of fatalities, I would have chosen a day in the summer, for children are most likely to be shot when the sun is shining and they are in the street.)

There were other days earlier or later that week when at least seven children and teens were shot dead. But they were not the days I happened to choose. This is not a selection of the most compelling cases possible; it is a narration of the deaths that happened. Pick a different day, you get a different book. Fate chose the victims; time shapes the narrative.

And so on this day, like most others, they fell – across America, in all its diverse glory. In slums and suburbs, north, south, west and Midwest, in rural hamlets and huge cities, black, Latino, and white, by accident and on purpose, at a sleepover, after an altercation, by bullets that met their target and others that went astray. The youngest was nine, the oldest nineteen.

For eighteen months I tried to track down anyone who knew them – parents, friends, teachers, coaches, siblings, caregivers – and combed their Facebook pages and Twitter feeds. Where official documents were available regarding their deaths – incident reports, autopsies, 911 calls – I used them too. But the intention was less to litigate the precise circumstances of their deaths than to explore the way they lived their short lives, the environments they inhabited and what the context of their passing might tell us about society at large.

The *New York Times* quotation for that day came from California Democratic congressman Adam B. Schiff, who found twenty minutes to meet with Faisal bin Ali Jaber. Jaber's brother-in-law and nephew were incinerated by a US drone strike in rural Yemen while trying to persuade Al Qaeda members to abandon terrorism. Schiff said after the meeting, 'It really puts a human face on the term "collateral damage".'[5] My aim here is to put a human face – a child's face – on the 'collateral damage' of gun violence in America.

*

I am not from America. I was born and raised in Britain by Barbadian immigrants. I came to the United States to live in 2003, shortly before the Iraq War, with my American wife, as a correspondent for the *Guardian*. I started out in New York, moved to Chicago after eight years, and left for Britain during the summer of 2015, shortly after finishing this book.

As a foreigner, reporting from this vast and stunning country over more than a decade felt like anthropology. I saw it as my mission less to judge the United States – though as a columnist I did plenty of that, too – than to try to understand it. The search for answers was illuminating, even when I never found them or didn't like them. For most of that time, the cultural distance I enjoyed as a Briton felt like a blended veneer of invincibility and invisibility. I thought of myself less as participant than onlooker.

But, somewhere along the way, I became invested. That was partly about time. As I came to know people, rather than just interviewing them, I came to relate to the issues more intimately. When someone close to you struggles with chronic pain and has no health care or cannot attend a parent's funeral because she is undocumented, your relationship to issues such as health reform and immigration is transformed. Not because your views change, but because knowing and understanding something simply does not provide the same intensity as having it in your life.

But my investment was also primarily about my personal circumstances. On the weekend in 2007 that Barack Obama declared his presidential candidacy, our son was born. Six years later, we had a daughter. I kept my English accent. But my language relating to children is reflexively American: 'diapers' instead of 'nappies', 'stroller' instead of 'push chair', 'pacifier' instead of 'dummy'. I have only ever been a parent in the United States – a role for which my own upbringing in England provided no real reference point. For one of the things I struggled most to understand – indeed, one of the aspects of American culture most foreigners find hardest to understand – was the nation's gun culture.

In this regard, America really is exceptional. American teens are seventeen times more likely to die from gun violence than their peers in other high-income countries. In the United Kingdom, it would take more than two months for a proportionate number of child gun deaths to occur.[6] And by the time I'd come to write this book, I'd been in the country long enough to know that things were exponentially worse for black children like my own.

It ceased to be a matter of statistics. It was in my life. One summer evening, a couple of years after we moved to Chicago, our daughter was struggling to settle down, and so my wife decided to take a short walk to the local supermarket to bob her to sleep in the carrier. On her way back, there was shooting in the street, and she sought shelter in a local barbershop. In the year we left, once the snow finally melted, a discarded gun was found in the alley behind our local park and another in the alley behind my son's school. My days of being an onlooker were over. Previously, I'd have found these things interesting and troubling. Now it was personal. I had skin in the game. Black skin in a game where the odds are stacked against it.

Around the time of my departure, those odds seemed particularly bad. The children and teens in this book were killed four months after George Zimmerman was acquitted for shooting Trayvon Martin dead in Sanford, Florida (which was when the hashtag #BlackLivesMatter was coined) and nine months before Michael Brown was shot dead in Ferguson, Missouri (which was when #BlackLivesMatter really took off). In other words, they occurred during an intense period of heightening racial consciousness, activism and polarisation. The deaths covered in this book don't fit neatly into the established #BlackLivesMatter narrative. None of the victims was killed by law enforcement, and where the assailants are known they are always the same race as the victim. The characters in this book cannot be shoehorned into crude morality plays of black and white, state and citizen.

But that doesn't mean race is not a factor. For in the manner in which these fatalities are reported (or not reported), investigated (or not investigated), and understood (or misunderstood), it is clear that whatever American society makes of black lives, in many if not most instances black deaths such as these don't count for an awful lot. On a typical day, of the seven children and teens who die, one would be female, three would be black, three white, one Hispanic, and, every five days, one of those seven deaths will be a child of another race (Asian, Pacific Islander, Native America, Native Alaskan).[7] But precisely because the day was random, it was not typical. Of the ten who died during the time frame of this book, all were male, seven were black, two Hispanic, and one white. In other words, black men and boys comprise roughly 6 per cent of their cohort but 70 per cent of the dead on the day in question.

You won't find another Western country with a murder rate on a par with that in Black America – for comparable rates you have to look to Mexico, Brazil, Nigeria or Rwanda.[8]

This is not a book about race, though a disproportionate number of those who fell that day are black, and certain racial themes are unavoidable. It is not a book that sets out to compare the United States unfavourably with Britain, though it is written by a Briton to whom gun culture is alien. Finally, it is not a book about gun control; it is a book made possible by the absence of gun control.

This is a book about America and its kids viewed through a particular lens in a particular moment. 'Whether they're used in war or for keeping the peace, guns are just tools,' wrote the late former Navy Seal Chris Kyle in *American Gun: A History of the U.S. in Ten Firearms*. 'And like any tool, the way they're used reflects the society they're part of.'[9] This book takes a snapshot of a society in which these deaths are uniquely possible and that has a political culture apparently uniquely incapable of creating a world in which they might be prevented.

*

For a relatively brief moment, there was considerable national interest in the fact that large numbers of Americans of all ages were being fatally shot on a regular basis.

It followed the shootings in the small Connecticut village of Newtown. Less than a year before the day on which this book is set, a troubled twenty-year-old, Adam Lanza, shot his mother, then drove to Sandy Hook Elementary School and shot twenty small children and six adult staff members dead before turning the gun on himself. Even though mass shootings comprise a small proportion of gun violence in any year, they disturb America's self-image and provoke its conscience in a way that the daily torrent of gun deaths does not.

'Individual deaths don't have the same impact and ability to galvanise people because mass shootings are public spectacles,' *New York Times* journalist Joe Nocera told me. 'They create a community of grief. So it stands to reason that Newtown would be the thing that wakes people up . . . I was galvanised by Sandy Hook.'[10]

Sandy Hook's political impact was not solely about the numbers. It was also about the victims' ages (most of the victims were first-graders – aged six and seven); the pathos of hearing how Lanza picked them off one by one, how they cowered in bathrooms and teachers hid them in closets. These facts forced a reckoning with what could and should be done to challenge this ever happening again. 'Seeing the massacre of so many innocent children . . . it's changed America,' said West Virginia's Democratic senator, Joe Manchin, who championed a tepid gun-control bill that would not even come to a vote in the Senate. 'We've never seen this happen.'[11]

The truth is it's happening every day. Only most do not see it. 23 November 2013 was one of those days.

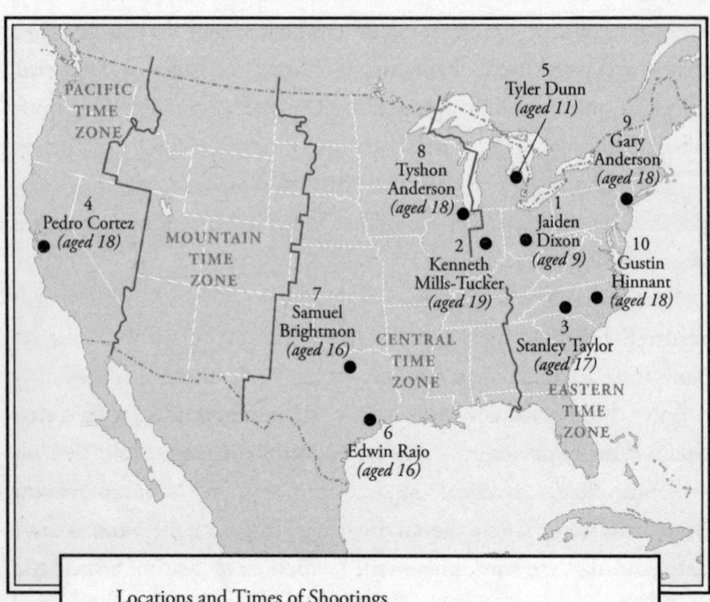

Locations and Times of Shootings

1 Grove City, Ohio, 22 November, 7:36 a.m. EST

2 Indianapolis, Indiana, 23 November, 3:13 a.m. EST

3 Charlotte, North Carolina, 23 November, 4:17 a.m. EST

4 San Jose, California, 23 November, 4:22 p.m. PST

5 Marlette, Michigan, 23 November, 8:19 p.m. EST

6 Houston, Texas, 23 November, 7:15 p.m. CST

7 Dallas, Texas, 23 November, approx. 11:00 p.m. CST

8 Chicago, Illinois, 23 November, 11:05 p.m. CST

9 Newark, New Jersey, 24 November, 1:00 a.m. EST

10 Goldsboro, North Carolina, 24 November, 3:30 a.m. EST

Author's Note

To save us all from straw men and confusion, a project such as this must be as transparent and clearly defined as possible. To that end, I want to make explicit three basic parameters on which this book is based.

First, although the time frame spans twenty-four hours, it is not a calendar date. This allows for more flexibility but not more time. A US calendar day, spanning from the East Coast to Hawaii, is longer, stretching twenty-nine hours. This book covers the gun deaths that occurred between 3.57 a.m. Eastern Standard Time (EST) on 23 November 2013, and 3.30 a.m. EST on 24 November.

Second, the book covers the gun deaths that occurred within that twenty-four-hour period – which is not quite the same as including those who were shot on that day and then died on a later date. Jaiden Dixon was shot on Friday, 22 November, but not pronounced dead until Saturday, the 23rd. He's in the book because he died within the time frame in question. Quindell Lee, who was shot in the head on 23 November in Dallas by his thirteen-year-old brother while his stepfather 'stepped out for 15 minutes'[1] is not in the book, because Quindell wasn't pronounced dead until Monday, 25 November.

Finally, the book includes children and teens. That is not the same as minors. Some are legally adults; more than half are over 16. The median age is 17.5; the average age 14.3. You can slice and dice the data and definitions anyway you want. But once you've seen their pictures, encountered the braggadocio on their Facebook pages, and seen the peach fuzz referred to in autopsy reports, the arguments become moot. It's not complicated. They're kids.

But perhaps the most important thing for you, the reader, to know is that these were not necessarily all the gun deaths of young people that day. They are all the gun deaths I found. I found them through Internet searches and on news websites that tracked gun deaths on a daily basis. There was no other way.

Each of the more than three thousand counties in the United States collects data in its own way and has different rules for how the information can be disseminated. Some will tell a reporter if there have been any gun-related fatalities in the last week; others refuse. Meanwhile, it takes more than a year for the numbers to be aggregated nationally by the Centers for Disease Control and Prevention. So a project like this, which seeks to report on the cases in a more timely manner, is necessarily reliant primarily on local media. These are the gun deaths that I found that got reported.

As such, one important and sensitive category is absent: suicides. On average, around two of the seven gun deaths that occur in the United States each day involve young people taking their own lives.[2] (They tend to be disproportionately male, white, Native American or Native Alaskan.) Unless these tragedies are emblematic of some broader issue – online bullying, academic pressure, or a mass shooting – they are generally not reported. It is, apparently, in no one's interest for suicides of any age group to become public knowledge. For the family the pain is compounded by stigma. For the media it is considered too intrusive and inherently unappealing to ask; mental health professionals fear publicity will encourage the vulnerable to follow suit. 'They don't like to report them on the television because it's bad for advertising,' a representative of C.A.R.E.S. Prevention, a suicide-prevention organisation based in Florida, told me. 'They're too much of a downer.' So more children and teens were almost certainly shot that day. These are just the ones we know about.

1

Jaiden Dixon
(aged nine)

Grove City, Ohio
22 November, 7.36 a.m. EST

School mornings in Nicole Fitzpatrick's home followed a predictable routine. As soon as her three boys – Jarid Fitzpatrick, aged seventeen; Jordin Brown, aged sixteen; and Jaiden Dixon, aged nine – heard her footsteps, they would pull the covers over their heads because they knew what was coming next: the lights. The older two would take this as a cue for the inevitable and get up. But Jaiden, who had a loft bunk bed in the same room as Jarid, would try to string out his slumber for as long as possible. Rubbing the sleep from his eyes, he would first migrate to his mother's room, where his clothes hung, and climb into her bed. Then came the cajoling. 'I'd tickle him to try and get him to get up,' says Nicole. 'And goof him around. I'd pull him by his ankle to try to get him to get dressed.' They had a deal. If he could get himself ready – 'all the way ready. Socks, shoes, shirt, everything' – the rest of the morning was his. 'He could play on the computer, play Minecraft, watch *Duck Dynasty* or a DVR from the night before,' she explains. 'You get all the way ready to go, [ready to] walk out the door, and you can do what you want for that time frame.'

It was Friday, 22 November 2013, the fiftieth anniversary of John F. Kennedy's assassination. The morning papers were full of nostalgia for the nation's lost innocence. They might have found it on Nicole's street in Grove City, a dependably humdrum suburb of Columbus, which had been crowned 'Best Hometown' in central Ohio for that year. It was precisely its dependability that convinced people to stay. Nicole went to school with the parents of the children her kids go to school with. Amy Baker, whose son Quentin hung out with Jaiden, was one of Nicole's good school friends, and they remain close. Baker was the third generation of her family to go to

Grove City High School; her daughter is the fourth. When Nicole and Amy were growing up, Grove City had a reputation as a hick farming town. Some disparagingly and others affectionately nicknamed it 'Grovetucky' – a Midwestern suburb that owed more to the rural ways of Kentucky than to its status as a suburb of Ohio's biggest city. Back then the town's border, appropriately enough, was marked by a White Castle restaurant. There was no cinema. The Taco Bell parking lot was the main hangout for youngsters. 'You had to leave Grove City to get a decent pair of shoes,' says Baker. 'Otherwise you were shopping at Kmart.'

The population has more than doubled in Nicole's lifetime and now stands at 38,500.[1] Nicole and Amy remember much of the development, including the large strip mall where I met Nicole for dinner one night. At just thirty-nine, she can sound like an old-timer. 'There was nothing there,' she told Jordin, trying in vain to evoke the limitations of the world she grew up in. 'It was all farmland. Corn. Farmland. Soy.' Nicole, Jarid, Jordin and Jaiden lived on Independence Way, off Independence Street and past Independence Court, three thermometer-shaped streets – culs-de-sac, each with a circular bulb at one end – without picket fences but with a hoop in almost every yard and a flag flying from many a porch. A yellow traffic sign stood by the house, warning, 'SLOW – CHILDREN AT PLAY'. On a breezy weekday morning it's so quiet you can hear the wind chimes.

They'd been there for three years, and Nicole had recently signed another two-year lease. 'I knew the people next door, the people at the end of the street. Everybody knew everybody. There wasn't any crime. I had no problems with Jaiden being outside playing. The rule was I had to be able to walk out of the front yard and be able to see him. I never really needed to worry in that regard.' Jaiden was ready that morning with time to spare for high jinks. When Nicole threw him his socks, Jaiden wound his arm around and threw them back before telling her he wanted to try out as a pitcher for his Little

League baseball team. He was playing on his Xbox and Nicole was packing his bag when, shortly after 7.30, the doorbell rang. This was not part of the routine. But nor was it out of the ordinary. At the end of the street lived a woman Nicole had gone to high school with. Every now and then one of her two teenage girls, Jasmin or Hunter, might pop around if their mom was short of sugar or coffee or they needed a ride to school. Usually, they would text Jarid or Jordin first. But occasionally they just showed up.

So when the bell rang, Nicole called for someone to answer it and Jaiden leapt up. He opened the door gingerly, hiding behind it as though poised to jump out and shout 'Boo' when Jasmin or Hunter showed her face. But nobody stepped forward. Time was suspended for a moment as the minor commotion of an unexpected visitor's crossing the hearth failed to materialise. Nicole craned her neck into the cleft of silence to find out who it was but could see nothing. She looked to Jarid; Jarid shrugged. Jordin was upstairs getting ready. Slowly, cautiously, curiously, Jaiden walked around the door to see who it was. That's when Nicole heard the 'pop'. Her first thought was, 'Why are these girls popping a balloon at the door? What are they trying to do, scare me to death?'

But then she saw Jaiden's head snap back, first once, then twice before he hit the floor. 'It was just real quiet. Jarid was standing there in the living room and it was like everything stopped. And I remember staring at Jarid.' And in that moment, though she had seen neither the gun nor the gunman, she knew what had happened. It was Danny. 'I didn't need to see him. I knew it was him.' Jarid didn't see his face or the gun either. But he saw the hoodie making its escape to the car. He too knew immediately who it was.

Danny Thornton was Jarid's father. Nicole had met him years before at Sears, where he made keys. She was nineteen; he was twenty-eight. 'We were never really together,' she says. 'It was really a back-and-forth kind of thing. And that has just been our relationship ever since.' Amy Sanders, Nicole's best friend, never liked Danny. The first time she met him, Jarid couldn't have been more than three. Danny knew she was Nicole's best friend, and he hit on her anyway. 'He was gross and he was mean,' Amy says.

Nicole hadn't seen him since July. He'd found her over a year earlier, in January 2012, when he was in need of help. 'He didn't have anywhere to stay,' she recalls. 'He was getting ready to be evicted, and we kind of decided to let him stay with us with the intention that we could help each other out. He could spend time with Jarid and keep him under control, and I could help him get a job and get him back on his feet so he could give us some money.' She gave him Jarid's room, and the boys all shared a room. She put together his résumé and emailed places where he might work. He got one job for a month and was fired. He didn't find another one.

While he was staying with the family, he got to know Jaiden. He took him bowling. He once told Nicole he liked Jaiden because Jaiden made him laugh. He even said he preferred him to his own son, Jarid. The arrangement didn't work out. Money and space were tight, and so long as he was jobless Danny had little to offer. Nicole needed the room. She tried to let him down gently. But any way you cut it she was kicking him out. That made Danny angry. And Danny didn't deal with anger well. According to court records, his criminal history dating back eighteen years included charges of felonious assault, domestic violence, aggravated menacing, disorderly conduct, assault, attempted possession of drugs, having a weapon under disability, and carrying a concealed weapon. He was also a semi-pro, super-middleweight boxer – five feet eleven and around 160 pounds – who favoured the southpaw stance: right hand and right foot forward, leading with right jabs, and following up with a left cross, right hook. He'd fought as far afield as Canada and Florida and had acquitted himself respectably – in fifteen wins and fifteen losses, he'd delivered eleven knockouts and been knocked out fourteen times himself.[2]

'He was pissed,' says Nicole. 'He moved all his stuff out. I don't know where. I didn't care.'

What she didn't know for some time was that as he was packing up he told Jarid, 'I have no problem making you an orphan. I'm not going to be living out of my car at forty-seven years old. I have no problem shooting your mom and shooting your brothers.' When he'd done with his shooting spree, he told his son, he'd end his life in a shoot-out with the cops.

Although he'd never directly threatened to shoot Nicole's family, Danny had talked to her about shooting others. 'We'd had this discussion before. He had twins. I don't even know how old they are. He was pissed off with the mom for filing child support on him. He already had two other child support orders on him, and he didn't work, didn't have a job, already had a couple felonies on his record, so he couldn't get a job. And he talked about if he knew where she lived he'd go over there and shoot her and shoot the babies. And I remember telling him, "Don't shoot the babies. Why are you going to shoot the babies? They didn't do nothing to you." And he said, "No. They don't love me. I don't love nothing that don't love me back."'

He'd once come close to shooting another ex-partner, Vicki Vertin. He'd told Nicole he had been on his way to shoot Vicki, their daughter and her family when he got a phone call from a friend he hadn't spoken to in years. 'He took that as a sign not to do it that day.'

'He had a list,' says Amy Sanders. 'An actual, physical list of people he wanted to kill . . . He would talk about it whenever he met up with Nicole. Nicole was afraid of him. She always thought if she was nice to him she wouldn't be on his list. And unfortunately she was the first one.'

Jarid was shielded from much of this. 'They never said anything bad about him in front of us,' says Kayaan Sanders, Amy's son, who effectively grew up with Jarid. 'I never saw Danny get angry and aggressive in front of us. He'd always be the cool dad, that would be funny, said inappropriate things sometimes that would make you laugh. Jarid never said anything bad about his dad in front of me.' So when Danny talked about making him an orphan, Jarid thought he was just running at the mouth. He didn't tell his mom about it until September. Danny had been absent for much of Jarid's life. 'He didn't know what Danny was capable of. When Jarid told me [what Danny said], I stopped dead in my tracks,' says Nicole. 'I said, "Jarid, he's going to kill me. He's going to kill me." And Jarid said, "No, he's not, Mom. He's just blowing off steam." I was petrified. Petrified. I told my friends if something happens to me go after Danny, make sure my kids are taken care of. I was preparing for it to be me.' But time passed. They didn't hear from Danny, and she began to wonder if Jarid was right. Maybe he was sounding off.

Then Danny's mobile phone subscription expired. He'd been on her plan. She'd continued paying for his mobile after he'd left in order to placate him. But Christmas was approaching and she could no longer afford to. She hesitated, mindful of what Jarid had told her and fearful of Danny's response. On 20 November she sent him a text telling him his contract would end on Monday, the 25th. 'I can't pay it any more,' she wrote. 'But the phone's yours. You can go and turn it on at any provider.' The message sat on her phone for a while unsent. 'I knew what he was capable of,' she says. 'But I had to look out for my kids. I had to look out for me.' She pressed send. He replied within an hour: 'What fucking took you so long?'

Nicole forwarded the message to Amy Sanders. 'I swear he's gonna kill me one day,' Nicole texted. 'In two years, when nobody suspects him, I know he's gonna kill me.'

'We were serious,' says Amy. 'But somehow it was still more like a joke. Who can wrap their minds around a reality like that until it really happens? It's not really real until it happens.'

And then it happened. Two days after the exchange, this was the man who sped away from Independence Way in a blue Toyota, leaving Jaiden with a bullet in his skull as Danny's biological son desperately tried to revive his brother. 'And I struggle to try and understand,' says Nicole. 'Did he shoot whoever answered the door, or was Jaiden his target? Because honestly he could have stepped one foot in that house and shot me, shot Jarid, shot Jordin. We were defenceless. We opened the door and let him in. There was nothing to stop him taking us all out.'

Danny left a grey, circular hole on Jaiden's temple and chaos all around. Jarid fled out of the house, screaming and crying, asking a neighbour, Brad Allmon, to call 911. 'He just shot my brother in the face. He shot my brother in the face,' he told Allmon.[3] Once he got the emergency services on the phone he could barely make himself understood through the pandemonium.

'Sir, please calm down so I can understand what you're saying,' says the operator. 'We've got to learn what's going on.'

'My dad just shot my baby brother,' says Jarid.

'What happened? What happened?' Trying to make out the pattern of events over the mayhem in the house, the dispatcher says, 'Calm down, sir. Please tell me what happened.'

'I don't know. I don't know.'

'Who shot him?'

'Danny Thornton. D-A-N-N-Y T-H-O-R-N-T-O-N." Jarid alternates between trying to communicate with the dispatcher and trying to revive Jaiden. Desperation and the occasional expletive interspersed with formal niceties – 'sir', 'ma'am', 'fuck', 'please God' – in an exchange between a public servant and a fraught teenager whose baby brother is dying in his arms.

'C'mon, Jaiden. C'mon, baby. C'mon, Jaiden. C'mon. C'mon.'

'Where are you now?'

'Oh my God. I'm going to fucking kill him. I'm going to fucking kill him. I'm going to fucking kill him.'

'Sir, that's not going to help your brother.'

'Listen, he said he wants suicide by cop.'

'Where is he?'

'Oh God, please come. Please.'

'Do you know where he is?'

'Oh, please stay with me. Please. Please.'

'I need you to tell me where the guy is with the gun. Where did he go?'

'I don't know. He walked up to the fucking door. Shot him and then took off.'

'Walking or driving?'

'He was driving a blue Toyota Camera, uh, Camry. C'mon, Jaiden, please stay with me.'

'Sir, you've got to talk to me, OK?'

'Yes,' said Jarid, and then turned to someone in the house and said, 'Hold his head. Hold his head. Hold his head.'

'Sir, listen to me. You need to answer my questions.'

Jordin also calls 911 and is on the other line.

'1916 Independence Way. My brother got hurt, I need somebody now, please.'

'Was he hurt from somebody or in a fall?'

'I don't know. Just please get somebody here. Please.'

'Where is he bleeding from?'

'The head. There's blood everywhere.'

'Did he take some kind of drugs or medication?'

'No, no, no.'

'Sir, how old is he?'

'He's nine. Nine, nine, nine, nine.'

'He's nine? Is he breathing?'

'I don't know. I don't know. Is he breathing, Mom? Is he breathing? I don't know.'

'Is he inside?'

'Yes, he's inside.'

'OK, I want you to get right down beside him and tell me if he's breathing.'

'Mom, is he breathing? No, he's not breathing.'

'Was he shot? Are you right there beside him, sir?'

'Yes, ma'am.'

'I want you to lay him down on his back, remove his clothes, and place your hand on his forehead. Put your hand under his neck, tilt his head back, put your ear next to his mouth. Tell me if you can hear breathing. Sir, was he shot? Where was he shot?'

'In the door. He answered the door.'

'Where in his body was he shot?'

'In his face.'

'In his face?'

'In his head.'

'In his head? The front or the back? Can you feel any air moving?'

'I don't know.'

'All right. Stay calm. Is he in the house?'

'Yes.'

'Where's the man who shot him?'

'I don't know.'

'Do you know him? Do you know where he went?'

'I don't know. Danny Thornton.'

'Did they do it on purpose?'

'I don't know. I think so.'

'The person with the gun. Did they leave or are they still there?'

'They left.'

'Did he leave in a car or on foot?'

'I don't know.'

'Sir, what's your name?'

'Jordin Brown.'

'Stay on the phone with me. Who shot him, do you know?'

'Danny Thornton, I guess.'

'Do you know where he went?'

'I don't know.'

'OK, Jordin, stay on the line with me.'

Jordin is sobbing. The dispatcher is calm and tries to be calming. 'Do you know who shot him, Jordin? Do you suspect who shot him?'

'I don't know. Can you please get me the police?'

'They're on their way, sir. Jordin, I know this is very hard but I need you to tell me. Tell if you know where they went, OK?'

'I don't know. I was upstairs, then I heard shooting and I came downstairs.'

'All right, Jordin. Is this your little brother?'

'Yes, yes.'

'Can you feel any airwaves moving in and out of his mouth? Are you there with him?'

'Airwaves? No, no, no, no. Please. Please,' says Jordin, pleading for the police to hurry up.

'They're on their way, Jordin, OK? Do you know where the person went?'

'I don't know. Please, please.'

'They're on their way, Jordin, OK?'

'They're here. They're here.'

'They're right there, Jordin. Stay on the phone until they're with him, OK?'

'They are. They're here. Yes. Yes.'

'OK, Jordin, I'm going to let you go, OK? Jordin. They're right there. Jordin.'

'Yes.'

'Who is with you?'

'My mom and my brothers and two cops.'

'The cops are there with you. I'm going to let you go now, Jordin, OK?'

'Yes, yes.'

Throughout, Nicole did her best to focus despite the hysteria. She put one hand over the wound and the other on the back of Jaiden's head, where she could feel the bullet. She scooped Jaiden up, hugged him, rocked him, and then laid him back down. His eyes were closed the entire time as he lay straight with his hands down by his sides. Then, still unconscious, Jaiden lifted his left arm three or four inches off the ground and let it fall again.

'I freaked out,' she says. 'I said, "Jerry, Jerry [her nickname for Jarid]. He's still alive. He's still OK." We felt his heart, his pulse. He was never just dead. So after he lifted his arm up I was thinking this is what they do on TV. CPR. Mouth to mouth. And all it was, was just gurgle . . . And I scooped him up again. And was holding him against my chest.'

The emergency services arrived and took over as the boys cried in the front yard and Nicole shook with shock. The fact that he had raised his arm, she felt, signalled there was still hope. 'Now I know. But we felt his pulse and his heart beating. We could feel him alive. I hugged the boys and was saying, "Be strong. We'll get to the hospital and get him fixed." Because I kept thinking the whole time, "Just get him in there, get him to surgery, get the bullet out, and get him fixed. We'll fix him. Let's go, let's go, let's go."'

'The amok man', writes Douglas Kellner in *Guys and Guns Amok: Domestic Terrorism and School Shootings from the Oklahoma City Bombing to the Virginia Tech Massacre*, 'is patently out of his mind, an automaton oblivious to his surrounding and unreachable by appeals or threats. But his rampage is preceded by lengthy brooding over failure and is carefully planned as a means of deliverance from an unbearable situation.'[4]

Such was Danny, gaining his power from the fear he instilled in others as the full extent of his inability to cope with adult life – an inability to keep a job, a home, a relationship, or to support himself or his many children financially – overwhelmed and enraged him. Humiliation came easy to Danny. When Jarid was about eight years old, Danny took him to buy a new pair of shoes. Danny wanted Jarid to stay the night with him afterwards, but Danny's visits had been irregular and Jarid didn't feel comfortable going back to Danny's house. In retaliation, Danny returned the shoes and told Nicole he didn't love anyone who didn't love him back. When Nicole asked how he could say that in front of his own son, Danny responded, 'I wouldn't care if he got hit by a car in front of me . . . I wouldn't even stop.'

'He was a sociopath,' Amy Sanders told me, as I sat with her and her four children in the living room of her home in Houston, where she'd moved in August 2013 to be closer to her father. 'He never took responsibility for anything. He never had any conscience when it came to hurting other people. He'd say and do anything.'

'The amok state is chillingly cognitive,' writes Kellner. 'It is triggered not by a stimulus, not by a tumor, not by a random spurt of brain chemicals, but by an idea.' The idea, argues Kellner, was best described by a psychiatrist in Papua New Guinea who interviewed seven men who'd run amok and summarised their self-images thus: 'I am not an important or "big" man. I possess only my personal sense of dignity. My life has been reduced to nothing by an intolerable insult. Therefore, I have nothing to lose except my life, which is nothing, so I trade my life for yours, as your life is favoured. The exchange is in my favour, so I shall not only kill you, but I shall kill many of you, and at the same time rehabilitate myself in the eyes of the group of which I am member, even though I might be killed in the process.'[5]

If such men can be found in Papua New Guinea, there is no reason why they might not be found in the suburbs of Columbus. But when they do appear, they are of, course, a shock to the system. 'That doesn't happen here,' says Nicole. We're sitting in the house she moved to after leaving Independence Way – a spacious place with a porch and a garden. 'It never has. I'm not living in the 'hood. It happens in Columbus. It happens in Reynoldsburg. It doesn't happen in Grove City. It's boring. It's secure.' Of all the places where children were shot that day, Grove City had the lowest homicide rate that year – 2.7 per 100,000 inhabitants,[6] the same as Bangladesh.[7] The crimes

Grove City residents are used to are mostly petty – car break-ins, burglaries maybe. When I ask Nicole and Amy Baker about violent crime in the town, they struggle to work out the last time anyone got murdered and settle on a domestic dispute two years earlier. As though to illustrate what qualifies as a nuisance, the police arrived during our interview to ask if Nicole could get her dog, Jango, to stop barking so loudly – it was 9.30 p.m.

But if a man like Danny running amok is a shock to the system, the system is nonetheless built to contain it. With the facts of Jaiden's shooting both partial and evolving, and Danny's whereabouts still unknown, the suburb's security apparatus curled reflexively into a tight foetal ball. Within five minutes of the first 911 call, Highland Park Elementary, just one block from Nicole's house, went into lockdown. School hadn't started yet, so the Grove City Police Department secured a perimeter around it, diverted buses and told parents arriving in cars to take their children home, while ushering in kids who'd arrived early.

By that time Danny was long gone, heading eastbound on Interstate 270 to Groveport, twenty minutes away, where his ex-partner, Vicki Vertin, with whom he had an eighteen-year-old daughter, worked as a dental hygienist. Vicki, unaware of what had just happened, came out to meet her unexpected visitor in the lobby.

She hadn't seen Danny for twelve years but, like Nicole, lived in fear of his temper. 'He told me one day he'd kill me,' she told a local news channel. 'The day he walked in, I knew it was that time.'[8] Danny was wearing a grey hoodie and had his hands in the front pocket. 'Haven't seen you in a while,' Vicki told him. Danny took out his gun, shot her in the stomach, and raced off again.

By this time, the 911 dispatch office was in overdrive. Calls were pouring in from all over. On the recordings you can overhear new information being received even as dispatchers struggle to process the facts they have. The dispatchers were not long finished with Jordin and Jarid when one of Vicki's co-workers was on the line. With

Danny now identified as the gunman in both locations, it took them six minutes to link the two shootings and realise they were dealing with an assailant committed to both murder and havoc: an amok man.

Two of Danny's friends also called the police. He'd told them that he'd 'killed two people and that he's not going back to jail',[9] and 'he will not go down without a fight with police'.[10] More schools went into lockdown. Vicki's family, who had been notified of the shooting, were taken to a protective room.

Nicole, meanwhile, had arrived at the hospital, where they paged for a neurologist to come to the trauma unit. As they took Jaiden for a CT scan, more doctors and a pastor came in. Detectives pulled Nicole aside to ask if she had any idea where Danny would be going or anyone else he might be targeting. That was when she found out he'd shot somebody else.

She told them that although she hadn't seen the shooter she knew who it was. 'Who would the gunman be targeting?' 'Where would he be going?' 'Where would he be staying?' Her mind was blank. Her thoughts were with Jaiden; she couldn't get into Danny's head to divine his intentions at the best of times. And this was not the best of times.

Had Jarid googled 'suicide by cop' after the conversation he'd had with his father a few months earlier, he'd have found a 1998 paper published in the *Annals of Emergency Medicine.* It was written by several academics and medical practitioners who reviewed all the files of officer-involved shootings investigated by the Los Angeles County Sheriff's Department from 1987 to 1997 related to the phenomenon. It is a term used by police to describe incidents in which people ostensibly deliberately provoke law enforcement into fatally shooting them.

Not surprisingly the term is hotly contested since it can provide one more justification for police killings on the basis of a psychiatric state they can generally only guess at when they shoot someone. Quite what Danny had in mind when he mentioned it we shall never know.

The paper's authors argue that to qualify a case must meet four criteria: '(1) evidence of the individual's suicidal intent, (2) evidence they specifically wanted officers to shoot them, (3) evidence they possessed a lethal weapon or what appeared to be a lethal weapon, and (4) evidence they intentionally escalated the encounter and provoked officers to shoot them.' By that definition they concluded suicide by cop accounted for 11 per cent of all officer-involved shootings and 13 per cent of all officer-involved justifiable homicides during that time frame. 'Suicide by cop', they concluded, 'is an actual form of suicide.'[11]

'People who sought suicide by cop have to be in some kind of depression,' Dr Harry Hutson told me in a phone interview. Hutson, who wrote the paper, is assistant professor in the Department of Emergency Medicine at Massachusetts General Hospital, Harvard Medical School. 'The police shoot over four hundred people every year, and people know that if you brandish anything that looks like a weapon the police will act in self-defence or in defence of the community. So if you want to die, these people will do it for you.'

The subjects of the study were all between the ages of eighteen and fifty-four, 98 per cent were male, most had a criminal record, and a third were involved in domestic violence cases. As such, says Hutson, Danny's case sounds 'pretty classic'. 'He was depressed. He didn't want to live any more. He didn't think he could carry on.'

An hour and forty-five minutes after he shot Vicki, Danny was traced to a Walmart parking lot in Easton town centre, a twenty-minute drive from her workplace and not far from the motel where he'd been staying. At 9.46 he sat in his car trapped by two police vehicles. 'Most of these incidents are over pretty quickly,' explains Hutson, with 70 per cent of shootings taking place within thirty minutes of the police arriving. Sure enough, a shoot-out soon ensued in which one policeman was injured and Danny finally got his wish: suicide by cop.

Vicki's first thought when she woke up from surgery was that he could still be out there. 'Did they get him?' she asked her dad. 'No,' he replied. Vicki tried to get out of bed. 'Oh my God, he's coming back to get me,' she thought. Her father clarified that Danny hadn't been arrested but rather had been shot dead. She sank back down into the bed. She said it was the first time in years she'd felt safe.

Across town, Nicole was told that Jaiden wouldn't make it. 'His injuries aren't survivable,' the neurologist told her. 'There's nothing we could do.' The neurologist said that Jaiden's CT scan was one of the worst she'd ever seen. The bullet had taken a path straight to the back of his brain, where it had ricocheted around, causing irreparable damage. They put Jaiden on a ventilator while a decision was made about organ donation. 'I don't remember feeling anything,' says Nicole. 'I don't know if I cried. I was in shock and numb. "This cannot be real. It cannot be real. This is not happening right now." All I remember is having this image of him in his shoes. He'd just put his shoes on, and his T-shirt was on the floor. And now he's in a hospital gown with a thing down his throat and a patch on his head. All in about an hour or so.'

Her last entry on Facebook, the night before, had been a link about Merrick McKoy, a Colorado man who, four days earlier, had posted a picture of himself and his nineteen-month-old daughter on his page shortly before shooting both her and himself. 'This is the very definition of a monster . . .' wrote Nicole. 'What is wrong with people?!!' Her first posting after the shooting read simply: 'I love you, Jaiden. I love you so much.'

News of Jaiden's shooting spread through Grove City like a bushfire. When convoys of police cars and news trucks roll up on a street like Independence Way, people inevitably start talking. For most of the morning few knew the names of either the victim or the assailant or their fates. All they knew was that a child had been shot. Jimmy Lewis, who lived across the road from Jaiden and worked at his after-school club at the local YMCA, had gone in early to work out. The Y is a bustling facility where children are fed, do their homework, and participate either in sports, arts, nature class or in 'brain work' while they wait for their parents to pick them up. Jimmy got a call from his mother alerting him to the commotion taking place at the end of their street. His colleague Pamela Slater knew that Grove City was a small enough community that, whoever the victim was, the YMCA would be impacted somehow. 'There was a 90 per cent chance that it was one of our kids,' she said. 'The age and the connections we have in the community, whether or not it was an actual YMCA kid, it could have been a previous kid or a sibling. Somehow, some way we were going to be affected, and our kids would be affected because they would have known.'

Within hours, Jaiden's teacher, his baseball coach, Nicole's sister, and many others were at the hospital. They had to give the security desk a password to stop the media from sneaking in. At around noon, Pamela was pulled out of a meeting and told that the victim was Jaiden. With only a few hours before the children were supposed to arrive for after-school care, she had no time to process her grief or shock as she pulled the YMCA's various departments together to draft a letter to give to the parents. Their priority was to protect the children from rumour and let their parents break the news to them. When the children arrived, the staff said nothing. So, when parents came to pick up their children, they were given the letter.

'I know you heard about the shooting,' Pamela would tell them. 'I know, it's terrible,' they'd reply. 'But there's a little bit more detail,' Pamela would interject. 'I know, it's terrible,' the parents would repeat. 'And then,' says Pamela, 'you hand the letter to the parents. And you say, "He was in our programme." And they'd say, "Oh no. It was Jaiden."

'It was tough. It was difficult to have to repeat and repeat and repeat over and over. You could just see these levels and layers of the immensity of what we were talking about as I broke it to them. But we wanted the parents to be able to talk to the kids, especially because it was the weekend.'

Most children found out that night or over the weekend. Jaiden's baseball coach, Brady – a mild-mannered man who clearly understood his role as primarily coaching children rather than coaching a sport – says he knows of some who were never told. When the YMCA opened again on Monday there were extra staff to help with counselling.

'I can remember that there were some kids who were just devastated coming right in off the bus that Monday,' recalls Jimmy. 'Our staff coached us on how we could support them. It was off and on all week. We serve meals every evening, and for a good week or so they kept an empty chair for Jaiden and even put a meal out for him. Probably wasn't until after Christmas that you didn't say "Jaiden" and everyone starts crying.'

Several months later, while wandering through the YMCA before the summer break, Pamela was struck by how many art projects were devoted to Jaiden. 'There'd be these hearts with "Jaiden" on them or little wings with his name or crosses that say, "Rest in Peace, Jaiden". I wasn't even really looking for them. But once I started noticing them they were everywhere.'

Amy Sanders and Nicole are like sisters. 'We have a lot in common,' Amy explains. 'We are both single moms. We both have biracial children. We were both struggling. She didn't have family she was close to in Ohio and neither did I. So we became like this team.' It was a very modern family. Two white women, co-parenting their multiracial brood, who effectively grew up with two straight moms.

Sometimes Nicole might work two jobs and Amy would have the kids overnight and during the day, or vice versa. They kept them in the same schools. If any of them were in trouble the school would call either mom. They raised the boys together like brothers. They didn't need to pack bags to go to each other's house – they always had stuff there. Amy had an older daughter, and shortly afterwards Nicole fell pregnant with Jaiden. They were close in every way until Amy's move to Houston.

Back in Grove City, Jaiden was being kept on life support until the doctors could remove his organs for donation. They wouldn't declare him dead until they had done a test for brain activity. Nicole asked the doctors to put it off until Amy could get there from Houston. That would also give Jaiden's paternal grandmother time to arrive from Akron. It was only a two-hour drive, but she kept having to pull over to cry.

When Amy broke the news, Kayaan started hitting things. Kayaan called Jarid. 'Bro,' said Kayaan. 'Bro,' said Jarid. 'Literally me and him don't talk,' explains Kayaan. 'We just say, "Bro".' But after a while they couldn't even say that. They just sobbed until Jarid could get it together to ask, 'When are you coming?' 'We'll be there right now,' said Kayaan. 'Right now, man.'

It takes nineteen hours to drive from Houston to Grove City. They stopped for gas and one meal. Almost a full day of silence and grief jammed in a car. They made it to the hospital by early morning. When they walked into the hospital room, it was packed. 'Everyone's looking at us. Everyone's crying. No one says anything,' recalls Kayaan. 'After that brief pause they cried and hugged. Finally someone said something and conversation started.' Jaiden looked like he was sleeping, says Amy. 'He was breathing. His heart was beating. The swelling had gone down. His flesh was warm. It was hard to believe he wasn't going to go home with us.'

Jaiden was pronounced dead at 3.47 p.m. on Saturday, 23 November. Once his death was official they could start seeking out recipients for his organs. It took a day for all the different medical teams from as far afield as Delaware and California to get to the hospital. (His lungs found a home in a girl from St Louis.) The long wait evolved into an affair similar to an Irish wake – only without the coffin. Nicole and the boys were with him on and off the whole time. Nicole would lie with him until she couldn't bear the fact that his eyes would no longer open, and then she would ask Amy to take over while she went for a walk. By the time they took him away to the operating room to remove his organs the whole family was there.

Jaiden hadn't had much of a relationship with his father, Rosell Dixon III, said Nicole, but the relationship he did have was pretty good. (Rosell didn't respond to requests for an interview.) They were never close but he would go over sometimes to play with his sisters, who were the same age. 'His dad loved him and he did care for him,' she told me, 'but it wasn't the type of thing where he'd go over just to hang out with his dad.' But Rosell was at his side that night, as were his paternal grandparents, cousins, brothers and sisters from his father's side – all telling stories and saying their goodbyes.

Up until the moment they wheeled him away for his final journey to the operating room, Nicole kept it together. 'She held up really well,' says Amy. 'It was like she was on automatic.'

But witnessing that final journey was too much to bear. 'I wish I would have,' says Nicole. 'But I couldn't see the doors close. It was surreal. It was almost like they were taking him to have his tonsils taken out.'

It was around 3 a.m. on Sunday. Nicole had been up for forty-five hours, during which time her life had been turned upside-down and then crushed underfoot. What happened next was a blur. 'I just remember breaking down and crying and all these people hovering over me, and then somebody put me in a wheelchair and took me out of the hospital. I didn't go back to his room to pick anything up or to get anything. I didn't go back to the hospital at all.' The fog did not clear until the viewing. 'It was maybe a week after he died,' she recalls. 'He was laying in his casket. And I remember that because I'd been able to touch him so much at the hospital I went right up to him and I kissed him on the forehead, and I grabbed his hand and it was cold as stone and hard. And that was when the reality hit me. Oh my God. My baby's gone. Until I saw him go into the ground it was like going through the motions.'

Nicole never went back to the house on Independence Way. She went straight to the Drury Inn and stayed there until Christmas, when she went to Dallas to stay with a cousin and then to Houston to stay with Amy before coming back to Grove City for New Year.

When Nicole was pregnant with Jaiden, she was convinced he would be a girl. She was going to call him Olivia, and then he could lyrically double up with Amy's youngest, Khiviana: Livvy and Kivvy. But she was relieved he was a boy. 'God gave me boys for a reason,' she says. At school she had been an avid and, by all accounts, excellent softball player, pitching for the Grove City High School team, which won the league every year and the state championship in 1983.

Tall and hefty, she was often teased about her weight during her youth. 'I've never been a girly girl. I was a tomboy. My hair's thrown up in a bun. I'm out there watching football games and yelling. I'm that mom in the basketball stands yelling at the ref because he made a bad call. So I'm glad I had boys.'

Jaiden's home life sounded quite familiar to me. Like him, I was by far the youngest of three boys with a single mom at the helm. Jaiden was indulged; Jarid, the eldest, took on a lot of responsibility for him; Jordin, the middle child, was caught between the two; and Nicole ran from pillar to post trying to keep it all together. Like mine, theirs was a loving household full of camaraderie, tough love, rough and tumble, and considerable autonomy – *Lord of the Flies* meets *The Brady Bunch* with a touch of *Roseanne*. 'They would fight. They would torture him. They'd torment him. They'd call me all the time at work. "Mom, they won't let me play on the Xbox." "They won't let me do this or that." And I'd just say, "Well, figure it out, boys."' Jaiden was mixed race – Nicole is white, Rosell is black – but much lighter skinned than his brothers, whose fathers were also black. His skin was the colour of straw. If Nicole was out with him alone he could pass as white, though he was often mistaken for being Middle Eastern.

The baseball coaches collectively called him Smiley. 'Every kid has a bad day,' says Brady, his coach. 'But he was always smiling. It just never seemed like the kid was in a bad mood.' In most pictures he wears a grin so wide it can barely fit on his face. At the after-school club at the YMCA, not far from his house, he was into pretty much everything. 'He was the kind of kid I would love to coach,' said Justin Allen, who spent the most time with Jaiden of anyone there. 'I would love to have him on my team. He was like a leader. Not in a vocal way. But just in the way he'd play the game. He was real enthusiastic and would get all the other players involved.'

Although Jaiden clearly enjoyed baseball, says Brady, he wasn't a stand-out player. 'He had the best attitude. But I don't think he'd ever really been coached a lot. You could tell he was really interested and wanted to learn. But he hadn't been exposed to it that much so he just wasn't as familiar with the game as some kids his age might be. He was at that age where kids just start to catch fly balls. And Jaiden was one of those where it took a little longer to judge the fly ball.'

But the time he made the game-winning catch still sticks in everyone's mind. 'At the very last second he stuck his glove out,' recalls Brady, whom I met at Nicole's house. 'It reminded me of *Sandlot*. That movie. "Just hold your glove up and I'll take care of the rest." He's just standing there. And we're thinking, "It's over his head. It's over his head. It's over his head." And just at the very last second he stuck his glove out and caught it. It was third out so it ended the game and everybody just lost it. It was like they just won the lottery. They lost their mind.'

'He had the biggest grin on his face,' says Nicole. 'In the car on the way back he kept saying, "Did you see me catch the ball?" "Yes,"' she repeated as her eyes welled up.

As well as most sports, Jaiden liked playing Battleship, hide and seek, and cops and robbers at the YMCA. He played Transformers with Ethan – he was Optimus Prime, leader of the autobots, and Ethan was Bumblebee, with the altmode of a compact car. They also acted out wrestling moves they'd seen on WWE.

His best friend there was Sidney, who was one year older. Sidney bears a slight resemblance to Olive in *Little Miss Sunshine*, the affectionate granddaughter who enters the pageant. There was no play fighting when Jaiden hung out with Sidney – though he did teach her to play 'glide', which involved jumping off a raised platform in her back yard with an open umbrella and 'floating' to the ground. Most of the time, at the Y, they would sit on the benches in the gym, do their homework and chat. She was his first valentine and he hers. They weren't boyfriend and girlfriend, Sidney explained, but they were nonetheless betrothed. 'This might sound silly,' she confessed. 'But we said we would marry each other when we got older.' In the life they planned together he was going to be in the army and she was going to be a singer.

Jaiden was a giving soul. When he saw beggars he wanted to give them money. When it was hot he was always the last off the bus at the after-school club because he went up and down the aisle closing all the windows that other kids had left open. A day after his school book fair he came home with just one book and asked Nicole for a few more dollars. When she asked him what he'd done with the money she'd given him, he told her he'd given it to a girl who wanted a bookmark but couldn't afford it.

He was also a big animal lover. Dogs, kittens, turtles – you name it. With his brothers preparing to leave home in a few years Nicole had promised they would get a dog once it was just the two of them. 'He was super stoked and ready for them to be gone,' she says. 'And when the boys would tease him he'd taunt them back: "When you move we're getting a dog."'

At home, when he wasn't playing computer games, particularly Minecraft, he'd be out creating his own adventures. The back of the house led to a small wooded area that ran down to Marsh Run Creek, where he would join his friends to play 'soldier army' with their Nerf guns. He once made a survivor video on his phone, narrating his abandonment in enemy territory. 'Here we are out in the woods,' he said, like Captain Kirk dictating the ship's log. 'We don't have many supplies. I have a cell phone but the battery's low and I don't have much service.' Then there was TV – Cartoon Network was his default channel. He knew the movie *Cars* by heart, and Jordin would often come downstairs to find him mouthing the words to nobody in particular. Finally, there were bikes. 'Riding bikes, fixing bikes, swapping out tyres,' recalls Nicole. 'They'd just be at it all day – little boys working on bikes.'

His transgressions, like his passions, were very much those of a nine-year-old boy. 'Not listening. Ignoring me. Staring into the computer world,' says Nicole, listing the things he'd get in trouble for. 'Nothing serious. Nothing bad. Normal little-boy stuff. He went to his friend's house without asking once. Another time he didn't tell me or Jarid that he wanted to go out and play.' She went out, looked left and right, and couldn't see him. It turned out he was down by the creek. 'That was as bad as it ever got.' That was why it was particularly hard to make sense of his shooting, explains Kayaan. 'I think I put myself in more danger every day than Jaiden did in his whole life.'

When I asked Ethan, his nine-year-old friend at the Y with whom he played Transformers, how he heard about Jaiden's death, he said his mom told him in the car on the way home. He knew a child had died that day but he didn't know it was Jaiden. 'That's why he wasn't at the Y,' he told his mom and then he threw his head back on the seat and cried. 'But one thing I do know', he says, 'is that he will come back alive. My mom told me if you die you come back alive.'

When I asked Sidney, his valentine, how she found out what happened, she started to cry. 'You think about him a lot still,' I said. I put my notepad down and suggested we stop for a moment.

She nodded and sniffed the tears away. 'I write songs about him,' she said, reaching in her bag for her mobile, on which she'd written one. 'It's called "Stars". It's about how I see him at night. It's kind of like a poem but it doesn't rhyme.'

I saw you in a shadow by the woods
I saw your face in all my dreams when I go to the meadow
I see you by the flowers and when I go to bed
I can't think at all, but then I thought you were there holding my hand
And now I see you in the sssstttaaaarrrs
They made me think of you when you shine bright
When you bow down on my window
I see you everywhere ya in the stars
I saw you by my house throwing pebbles
Then I went down to the meadow and then I saw you
And then I saw you in the sssstttaaaarrrs ya the sssstaaarrrs
Don't know if I'm crazy, don't know anything
Think I'm losing my mind
But then I see you in the stars ya the sssstttaaarrrssss
Oh sssstaaaarrrsss yaaaaaa ya.

Nicole's homecoming, following her post-funeral trip, was no easy process. She moved to another part of Grove City so she wouldn't have to live in the same house where it all happened or even pass that side of town. Now she had to pick up the pieces and carry on. The trouble was when she got back from Texas in the New Year there were far fewer pieces of her previous life waiting for her than she'd expected. The friends – 'Well, I thought they were friends' – who'd offered to take her things from the old house to the new one got tired of moving them, she says. Three-quarters of her belongings were left in the house and then thrown out by the landlord. Much of what was discarded had great emotional value. There were heirlooms, including a handmade stool her great-grandfather had made for her grandmother. And then there were the boys' 'boxes'. Whatever the boys had created, gathered or produced in a given year she would put in a box and write their school year on it: 'Jarid 7th grade', 'Jordin 6th grade', 'Jaiden kindergarten'. She stored them under the hutch in the basement. They had all been thrown out. 'I felt like the last ten years of my life were erased. I had to start all over again.'

For Nicole, 'all over again' meant starting from scratch. She had never been rich. She grew up in a solid blue-collar family. Her father, who'd moved to Arizona and died in 1999, had been a truck driver. Her mother, who looked after the house and the kids, and volunteered at school, has been severely disabled since suffering a stroke in 1993 and is cared for by her brother. Growing up, Nicole never had everything she wanted, but she had pretty much everything she needed – everything except self-esteem. Her dad was a verbally abusive alcoholic who used to reinforce the taunting she received in school about her weight and boyish ways. 'She went from one extreme to another looking for acceptance,' says Amy. 'And she found it in the wrong places with these guys who were real jerks to her. They would say horrible things, take her money, basically take what they wanted, and leave without ever committing to her. That's how she came by Danny.'

By Nicole's early twenties, she was in a tight spot, with two infants and nowhere to stay. 'Sixteen years ago, when Jarid was seventeen months and Jordin was four weeks old, I was homeless,' she says. 'We were legit homeless in a homeless shelter. We had nothing but the clothes on our backs. It wasn't like I wasn't intelligent or didn't have the education like a lot of the other people in the homeless shelters. It was because I simply didn't have anywhere to go. I had two kids. I had no family. Nobody could take us in. No money. I didn't have a job. I couldn't get a job because I was pregnant. It was a circumstantial homeless situation versus being an uneducated crackhead situation. We had nothing. And I busted my ass to get out of there and move up. Jordin's first Thanksgiving and first Christmas were in a homeless shelter back in 1997, and I swore to myself it would never be like that again. They were so little they had no clue. But it still bothers me. And I built what I had. And everything was for them. And I got to the point where I was starting to be a mom.'

She became a paralegal at a small law firm and gradually pulled her life together. Coming back from nothing gave everything she did have greater value. 'Once you've been homeless you hold on to too much because when you have nothing you try to keep every single thing you can.'

When she came back to Grove City to find most of her things gone, she felt as though she was back at square one. 'It was like moving back into the shelter. It seems like every day something is gone.' Her grief counsellor said that given her personal history and the circumstances of her return, she was probably suffering from post-traumatic stress disorder.

'Whether a son or daughter died in a muddy rice paddy in Southeast Asia or in an antiseptic hospital ward, in a sudden accident or after prolonged illness, the result is the same,' writes Harriet Sarnoff Schiff in *The Bereaved Parent*. 'You, the child's mother or father, seem to have violated a natural law. You have outlived your child.'[12]

Schiff, who lost her ten-year-old son, Robby, to heart disease, offers a mix of anecdote, homely advice and wisdom from the experiences of bereaved parents she interviewed. Her basic message is that nobody but those who have lost children can really understand what such a loss feels like, which makes the grief isolating. Still, Schiff insists, life will, in time, regain meaning. Nicole's world is now divided into 'before' and 'after', with Friday, 22 November as point zero. 'It was like before then I was in a theatre watching this movie, and since then it's been like walking into a parking lot and trying to adjust to the bright lights from being so engrossed in this movie for so long. It's like the places I used to go to look different to me because it's this post-movie kind of thing.'

It's not as though the movie she was watching was necessarily uplifting. As a single mother of three she remembers being exhausted, overwhelmed, and, at times, very down. 'I wish I had done more with the boys. I wish I wasn't so stressed and depressed all the time,' she says. 'There were a lot of nights when I would come home from work and just order pizza because I didn't feel like cooking anything. And I would stare at the TV, and Jaiden would either be at Quentin's or he'd be upstairs or whatever. And I feel like I wish I'd gone outside and played with them. And I regret not doing those things with all my kids.'

But it was nonetheless a movie with a complete cast of characters, and it felt whole. 'For the most part now it's still just me trying to figure things out. Like I've always done. It's nothing new. Except now instead of being a single mom of three I'm a single mom of two.'

The first time I met Nicole was in her office four months after Jaiden's death. It was her birthday, but she hadn't let on to her co-workers and had no plans to do anything special that night. She was wearing a hoodie bearing Jaiden's name and face and the word LEGENDARY. Her friend had set up a website so they could sell them to raise funds. She has one in every colour and at the time was wearing one every day. She also wore a necklace spelling Jaiden's name in curly script. She has another made from his thumbprint, which was taken at the funeral home. An image of Jaiden accompanied her pretty much everywhere she went. And yet at home she found it difficult to see him. 'I can't look at any of his pictures right now. I have school pictures in the living room over the mantel. I know where the picture is. I catch myself diverting my attention so that I don't have to look in that area because it hurts too much to see him.' She's in therapy, but struggling with the advice. 'The only thing they keep saying is that grief is different for everybody. And they keep saying that there's a light at the end of the tunnel. They keep saying,

"It'll get better, it'll get better." But I'm kind of at the point where I don't see it.'

Five months later, when I saw her again she still couldn't see it. We had dinner at the Longhorn Steakhouse and then went back to her house to meet friends who knew Jaiden. If anything, she was in a darker place. Most evenings she stayed up as late as possible to avoid going to sleep so that she could avoid the nightmares. Her mind whirs – an apparently endless loop of what-ifs and horror sequences that she can't bear but also can't prevent. 'I keep replaying seeing him falling to the ground. I keep replaying, "I should have done this, I should have done that. I should have been there. I should have opened the door." I don't want to sleep because I don't want to think about it.'

So she stays up and tries to engross herself in a game or the TV or a book. Anything to keep her mind off her melancholic, self-flagellating regret. 'When I go to sleep it's because I absolutely can't even keep my eyes open any more. And I'm so hoping the dreams won't even follow.' Three to five nights a week the nightmares come anyhow. Being awake is not much fun either. 'If I don't think about him, then I'm OK. But the second I start thinking about him and my brain starts going, then I just go crazy. It feels like I'm watching everybody else live their life in a TV show. And it's like I'm going through the motions – talking to people and interacting with people – but I'm not really there.'

Schiff writes: 'Far worse than lying awake all night were the mornings. There seemed to be daily a brief period shortly after I opened my eyes when I completely forgot Robby was dead. Then, like a tidal wave, remembrance would come and engulf me and make me feel as if I were drowning. I had to fight my way out of bed every day – and I mean every day. This went on for several months and was probably my toughest battle.'[13]

So it has been for Nicole. Moreover, for every night she stays up trying to stave off nightmares, there follows a morning where she's too tired to get herself together at a reasonable hour. Sometimes she simply can't get out of bed: 'I wish I could just get up and leave my problems at home, but I can't.'

She has worked at the same small legal firm for some time and is on good terms with her boss. She says he has been very understanding since Jaiden died. But when she struggles, so does he. And she's been struggling a lot. 'I've had a lot of breakdowns and meltdowns.' Some days she doesn't get in until noon. On others she doesn't go in at all. 'Sometimes I'll just text him and say, "I'm not getting out of bed today. I just can't do it."'

'To bury a child', writes Schiff, 'is to see a part of yourself, your eye colour, your dimple, your sense of humour, being placed in the ground . . . In reality, when children die, not only are we mourning them, we are also mourning that bit of our own immortality that they carried.'[14]

In the reception area of St Joseph's Cemetery, where Jaiden is buried, a range of small pamphlets is assembled to assist the bereaved: 'Losing Your Mom', 'Losing Your Dad', 'Losing Your Husband', 'Losing Your Wife', 'When Mom or Dad Dies', 'Talking with Your Kids about Funerals', 'Death of a Parent', 'When Death Comes Unexpectedly', and 'Grieving the Death of a Grown Son or Daughter' – to name but a few. There is pretty much every permutation of grief possible but one – a pamphlet titled 'Losing Your Young Child'. Because that's not supposed to happen. It goes against the natural order of things that a parent would ever have to bury her child. When that child is as young as Jaiden, the tragedy is so unthinkable not even a cemetery has a leaflet for it.

'You know what I find interesting?' Brenda asks her undertaker boyfriend, Nate, in the TV series *Six Feet Under*. 'If you lose a spouse, you're called a widow or a widower. If you're a child and you lose your parents, then you're an orphan. But what's the word to describe a parent who loses a child? I guess that's just too fucking awful to even have a name.'[15]

2

Kenneth Mills-Tucker
(aged nineteen)

Indianapolis, Indiana

23 November, 3.13 a.m. EST

A rapid, repetitive barrage of shots had pierced the night like the clacking of an almighty typewriter echoing through a dark, empty office. It was 3.13 a.m. when a woman, woken by the noise but still with the weight of sleep in her voice, called 911 and told the controller what she'd heard. 'Some kind of gunfire,' she said, before deferring to her husband, a muffled presence on the line. 'My husband says it's automatic.' The controller asks which direction the gunfire is heading. 'Going north. From just down to the street,' she says before her husband corrects her. 'He says it's going east. Going toward the main office.'

'How many did you hear?'

'Repeated fire. It's more than six.'

'Six?'

'*More than six*. I'm in my bed, I didn't get up. Cos they woke us up. It woke me up. I never heard this kind of fire before.'

The second caller was matter-of-fact and brief. '911? The police are round here now. But someone got shot outside my house.' As the drama unfolded in real time, residents in a patch of northwest Indianapolis offered what they could by way of information. Stray bullets peppered the area. One hit a bedroom wall, two others went through bedroom windows. The calls were partial, occasionally panicked accounts from residents whose slumber had been disturbed by the high-powered crackling of a weapon of war and who were now disoriented as they struggled to relate their versions of events to the dispassionate voice of a civil servant seeking hard, actionable information on the other end of the line.

'I'm at Three Fountains West apartments. And I think I heard gunshots. And then people running through right past my house,' a third caller says in breathless, abrupt sentences. 'I heard the shots. And as soon as I looked out the window there were two gentlemen running right past my house. And I saw them stop.'

'OK. Are they white, black, Hispanic?' asks the controller.

There's a long pause.

'They are black. And they're wearing black.'

'Both wearing black?'

'So my roommate says. The victim was shot right in front of his room.'

'He saw this happen?'

'He didn't see it. He heard it. And looked out the window. He saw that he fell.'

The next caller is clearly terrified. 'Me, my baby, and my boyfriend were in the house and then we heard a gunshot. My window . . . My wall is just . . .' A bullet had just gone through her window. As she loses her train of thought, her boyfriend takes over, his tone more fretful and urgent. 'They're shooting from my house. We're at Falcon Crest watching TV. I need to get out of here. Can you get a car so I can get out of here? I don't want to be in this area.'

'I think there's several officers already over there,' the dispatcher says.

'I don't want to be in this area. What the hell.' He's breathing hard.

'There are so many officers over there,' the controller says, trying to reassure him. 'You're going to be OK now. OK. There's a lot of them over there.'

He's not listening. He's instructing his girlfriend to gather their things. 'Put the stuff in the baby bag. Find it tomorrow. We'll carry it to a hotel.' His breathing is still laboured.

'We're going to let them know,' says the controller.

'How long is it going to take?' he asks.

'You want to leave now?'

'Yeah, we just want to sleep in a hotel.'

His girlfriend returns to the phone. 'Hello, ma'am. We've got a young two-month-old baby.'

'I understand.'

'So we really want to leave now, OK?' she says. 'We really want to leave.'

The controller is getting testy. 'I understand, ma'am. I've already told you that we're going to get an officer inside your house, OK? They're really busy out there. There's a lot going on out there. They'll be with you as soon as they can. But I'll let them know that you want to leave and you want to go to a hotel. They'll be there as soon as they can, all right? As soon as they can? As. Soon. As. They. Can. To talk to you, OK? Just stay inside your apartment. Do not go out. We'll get an officer to you.'

'All right. Thanks.'

Three Fountains West is in a curious part of Indianapolis where country, town and suburb meet but don't match. Within a three-minute drive you can be on the interstate, on a horse, in a box store, in an apartment, or in a town house. But Three Fountains West, a housing cooperative, is pleasant. It reminded me of the English new town that I grew up in during the seventies: newly built, affordable, identical homes, with gardens front and back, decent amenities – a few playgrounds, a community centre, a swimming pool with a slide – and well-tended green space. A three-bedroom town house here goes for $620 a month, with management promising to 'provide that "at home" feeling without the hassles of home ownership'.[1] According to the census tract (a relatively small area usually comprising a few thousand people), this was the most diverse of all the places where kids got shot that day (62 per cent black, 15 per cent white, 20 per cent Latino).[2]

The police got to Three Fountains West very quickly. They had been setting up for an unrelated detail nearby when they heard the shots reported in the 911 calls. Still, by the time they arrived, the shooters had fled, leaving what looked like a scene from a David

Lynch movie. A green 2002 Honda Accord had struck a utility pylon and flipped onto its roof. Its four occupants were now scattered. Wayne Wilson, aged twenty, the driver, was on the grass complaining of a pain in his back. Jaylen Grice, twenty, who was with him in the front, felt pain all over his body. Both were taken to the hospital. Tarell Davis, nineteen, was not there when the police arrived but returned later, apparently uninjured. Kenneth Mills-Tucker, nineteen, lay still, not complaining at all. He had staggered a short distance and fallen about a hundred feet from the car. He'd been shot in the left side of his torso; another bullet had grazed the right side of his abdomen. Police believe the gunfight took place right outside the administrative offices of Three Fountains West because casings were found in the parking lot there. Kenneth and his crew did not get very far. The car overturned yards away as they tried to head south on Moller Road, leaving the area in darkness for several hours after it struck the utility pole. The coroner's verdict report reads, 'Medical intervention was unsuccessful and the decedent was pronounced non-viable at 3.57 a.m.'

Around the time Amy Sanders and her family were crossing the Mason–Dixon line on their way from Houston to Grove City to see Jaiden inert but still technically alive, Kenneth became the second person whose story is told in this book to be shot and the first to die over the twenty-four-hour period covered. Jaiden was the youngest; Kenneth was the oldest – only three days shy of his twentieth birthday.

In the picture used for his obituary, Kenneth, who was also known as 'KJ', looks quite the dandy, wearing a white shirt and bright white hat, tilted slightly to the right, and a matching bow tie and waistcoat with grey and white diagonal stripes. His closed-mouth smile makes the most of a prominent chin and the goatee growing on it. Formal and handsome in his bearing and playful with his clothing, were he not black he could be an extra in *The Great Gatsby*.

Apparently, he had been looking forward to bidding farewell to his teens – his Twitter handle was his birthday, @Nov.26th. One of his last tweets, sent on the evening he died, read, 'Out with the gang Dooney Wayne n Rell what's going on tonight. My last weekend being a teenager.'[3] According to the coroner's report, the four had left a party at the Three Fountains apartment complex around 3.13 a.m.

As the sun rose, Twitter hummed with news of his death. In one exchange at 5.21 a.m., a friend commiserated with Kenneth's girlfriend, Denise: 'yu might be tha last voice he heard, no one can imagine what yu goin thru smh it's hard for everybody but keep ur head up.' Denise had not heard. 'What are you talking about,' she wrote. 'KJ dead' came the reply. 'No TF he's not what are yu talking about what's your number where's KJ.'

Those who know what the shooting was about have not come forward. If the police know, they are not saying. Meanwhile, Kenneth's assailant has not been found.

Dead men tell no tales. For each young person who fell that day there is a story beyond his death. The challenge, in compiling this book, was to unearth as many of those stories as possible. Finding family members was not always easy. There were short news reports, usually written by whichever general-assignment journalist was unlucky enough to be on the weekend shift. Occasionally, they included a quote from a family member. But often not. After that, there were online obituary notices, which provided names of parents, siblings, funeral directors and churches. If the shooting had happened in or near the home, families often moved away – as Nicole had done. So contacting people was a mixture of persistence and luck: trawling online phone directories for names listed in online obituaries in the hope that there might be an address; messaging people on Facebook; literally walking streets and asking if anyone knew the family; approaching the funeral directors who buried the victims and the pastors who eulogised them; asking local journalists if they would share leads.

If any of those attempts bore fruit, then came the tough part: approaching the families.

Talking to the relatives of bereaved children is inherently intrusive. The issue is whether the intrusion is at all welcome. It is no small thing to trust a person you don't know with the story of your dead child. Journalists are not entitled to such stories. But often parents are genuinely heartened to know that someone from outside their immediate circle is even interested. They are relieved to hear that someone, somewhere, noted that the young person whom they bore and reared has been summarily removed from the planet.

Conversely, there are others who not only do not want to speak but resent being asked. The relative of one child in this book responded to my request for an interview with this angry voicemail: 'Don't call my phone. You're a stupid son of a bitch. And I've got your number. And I'm gonna give it to my lawyer. And I don't want anything to do with your dumb ass. Don't you ever fucking call my phone. You bitch.' A family member, whom I'd already interviewed, had given me her number.

The truth is, you never know until you ask. I asked Kenneth's grandfather. I found his name through the list of family members on Kenneth's online obituary and then matched it to an identical name in the online phone directory. According to the census, his address was in a neighbourhood with a substantial black community. I figured that, of all Kenneth's relatives, his grandfather was most likely to have a landline. So I called.

A woman answered and said I'd called the right place but he wasn't home. I explained my idea for this book and she was very enthusiastic. 'Thank God. Somebody should write about this,' she said. 'They should teach children in first and second grade to stay away from guns. It's a waste. The guys who shot him weren't even looking for him,' she said. I asked if she had a contact number for either of his parents.

'Wait and I'll call him,' she said, referring to the grandfather. 'He's in. I just thought you were a collector,' she laughed. The grandfather gave me Kenneth's father's mobile number. In hindsight, I should have texted his dad. That would have given him time to process the enquiry in his own time. An unexpected call from an unfamiliar number in the middle of the day from someone wanting to talk about your recently murdered son would throw anyone off. I know that now. But I called. I told him how I'd got his number, what the book was about, and asked if I could see him when I came to Indianapolis in a few weeks.

'Where did you get my number from?' he asked. I explained again. 'How did you get their number?' he asked. I explained. 'How did you find our names?' he asked. I explained. And so it went on. Understandably, he couldn't see past being blindsided. I apologised for putting him on the spot and asked if we could talk at a better time. He said he'd call me back that night.

I immediately texted an apology and a further explanation of the project. He didn't call back that night. Nor the night after that. I left it for a couple of days and texted again and then once again before I left for Indianapolis. He never called back. When I arrived in Indianapolis five months later, I called the grandfather's house and left a message. When they didn't get back to me, I went to their home and left a note at their door. By the time I got back to the hotel, they'd left a voicemail while I was driving. It was his grandfather's partner. The message was four seconds long. She simply repeated her number and said, 'Don't call again.'

I'd gone to Indianapolis in April 2014, almost exactly five months after Kenneth's death, for the annual convention of the National Rifle Association, which was being held in the downtown convention centre, just twenty minutes away from where he was shot. The sense of fear and helplessness exhibited in those 911 calls the night Kenneth died – the infantilised man unable to defend his family and seeking protection from the state; domestic cocoons pierced by the chaos of the street; law-abiding citizens paralysed by vagabonds run wild – is the currency in which the NRA trades. The 911 dispatcher instructed the caller to sit and wait; the slogan for this NRA convention that year was 'Stand and Fight'.

When the NRA comes to town, it makes its presence felt. A huge banner straddling an entire block of the city centre promised 'NINE ACRES OF GUNS AND GEAR'. The displays inside didn't disappoint. In a cavernous exhibition hall showcasing the industry's finest killing machines, scores of white men (few other demographics were present) aimed empty barrels into the middle distance and pondered their purchases. All the big names were there: Mossberg ('Built rugged. Proudly American'), Smith & Wesson ('Advanced by design'), and Henry ('Made in America. Or not made at all').

The relationship some of the men walking these halls have with guns is romantic. At times it even borders on the sexual. The touch, smell and power of a firearm come together in their own erotic alchemy. 'Pick up a rifle, a pistol, a shotgun, and you're handling a piece of American history,' writes Chris Kyle in *American Gun*. 'Take the gun up now, and the smell of black powder and saltpetre sting the air. Raise the rifle to your shoulder and look into the distance. You see not a target but a whole continent of potential, of great things to come, a promising future . . . but also toil, trial, and hardship. The firearm in your hands is a tool to help you through it.'[4]

The convention hosts scores of seminars ranging from 'Wild Game Cooking: From Field to Table' to 'The Men and Guns of D-Day'. But by far the most popular are those premised on the notion that you are fighting for your life. In the 'Home Defense Concepts' seminar, Rob Pincus, a taut, muscular figure with a trimmed goatee, encouraged several hundred attendees to visualise the room in their house where they would barricade themselves in the event of a burglary and to 'recreate that emotional component' of a break-in by having a dry run with the whole family. Families should have a code word. 'Think about where you are in the morning and in the evening,' he told them as they imagined the best hiding place. Running through the arsenal that might be most appropriate, he suggested a 20-gauge for defence, or maybe a 9 mm, 'which can be a lot more manageable'. When thinking of the firearm you'd use, bear the following in mind: 'What's the practical distance? What's the predictable distance? What's the predictable size? What are the shooting skills?'

In other words, imagine a burglary in vivid detail, and then make sure you are always prepared for that eventuality. Rather than succumb to the complacency that it would not happen or is unlikely to happen, develop a state of alertness in which you have embodied and embedded the notion that it could happen to you at any moment, and develop the reflexes to respond effectively and accordingly. Basically, live your life in fear of threat and violation. Be stimulated by the possibility that someone, somewhere, might be poised to invade and attack. 'You have to do the drill,' he stressed. 'You have to create the stimulus.'

But the threat the NRA evokes is not only to an individual or even a family; it is to American civilisation itself. 'In order to justify the necessity for firearms, the gun-rights narrative must continually reaffirm the frontier spirit, which makes self-defence essential and militia duty compulsory,' writes James Welch, an assistant professor at the University of Texas at Arlington, in his essay 'Ethos of the Gun'. 'Despite the fact that the frontier has long ceased to be a common experience for Americans, the staunchest gun advocates go to great pains to maintain a sense of the world as a dangerous, insecure place.'[5]

The NRA defends the right to bear arms under the Second Amendment to the Constitution. Adopted in 1791, it states: 'A well-regulated militia being necessary to the security of a free state, the right of the people to keep and bear arms shall not be infringed.'

The assumption that this relates to the rights of an individual is widespread but by no means uncontested.

'The world of the Second Amendment is unrecognisable,' argues Michael Waldman in *Second Amendment: A Biography*. 'A world where every white American man served in the military for his entire adult life, where those citizen soldiers bought their own military weapons and stored them at home, and where the idea of a US Army would be enough to send patriots to grab their musket. When the militias evaporated, so did the original meaning of the Second Amendment.'

Five years after his retirement from the Supreme Court, Chief Justice Warren Burger, a conservative appointed by Nixon, insisted the Second Amendment 'has been the subject of one of the greatest pieces of fraud – I repeat the word "fraud" – on the American public by special interest groups that I have ever seen in my lifetime.'[6]

Back at the convention the NRA's executive vice-president and CEO, Wayne LaPierre, addressed a huge rally painting a dark picture of hydra-headed threats enveloping the country, leaving no person safe and no place uncontaminated by suspicion. 'We know, in the world that surrounds us, there are terrorists and home invaders and drug cartels and carjackers and knockout gamers and rapers, haters, campus killers, airport killers, shopping-mall killers, road-rage killers, and killers who scheme to destroy our country with massive storms of violence against our power grids, or vicious waves of chemicals or disease that could collapse the society that sustains us all. I ask you: Do you trust this government to protect you? We are on our own.'[7]

Apocalyptic in tone, demagogic in content, hyperbolic in scale, the dystopian vision conjured by LaPierre was of a nation not only under attack but in decline. 'Almost everywhere you look', he said, 'something has gone wrong. You feel it in your heart, you know it in your gut. Something has gone wrong. The core values we believe in, the things we care about most, are changing. Eroding . . . It's why more and more Americans are buying firearms and ammunition. Not to cause trouble, but because we sense that America is already *in* trouble.'[8]

Every NRA convention attracts a small but determined gathering of protesters from around the country. But this one was special. A few weeks earlier, the former New York mayor, Michael Bloomberg, had announced he would spend $50 million dollars developing a grass-roots network of gun control advocates that would bring together some of the main organisations campaigning on the issue, including Mayors Against Illegal Guns and Moms Demand Action for Gun Sense in America, to form a group called 'Everytown for Gun Safety'.[9] Its press conference in Indianapolis that day to protest the NRA convention was one of the first events it had ever held.

Given the initial reaction of Kenneth's grandfather's partner and the fact that the NRA convention was in his home town, I hoped that I might find Kenneth's friends or relatives among the gun control activists, galvanised by his death. Looking around the room at the press conference, that seemed unlikely. In a city where one in four people is African American, and more than half the homicide victims are black, there were precious few black people among the protesters – apart from a handful of women at the podium, all from other cities, who had lost their sons to gun violence. Indeed, despite Indianapolis having one of the highest homicide rates of any of the cities covered in this book, there didn't seem to be anyone from the city there who had suffered from gun violence.

When I asked one of the organisers if I could talk to a local person, I was steered towards a woman from Carmel, a nearby wealthy suburb. Like most attendees at the convention, she became involved in gun control after the shootings at Sandy Hook elementary school, in Newtown, Connecticut. If others I spoke to said they had been active on the issue before, they told me that this particular tragedy had reignited their passion. If they admitted they'd never paid it much attention before, then Newtown forced them to reckon with their ambivalence. Given the large number of mass shootings – in 2013 alone there were 254, including one on the day this book is set and four in Indianapolis[10] – what was it specifically about Sandy Hook that had prompted her to act?

'I have four little kids,' she said. 'When that happened I couldn't help thinking about my little kids in school. I'd been growing increasingly more concerned. Every time a shooting happened I thought, "Oh my God." But I didn't really know how serious it was. Few circumstances are as great as a mom trying to protect her children.'

Donna Dees-Thomases, who organised the Million Mom March in 2000 (the biggest protest in favour of gun control to date), spelled it out when I met her at the press conference: 'It was first-graders. Twenty-six Americans were slaughtered in an elementary school in five minutes. That could have been our school. They could have been our children. It's the innocence of children. It isn't any more terrible than when anyone else dies a gun death. But you can't deny the devastation of these innocent first-graders, and we didn't protect them.' All around the room the children who died at Sandy Hook were invariably described as 'angels', 'innocents' or 'babes'.

This emotional connection is easy to understand. The enduring image of that day, of distraught children being escorted by a police officer in an orderly line, their faces contorted with panic and trauma, was searing. The sight of parents waiting anxiously to learn the fate of their kids and the pen portraits of fledgling lives so senselessly destroyed were harrowing. It is also easy to grasp the potential political impact of the moment. If Sandy Hook was a tragedy, it was also an opportunity for gun control advocates to illustrate their case in the starkest terms. Rights come with responsibilities; all freedoms come with some restrictions. Do you love guns more than you love children? How does the freedom to bear arms measure up against the freedom to know that your children will be safe in elementary school?

On the same day, in China, Min Yongjun, a mentally ill thirty-six-year-old, took a knife into Chenpeng primary school in Henan province and stabbed twenty-three children and an elderly woman.[11] No one died. Whatever one makes of the NRA axiom that 'Guns don't kill people, people kill people', it couldn't be clearer that people can kill more people more efficiently with guns than with almost anything else that is commercially available in the United States.

In law, as in life, children comprise a special category: the most vulnerable and the most in need of protection, both by and from their parents and the state. The fact that they are children means they have had no say in how the world they live in has been constructed or what the ground rules are. There is pathos in their pain and thus more intense outrage at those who would torment or harm them. To raise this in an argument does not exploit an issue but contextualises it.

But dwelling on children can be calculated. In not only emphasising their vulnerability but also declaring their inherent innocence and insisting on their angelic nature, one moves them from a 'protected' to an elevated category: it shifts the emphasis from the availability of guns to the moral purity of those they might be used to kill. Dees-Thomases was right when she insisted, 'It isn't any more terrible than when anyone else dies a gun death.' And yet to dwell on the innocence of 'babes' and 'angels' suggests there are more guilty, less angelic victims out there more deserving of the fate. The pursuit and promotion of the 'ideal, worthy victim' is a staple for social justice campaigns. It can at times be effective. But it is always problematic.

In 1955, fourteen-year-old Emmett Till was fished out of Mississippi's Tallahatchie river with a bullet in his skull, an eye gouged out, and his forehead crushed on one side after he failed to show 'due respect' to a white woman in a grocery store. The two white men who killed him (they later confessed to a journalist) were acquitted by an all-white jury. In an editorial, *Life* magazine drew attention to the fact that Till's father, Louis, had died in the military during the Second World War: '[Emmett Till] had only his life to lose, and many others have done that, including his soldier father who was killed in France fighting for the American proposition that all men are equal.'[12] This attempt to sanctify Emmett as the offspring of a patriotic serviceman backfired when it turned out that Louis had actually been hanged in Italy after he was convicted of raping two Italian women and killing a third – an accusation he denied. But if Louis had been caught, on camera, diving on a hand grenade to save his platoon, it would still have been irrelevant to Till's fate. No child should have been so brutally slain whether his or her father was a pimp or a priest.

Not all attempts to establish the decency of a victim are executed in such a ham-fisted manner, but they are all underpinned by the same fundamental flaw. The argument's centre of gravity shifts from 'This shouldn't happen to anyone' to 'This shouldn't happen to people like this', suggesting that there are people out there who might deserve it. Emphasising the innocence of the child victims of Sandy Hook may clarify the obscenity of the injustice of young people being shot, but that doesn't make the injustice less obscene when it happens to someone who has lived long enough to be deemed guilty of something. When you take these empathetic shortcuts, a lot of people get left out on the way.

Kenneth Mills-Tucker was guilty of something. With his family being unforthcoming, I trawled the Internet to find out what I could about him, including publicly available police files. It was there I discovered that on 10 March 2013 at around 11.50 p.m., he was guilty of driving while black. Or, more specifically, of slowing down but 'failing to come to a full and complete stop' while approaching a stop sign. In the incident report, the officer who pulled him over writes, 'When I got out and approached the vehicle, I smelled the distinct odour of what, through my training and experience as a law enforcement officer, I believed to be marijuana. When I got to the driver's side window, a large billow of smoke rolled out of the window, which again smelled of marijuana.' He took Kenneth's licence and registration, went back to his car, ran Kenneth's details through the system, and called for a backup unit. When the other officer arrived, he ordered both Kenneth and the other passenger out of the car and 'placed them in handcuffs for our safety and due to the probable cause of the odour of marijuana'.

Searching the vehicle, he found a pipe with marijuana residue in it, just above the pull-out cup holders, as well as several cigarillo wrappers and loose tobacco. Kenneth said it was his pipe and was arrested for 'possession of paraphernalia' and given a citation for failing to stop at a stop sign. The car was towed, the pipe was confiscated, and Kenneth was dropped off at police headquarters.

This is how large numbers of black men in the United States are caught in the criminal justice system – with a dragnet. In *The New Jim Crow: Mass Incarceration in the Age of Colorblindness*, Michelle Alexander explains that 95 per cent of 'Pipeline' stops yield no illegal drugs.[13] (Operation Pipeline trains uniformed officers to identify indicators of drug-related illegal activity while engaged in traffic-enforcement operations.) This was one of them. But once they've stopped you for 'something' they'll settle for anything. In the words of one California Highway Patrol officer quoted in the book, 'It's sheer numbers . . . You've got to kiss a lot of frogs before you find a prince.'[14]

Kenneth's pipe made him a prince that night. Though he was killed nine days before he was due in court, one can assume, given that it apparently was his pipe and the likelihood of his affording a good lawyer was probably remote (he'd been assigned a public defender), that he would have been convicted of 'something'. This would have cast him out of the world of 'babes' and 'angels'.

To a sympathetic eye, it wouldn't take much imagination to cast Kenneth as a success story. In a city where 38 per cent of black kids did not graduate from high school in 2012,[15] he was, according to his obituary, a graduate of Arsenal Technical High School.[16] In a city where 74 per cent of black youth between the ages of sixteen and nineteen were not working (many, of course, were still in school),[17] Kenneth had a job at U-Haul. But, most significantly, he was loved. 'K.J. was like a Son to us all,' wrote one family friend on his online obituary page. 'I always enjoyed watching him in church . . . You always had them dressed so well, and they were so well mannered, and I enjoyed looking into his bright eyes.'

But had Kenneth's death been an issue of public concern, all of this would likely have counted for nothing. No media account could or would include the phrase 'never been in trouble with the law'; most would be sure to mention his 'recent drug-related conviction'. No longer innocent, no longer worthy. On some level it would be framed as though he had it coming.

As it happens, the handful of stories about the incident said nothing about Kenneth beyond his age and name. The circumstances surrounding his death earned a couple of hundred words; the fact of his death earned scarcely more than a sentence; to his life was devoted nary a word. But had anyone considered it worth denigrating him, they wouldn't have needed to trawl through his police records. They could just go through his Twitter feed and let him condemn himself. For although dead men tell no tales, many younger ones (including all the teens who died that day) do now have a voice beyond the grave – on social media.

One should be cautious when drawing conclusions about people's characters from social media. On Facebook, nobody's children cry, nobody's marriage is imperilled, and everybody has beautiful holidays under the bluest of skies. These are performance platforms where we present versions of ourselves that are curated for public consumption.

Such performances are ripe for misinterpretation. After policeman Darren Wilson shot Michael Brown, an unarmed eighteen-year-old, in Ferguson, Missouri, in August 2014, news organisations initially used a picture of Brown from his Facebook page holding his hands in a manner that some claimed was a gang sign and others said was a peace sign. Within days, hundreds of young African Americans tweeted contrasting pictures of themselves – one in which they could be perceived as threatening and another in which they would be deemed 'respectable' – with the hashtag #IfTheyGunnedMeDown. They wanted to show how easily a picture of black youth, taken out of context, could be distorted in order to fit a stereotype.

Tyler Atkins, for example, displayed one picture of himself in a black tux and white bow tie, holding a saxophone, and another of himself wearing a blue bandanna with his finger pointed to the camera in what could be the shape of a gun. The first was taken following a jazz concert in which he performed; the second was for a rap video he'd made for a school math project. 'Had the media gained ahold of this picture, I feel it would be used to portray that I was in a gang, which is not true at all,' Atkins, seventeen, told the *New York Times*.[18] That sentiment was clearly felt by many; within two days the hashtag had been used 168,000 times.[19]

But even if it would be a mistake to read too much into someone's social media output, it would be no less of a mistake to ignore it altogether, for it does, at the very least, tell a story of the image a person wants to project, and that itself can be revealing. And in the absence of any contact from the family, social media and public records were the only ways to find out more about Kenneth.

Kenneth was a prolific but sporadic tweeter: in September he sent only one, the week before he died he sent one hundred. His Twitter feed largely reads like a mixture of the banalities for which social media has become infamous – 'Man I hate cold toilet seats'; 'I hope they make a strong ass phone to the point when u drop it the screen dnt crack' – and the online swagger characteristic of young men with too much time on their hands. There are quite a few references to smoking marijuana – 'The kush I'm smoking got me sneezing'; 'I hate going to sleep high. I feel like its a waist of weed' – and a considerable amount of misogynistic cock-strutting: 'if good pussy dot make a nigga stay then nothin will'; 'I dnt trust NO bitch PERIOD'. At times, his adolescence comes through. He's clearly excited about his upcoming birthday, mentioning it three times in just a few days. And he publicly splits up and reconciles with his girlfriend in the same night – as only an adolescent could. Within four hours, he goes from 'Love dnt live here nomore fuck the bullshit' to 'If I'm single ima b single for a couple of years shit stressful' to 'even doe we mad at each other buuuuuut [heartshape emoticon]' and finally to 'Tough Love'.

But what emerges most markedly (and what distinguishes his timeline from that of his peer group in almost any other Western country) is that his bragging goes beyond women and weed to weapons and death. In the seven months before he died, Kenneth lost three friends. A posting on 2 October reads, '4/5/13 R.I.P ReggieMac 7/21/13 R.I.P Frank 10/2/13 R.I.P Rockhead'. Frank, a seventeen-year-old who appears to have been killed in an accidental shooting in a Marriott parking lot during a Black Expo celebration, was apparently someone Kenneth was particularly close to.[20] Frank's picture was the backdrop to his Twitter home page. 'I miss Frank man y u take my nigga away from us,' he tweeted. And then a few weeks before he died, Kenneth tweeted, 'Man it's been 71 days since u left bro we miss u not a second go by u not on our mind but we gone keep the dream alive R.I.P @ImFrank_GMG.'

That such a young person would be in the vicinity of so much death is shocking, but once you've read their tweets it's not that surprising. Frank tweeted, just an hour before he was shot, 'im one of da only yung niggas out here dats really thuggin and i could careless about catchin a murder charge.' A couple of days before Kenneth died he wrote, 'Most niggas carry guns n act scared to use them.' A couple of days before that he asked, 'Am I wrong for popping him when he wanna take my life that shit ain't right.' And a week earlier he'd quoted rapper Chief Keef: 'I get gwop [money] now that bitch remember me I send shots now them niggas hearing me.'

More than two years after Kenneth was shot police arrested nine suspected gang members belonging to the Get Money Gang[21] who they claimed had 'terrorised' Butler-Tarkington, a north-side neighbourhood, while trafficking drugs and guns through the city. They seized 17 guns, almost 6 grams of cocaine, 26 pounds of marijuana and more than $32,000 in cash. Police believe the group was connected to four homicides in the neighbourhood and beyond, dating back to 2012, as well the fatal shooting of a ten-year-old boy, courtesy of a stray bullet.

Two people they had arrest warrants for in relation to the gang but failed to catch in the raids were Jaylen Grice and Tarell Davis – two of the three passengers riding in the car with Kenneth the night he died. The neighbourhood they are accused of terrorising is just fifteen minutes from where Kenneth was shot. His Twitter feed is peppered with references to GMG – the Get Money Gang.

Whether it's guns, death, or themselves Kenneth doesn't take seriously is not clear – it's only Twitter. We don't know if he had anything to do with GMG, if his friends were guilty, if he ever touched a gun, was carrying a gun the night he died, or ever did anything more criminal than failing to come to a full stop at a stop sign with marijuana residue allegedly in his pipe. Young men like to strut, preen, and bluster, and a platform such as Twitter makes that easy. But one can't simply dismiss it all as venting on social media. Because both Kenneth and those he mentioned really are dead. The day he was buried @QueenofPetty apologised on Twitter for not attending his funeral. She'd had enough: 'srry I couldnt see you get buried today. I can't go to anymore funerals its heartbreaking. See you in Heaven soon R.I.P.'

A few days shy of his twentieth birthday, Kenneth was no more an adult than the average college sophomore, but no one was going to describe him as an 'innocent', 'angelic' or 'babe'. The elevation and canonisation of the 'worthy victim' has a significant bearing on why so many of those most affected by gun violence – the black, brown, and poor – do not align themselves with the gun control movement. 'Sometimes, in the past, that has held organisations back,' Julia Browder Eichorn, who has been a gun control campaigner since the nineties, told me. Julia, who is African American and lives in Columbus, Ohio, was in Indianapolis to protest the NRA. I'd met her at Ohio State University by chance a few weeks earlier when I'd been in Columbus to deliver a talk. 'To put someone out there who has had less than a stellar lifestyle – the opposition is going to tear that apart. They're already calling our children, who've done nothing, thugs. That's a huge piece of why you don't see more moms of colour in this movement. Maybe they knew their kids were doing these things, and they didn't stop them. Maybe they just prayed nothing would happen to them. We have to stand with that mom who maybe didn't make the best choice, or maybe she made the best choice that she could, but sadly her kid's not here any more.'

Many of the kids who would die in the next twenty-four hours were raised in tough circumstances and had messy lives. But so long as the gun narrative stops at protecting 'innocents' and 'babes', it's difficult to see who will ever speak out for them. 'The children who are dying are real kids,' said Clementine Barfield, who set up Save Our Sons and Daughters after her two sons were shot (one survived, one died) in Detroit in the same incident, in an interview with Deborah Prothow-Smith, the former Commissioner of Public Health for the Commonwealth of Massachusetts. 'They are real kids from real families. Some were doing foolish things. And some were just caught in the wrong place at the wrong time. But all kids have the right to make mistakes. All kids have the right to live. My child is dead. Your child could be next.'[22]

3

Stanley Taylor
(aged seventeen)

Charlotte, North Carolina
23 November, 4.17 a.m. EST

As a behaviour specialist in the Charlotte school system, Mario Black spent an awful lot of his time trying to persuade his young, mostly black students that there's more to life – or could be – than hanging out in the streets and getting in trouble. 'Three or four times a day I have to break it down for the kids that this is what's out there for them if they don't change their ways – prison or death . . . It's hard work at times. I hope I'm getting through. You gotta hope that they're going to carry these nuggets with them for years to come and use them when they need them.'

After Mario's younger cousin, Davion Funderburk, was shot down in July 2013, he felt compelled to take action beyond the classroom. 'Me and one of my classmates were talking about how nothing's being done. So we said we need to do something.' And so a fledgling youth movement was born: the Million Youth March of Charlotte (MYMOC). It aimed to mobilise Charlotte's teenagers and youth, as well as its civic leaders, to prevent the violence taking so many young lives in the city. Mario planned to mix community outreach with educational events like youth panels.

'I'm trying to light a fire in them,' he told me. 'That the streets are not your life. There's life beyond the streets. We want to bring positive things to the community as it relates to people who are thirteen to twenty-five years old. Because we always hear the negative. There's always someone in that age group who's getting gunned down here.'

I met Mario, aged thirty-two, in an Olive Garden in a mall the size of a village. He was casually dressed in combat trousers and a hoodie, and wore a head full of long dreads, most tied together and hanging in a clump down the middle of his back while the rest dangled around his face and torso.

Four months after Mario's cousin was shot, one of his former elementary school pupils, Stanley Taylor, seventeen, drove up to a Marathon petrol station with some friends. Located just off exit 38 on Interstate 77, the Marathon stands as the most viable venture in what is little more than a small collection of commercial units that includes a barbershop and a derelict building. Going beyond the offerings of a regular gas station – snacks, drinks, lottery tickets, and basic toiletries – it sells T-shirts and hats bearing the logos of most major basketball teams and has a small fast food outlet in the back called Hot Stuff Pizza. Just a few minutes after Kenneth Mills-Tucker's body had been pronounced 'non-viable' 585 miles away in Indianapolis, Stanley was walking into the Marathon with his friends when Demontre Rice pulled up in his car so close to them they thought he was going to hit them.

'High-homicide environments are alike,' writes Jill Leovy in *Ghettoside: Investigating a Homicide Epidemic*. 'The setting is usually a minority enclave or disputed territory where people distrust legal authority . . . The killings typically arise from arguments. A large share of them can be described in two words: Men fighting. The fights might be spontaneous, part of some long-running feud, or the culmination of "some drama".'[1] Here was some spontaneous drama, and given the volatile temperaments of the two men involved, it was never going to end well.

Stanley, says his friend Trey Duncan, had a quick temper. 'Once you bumped him, it's over.' On the Facebook page set up in his memory – a space generally reserved for tender reflections and biblical citations – Quan Jones posted, 'Was up cuz remember that time we was in middle school in you hit that nigga with a lock in the class room. That was good time in middle school r.i.p. Lil stan aka madmix we love u cuz.' Demontre, twenty-seven, was no paragon of self-control either. His criminal record includes, among other things – and there are many other things – arrests for domestic violence, reckless driving and aggravated unlawful use of a weapon.

Precise details of what happened next are sketchy. The two men exchanged words. As Stanley and his crew made their way into the petrol station, Rice pulled out his gun and started shooting. According to the autopsy, Stanley was shot four times. One bullet penetrated his right leg, another grazed his right leg and one hit his left leg. But it was what the coroner labelled 'Gunshot Wound #1' that killed him. 'A penetrating gunshot wound to the back,' reads the autopsy, tracing the trajectory of the bullet. 'Upon entering the body the projectile passes through the skin and soft tissue of the back fracturing left ribs #9 and #10. The bullet fragments perforating the upper and lower lobe of the left lung. There is extensive residual blood present within the chest cavity. Bullet fragments are recovered from the left lung and chest wall. Multiple grey bullet fragments are retained as evidence.'

The 911 call reporting the shooting came in at 4.17 a.m., with all the formality and restraint of someone trying to sell car insurance. 'Yes, ma'am, somebody got shot down here,' says the muffled voice of a man with a South Asian accent who sounds like he sees people getting shot all the time.

'Where?'

'Lasalle Street.'

'Is the person that did it still there?'

'He's gone with his car and the other ones followed him in the other car.'

'OK. Is the person that's shot still there?'

'No, he's gone. Somebody's taken him.'

'But it happened there?'

'Yes, ma'am.'

'OK. The person that was shot, what kind of car did he leave in?'

'I didn't get it.'

'What colour was it, do you know?'

'Brown car. Nice car. Brown car. I know him. I know him personal,' says the caller, exhaling in what is the only remotely emotional moment in the call.

'The dude, he shoot him.'

'OK. We'll get officers out there.'

'Thank you.'

'You're welcome.'

As the caller had warned, by the time the police arrived everybody had gone. Stanley's friends had bundled him into a car and driven him the mile between Interstates 77 and 85. Mario thinks they were trying to get him to University Hospital. Whatever their plan, en route they saw an ambulance, flagged it down, and helped Stanley into it. When he got to the hospital he was pronounced dead.

By Sunday, police issued an arrest warrant for Rice, warning the public that he was 'armed and dangerous'. The following Friday he turned himself in at the Mecklenburg County Jail, where he was charged with murder. Almost a year later, he pleaded guilty to second-degree murder and was sentenced to between 285 and 354 months in prison.[2]

Stanley was tall, lean, and dark. He had a high-top fade crowned with small dreads that earned him the nickname MadMaxx. Photographs on social media of him looking directly into the camera, baring a strong smile of straight, white teeth, are outnumbered by more self-conscious poses in which his mouth is only half open and his head at a tilt. 'He had a beautiful sense of humour,' his mother, Toshiba, told me. 'He was a good kid. He was always joking around. He wanted to see you smile. Always joking. Being silly.'

'He was goofy,' recalls Trey, shaking his head and smiling. 'Sometimes he was so goofy it could get aggravating.' Stanley, it seems, could aggravate folks quite a lot. 'He didn't get along with too many people, to be honest,' says Toshiba, whose recognition of her son's many positive qualities did not blind her to his faults. 'He was very outspoken,' says Shimona, Toshiba's friend, who'd known Stanley since he was an infant. 'He was a good kid, too. Smart, silly, loving, giving. He loved his friends. He *loved* his friends.' If Facebook postings are anything to go by, his girlfriend, whom he would visit after school most days, was besotted with him. For more than a year after his death, friends kept posting messages for him – not just at New Year, Christmas, and his birthday, but on random days when they just wanted to testify in his memory. Within a couple of months of his death, someone had scrawled graffiti on the side of the wall of the Marathon petrol station, where he was shot, declaring, 'R.i.P $tan #FordBound'. It referred to Beatties Ford Road, a long, nondescript street in West Charlotte where he and his friends spent much of their time. The only hobby anybody mentions is basketball. 'But what he really liked doing', says Toshiba, 'is hanging on the corner with his friends.'

Trey was one of those friends. Although Toshiba intimated that Stanley 'hadn't recently had any trouble with the law', it was Trey who pointed out, quite matter-of-factly, even if the precise facts were elusive, that Stanley went to jail for 'three or maybe six months' when he was 'sixteen or seventeen' for 'something'. Stanley attended Turning Point Academy, a charter school with a mission to 'redirect student behaviour through positive programmes that provide rigour, relevance and relationships'.[3] But when Stanley came out of jail, says Trey, he struggled to get back on track. 'After that, he went downhill. He got into the wrong crowd, and when he got into the wrong crowd he didn't even care about school after that.'

Trey can barely remember a time when he didn't know who Stanley was from the neighbourhood. But it wasn't until they were in their teens that they became friendly. Trey, a slender, unassuming young man, met me in a Burger King. He wore a picture of Stanley pinned to his shirt, under which appeared two Bible verses, Proverbs 3:1–2. 'My son, forget not my law; but let thine heart keep my commandments; for length of days, and long life, and peace, shall they add to thee.' He organised a balloon release for the anniversary of Stanley's death, which drew a good crowd.

He arrived carrying a pair of drumsticks and told me he used to play cymbals in the school marching band. Stanley decided to try out for the band and ended up playing bass drum. Trey says he was pretty good at it; but though Stanley lasted only a few months in the band before he gave it up, the two of them remained close. 'We used to chill on Beatties Ford Road,' says Trey. When I ask what 'chilling' consisted of, things get vague. 'Just chill, you know,' he said. But I really didn't. It is a pursuit that, though it consumed hours of their time, apparently defies description and needs no qualification or further explanation. Primarily it seems to involve standing around, talking about girls and thinking of ways to get money. Most of the time, they hung out at L.C. Coleman Park, a bucolic spot just behind Beatties Ford Road with a playground, picnic tables, grills, and basketball courts. 'We'd go to the park, go to my homeboy's house, play a game . . . chill,' Trey explained.

Those closest to Stanley had only a faint idea of what he wanted to do or be. He'd never mentioned anything to Trey about a future profession. At his funeral, a high-school teacher read one of his last assignments, in which he'd written that he knew he was not living the right lifestyle and wanted to make some changes so he could graduate and go to college. 'He was basically making little changes in the right direction,' says Mario. 'He was talking about going to community college,' says Toshiba. 'He wanted to take adult high-school class and start his own business.'

But when they were chilling on Beatties Ford Road, Stanley's and Trey's big dream was to go to Miami one day to 'chill' and 'sleep with some white girls'. Trey couldn't say what it was that attracted them to Miami. But the dream lived on in Stanley's absence. 'That was my main goal,' says Trey. 'If I got to Miami that's gonna be some shit.' He paused. 'I might cry.'

Trey doesn't know quite how to describe the group he and Stanley used to hang out with on Beatties Ford – like 'chilling', it defies definition. It was not so formal as to have a name but not so casual that it did not have a code. 'I ain't gonna say it was a gang,' says Trey. 'But it was a neighbourhood thing. Beatties Ford. We got our own little clique. We on the West Side. North Side is a whole different neighbourhood you don't even fool with. Everybody was together. This my brother, this my brother. We all in the same clique. We got each other's back. I'm not going to let nobody else touch you. If you hit him I'm gonna hit you. Cos I'm his brother.' At times, that made Stanley a liability. His recklessness became the responsibility of the group. 'You try to restrain him. But once I know it's past that and he swinging, I'm right beside him,' explains Trey. 'If he going out we're going out together. That's why I really wish I was there when it happened,' he says referring to the night Stanley died. But would his presence have really helped, given that Rice had a gun? I asked. 'You're right,' Trey admits. 'There's not a lot I could have done.'

Mario not only taught Stanley in elementary school; he also went to elementary school with Toshiba. He saw Stanley grow up, occasionally running into him around town. The last time he saw him was about a year before the shooting. 'It was always a pleasure to catch up with him,' says Mario. 'He wasn't an angel. But he wasn't the worst either. Not by a long way. He was just a typical teen. Just running around. Out with his peers. Out in the street. Even in his teenage years he had a little more energy than some of the teachers could handle. Once he left elementary school, I would run into him. He would always show me the utmost respect. "Hey, Mr Mario. Hey, Mr Black."'

By daybreak on Saturday, 23 November, Black was vaguely aware that another youth in town had fallen. 'On Facebook I saw a lot of 'RIP Stan', but it wasn't until Sunday morning when I saw it on the news that I realised just who it was. I'd started the Million Youth March for that particular reason, so it actually hit home hard. As educators, we get attached to these students. We're like their parents away from home. So that was like one of mine getting gunned down as well. I cried like a baby.'

He called Toshiba and helped her organise the funeral. A couple of weeks later was MYMOC's Community Give Back Day. They'd organised to collect toys for the needy and for barbers to give free haircuts to children. It had been planned long in advance, but given Stanley's recent passing they dedicated the event to him. The day was a success, with over one hundred in attendance and Toshiba there to receive a candle lit in her son's memory. But precious few of Stanley's friends came. Mario was deeply disappointed. That evening, he wrote on Stanley's memorial Facebook page, 'To all that claimed they loved Stanley, or his mom and family I find it sad that you did not come out and support Million Youth March of Charlotte today during our day of giving back as we honored Stanley's life.'

'It surprised me that so few showed up,' Mario told me a few months later. 'Everyone claimed they were crazy about Stanley, and they showed up at the candlelight vigil. But when it was taking a stand for him, they weren't there. It was discouraging, because these were the same friends who said they would be there for him and would be there for his mom. And his family was there and they weren't.'

In his behaviour classes, Mario used Stanley's death as a cautionary tale. A picture of him hangs on the wall. 'I want them to see it when I break it down to them. I say, "His mom got a phone call on the Saturday before Thanksgiving and had to go through Thanksgiving planning a funeral. Imagine your mom getting a phone call. That their baby had been gunned down and killed, or their baby's in jail for hanging out with the wrong crowd or being in the wrong place at the wrong time."'

'Sometimes tears are shed,' he tells me. 'I take time, because I want every kid that I come into contact with to know that Mr Black told [them]. I hope a light will come on and steer them in the right direction. Three or four times a day I have to break it down for the kids that this is what's out there for them if they don't change their ways – prison or death. I also tell 'em that, as a teacher in their lives, I don't want to hear what I heard about Stanley.'

Toshiba fears few of Stanley's peers are ready to heed Mario's lessons. When I ask her what it will take to get them to understand what's at stake, she says, 'I'm asking myself the same question, because they're still out there hanging out.' She imitates their macho intonation – a low, gruff drawl, '"He gone. But we're still gonna thug on the corner." I don't know. I just don't know. Mario is really trying to get the youth to understand: "You could really have a good life."'

A year after she received the candle, the MYMOC held its second annual Give Back Day. It rained heavily, and only around twenty children participated. This time the event was dedicated to one of Stanley's best friends, Ajewan Jones, who was shot dead six months after Stanley was shot. The night Stanley died, Ajewan's brother was with him, and Ajewan was in prison for a parole violation. This time, Ajewan's mother, Toshiba's friend Shimona, was there to take the candle.

When somebody gets shot dead in Charlotte, Judy Williams knows about it. The organisation she runs, Mothers of Murdered Offspring, has arranged vigils for murder victims for more than two decades. When they started, the police would contact them and let them know when there had been a shooting. Now MOMO is such an institution in the city that victims' families usually go straight to them.

Judy, a friendly, devout, engaging woman with a short crop of silver hair, organised a vigil for Stanley, which she remembers as a regular affair with a large crowd in Lincoln Heights Neighborhood Park. On the anniversary of Stanley's death, she helped Trey organise the balloon release.

Judy started the support group after her goddaughter, Shawna Hawk, was strangled to death by a serial killer and left floating in the bathtub at her home in Charlotte. The murder occurred on 19 February 1993, during the year with the highest number of homicides in Charlotte's history to date.[4] Judy was worried that Shawna's mother wasn't going to make it. Shawna was an only child, and mother and daughter had been more like sisters. Judy wanted to contribute in some way following Shawna's death, and she came up with the idea of holding candlelight vigils and balloon releases for bereaved relatives.

If a family needs funds for burial, then she might hold the vigil as soon as possible after the death and take up a collection. (They've collected more than a thousand dollars in one night.) If not, they try to stage the vigils the night before the funeral. That's when most relatives and friends are in town, and it offers a release before the more formal occasion. 'We thought people were gathering anyway, so why don't we take advantage of that,' she says. 'Why don't I get those people together, because they were still at the family's house, allow them to express what they were feeling while we light candles, and talk, cry, read poems, sing, whatever they wanted to do. Things they usually wouldn't be able to do at the funeral the next day.'

Judy is a deeply religious woman. One of the many posters on the wall of her office, where she works as an administrator for the housing complex in which she lives, declares, 'Your relationship with God is as strong as the person you like least.' The balloons they release have scripture printed on them as well as a phone number and an email address so that those who receive them can respond. One made it as far as Canada. When I met Trey, a couple of weeks after the balloon release he'd held for Stanley, he had yet to hear word from anyone who found one.

When it comes to the fallout from gun violence, Judy is in the trenches – dealing with bereaved families and friends at the very moment when their grief is most raw. She has assisted in several thousand vigils and, when reaching for an anecdote or illustration, can generally remember the name of the victim and the place where he or she fell. She is politically aware and engaged, and freely shares her views on everything from American foreign policy to the Constitution. Ask her what is the primary reason for gun violence, and she barely hesitates. 'People are not going to church any more.

People are not being taught God. You can tell that by the respect that's given when you pray. You have to remind people to take their hats off. You didn't used to have to do that.'

This failure, she believes, has its roots in a fundamental crisis within the black family. 'The homes are not the incubators they need to be. To actually nurture children and give them all the tools they need to begin in the world without robbin' and stealin' and killing. A lot of them are mimicking what they see. We have a lot of teenage mothers who don't know anything about parenting. Who don't have the help to help them parent because their mothers are very young. You've got grandmothers who are thirty-two and thirty-six years old because kids are having babies so young. And nobody knows anything about being a parent at that age. And these children aren't getting the help that they need, and they're growing up pretty much on their own and being taught that the world pretty much owes them something.'

It is an article of faith among right-wing commentators that African Americans refuse to take responsibility for the problems in their communities, preferring instead to blame their woes on racism and poverty. Obsessed with a sense of victimhood, the pundits claim, they refrain from the hard, introspective work of social and economic revitalisation in their neighbourhoods.

'I have a dream that today's black leadership will quit blaming racism and "the system" for what ails black America,' said Tea Party Republican Congressman Joe Walsh, mimicking Martin Luther King on his radio programme. 'I have a dream that black America will take responsibility for improving their own lives.'[5] Black political leaders who raise issues of racism are branded 'race hustlers' who 'play the race card' in a bid to leverage white guilt for their own ends and to their community's detriment.

Such arguments were particularly prevalent in the wake of disturbances and demonstrations after a series of police killings of unarmed black youth and men, including Michael Brown in Ferguson and Eric Garner, who was videoed being choked to death by New York police as he uttered, 'I can't breathe.' In both cases grand juries refused to indict the officers. 'President Obama should provide some leadership,' insisted Fox News anchor Bill O'Reilly, '[by saying], "You know what, we fight the injustice and we realise it's there, but we love our country, we applaud the progress we've made, and here is a pathway to success. You know, don't abandon your children. Don't get pregnant at fourteen. Don't allow your neighbourhoods to deteriorate into free fire zones." That's what the African-American community should have on their T-shirts.'[6]

In a discussion about Ferguson on *Meet the Press,* former New York mayor Rudolph Giuliani said, 'I find it very disappointing that you're not discussing the fact that 93 per cent of blacks in America are killed by other blacks. We're talking about the exception here . . . So why don't you cut [black-on-black crime] down so so many white police officers don't have to be in black areas? White police officers won't be there if you weren't killing each other 70 per cent of the time.'[7]

The notion that raising the issue of 'black-on-black crime' is taboo has gained currency beyond the Right. In her granular account of policing homicides in Los Angeles in *Ghettoside*, Leovy claims that African Americans avoid discussion of the topic precisely because they know how conservatives will distort such a discussion. 'Some black scholars and advocates fear providing white racists with further ammunition – of giving them yet more ways to stigmatise poor blacks', she writes.[8]

My research for this book suggests that, at a grassroots level, almost precisely the opposite is true. In the scores of interviews I conducted with family members, community activists and others, the shootings of children and teens in the black community by other black teens were often discussed, and those conversations made almost no reference to poverty, racism or other broader structural issues. They focused instead almost entirely on personal responsibility. 'White society' – whatever that is – didn't even get a look in. Most described things pretty much the way Williams did, though with less emphasis on religion and more on family.

They didn't frame it as a problem of 'black-on-black' crime. But that's because it is a nonsense term. America is very segregated, and its criminality conforms to that fact. The victims of most crimes are of the same race as those who commit them. Eighty-four per cent of whites who are killed every year are killed by whites.[9] White people who buy illegal drugs are most likely to buy them from white people.[10] So the fact that black people are killing each other conforms to, rather than contradicts, America's criminal patterns where race is concerned. What is particular to the black community is the level of violent crime. The rate of black-youth homicides is falling, but it remains four times the national average and ten times the rate of white-youth homicides.[11]

The source of this problem, most African Americans I interviewed argued, was the breakdown in parenting and the absence of basic values being taught in the home – a state of affairs, most concurred, that has deteriorated significantly since they were young. 'A lot of the problem is kids raising kids,' says Mario, echoing Judy's point about teenage parents. 'When I was at elementary school, my mother was active in my school. A lot of parents were active in my school. But today a lot of kids are raising themselves. Parents are younger these days. They're think[ing] they can get their support from their peers out on the streets, because they're not getting their support at home.'

I've always found this line of argument odd because, having been parented in England and been a parent in the United States, I don't think Americans make worse parents than the British or any other nationality. Indeed, in Britain, where public drunkenness is far more common, the culture feels both far more violent and far less deadly. But no other developed Western nation suffers child gun deaths at the level of the United States.[12] It's not even close. The United States suffers eight times the per capita rate of gun murders as the average for Western Europe.[13] The rate is four times as high as it in Switzerland, the nearest contender.[14] Even if Americans did make worse parents, they couldn't be *that* bad.

But this reasoning runs so deep that black parents say parenting is the problem even when they are criticised for being the very parents they themselves believe to be the problem. Shimona had Ajewan when she was fourteen years old, and he was in and out of prison before he was shot. On paper, certainly, she is the archetype that Mario and Judy are referring to. Ask her what she thinks the source of the problem is that took him from her at such a young age, and she says, 'I think it's got a lot to do with your home. Your parents. These kids, their mamas don't love 'em like that. The streets raise 'em. They don't have nobody to tell them. To say, "This ain't right. You know you can't go and take nobody's life like that. You know better. You know right from wrong."'

At times, the contradictions are painful. While I was in Indianapolis looking for Kenneth Mills-Tucker's family, I met DeAndra Yates, who wore a T-shirt bearing the face of her thirteen-year-old son, DeAndre Knox, who was paralysed after having been shot in the back of the head at a party just a few months earlier. DeAndra was at a Moms Demand Action for Gun Sense demonstration protesting the policies espoused at the National Rifle Association's national convention being held in the city at the time. So there's no question she had a view about the bigger issues at play and their connection to DeAndre's fate. When I asked her what she thought the problem was, she didn't mention guns. 'Parents,' she said. 'That's where it starts. With the parents.'

When DeAndre's shooting was reported on a local news website, at least one commenter, Terry Payne, agreed. It was the parents' fault. But he didn't mean the shooter's parents – he meant DeAndra. 'Where are the parents and why are there 13-year-olds out after curfew?' he asked. 'This problem starts well before someone brings a gun into it. If parents can't decide to raise their children properly, they should not have children, either voluntarily or sterilised!' Six readers gave the comment a thumbs-up.

Speaking to Toshiba, you can feel the burden of that vilification. I met her at a TGI Friday's a few months after Stanley was shot. Stanley was her eldest of four. Toshiba is a small, slight postal worker with high cheekbones framing a handsome, youthful face. She's just thirty-two. At that age, very few people in Western countries have buried a parent. She has buried a son. So although her face is unfurrowed, her voice and bearing are prematurely, and possibly temporarily, aged by grief. Mario suggested she speak to me. I doubt she would have granted an interview otherwise. She arrived in a check-print trapper hat, fur earflaps down against a Carolina cold spell. Throughout our forty-minute conversation, she did not take it off once.

Reflecting on Stanley's short life, she stops answering my questions at a certain point and starts unconsciously defending herself against the pervasive assumption – never explicitly levelled against her, but implicit in all criticism of black parenting in these circumstances – that, somehow, she was at fault for her own son's death. 'I tried so hard with my child,' she says, affirming her struggle to set Stanley on a different path and protect him from the streets. Her tone is melancholic – resigned, defeated, but insistent. 'I tried,' she repeats, abrupt sentences emphasising the battles fought, lost, unnamed and unrecognised. 'I mean *I . . . tried.* I tried to keep him home. Locked doors. I tried to move. *I tried.* So I don't know. There's nothing you can do. I tried everything . . . to keep him home. I told him, "Everybody's not your friend. They will shoot you down and not think nothing about it." But they're thinking about having fun, hanging out with their friends, going to parties, you can't tell 'em anything . . . *I tried.*'

The challenges of parenting in the environments in which many black youth grow up are not the kind that get showcased on *Supernanny*. Criticisms of parenting in these contexts must first acknowledge what it takes to be an effective parent in an area where schools are bad, gangs are rife, drugs and guns are easily available, resources are scarce and policing is harsh. The stakes are higher, the dangers more prevalent, and therefore the margin of error far narrower. Doriane Miller, a primary-care physician on the South Side of Chicago who also works at the University of Chicago, recalls having lunch with a successful, quiet, young black man who was doing an internship at the university. Explaining how he kept out of trouble, he told her, 'I live in this really quiet community where there are a lot of old people . . . My mom says it's a way for me to be safe. So I go to school, I go home, I do my homework and I don't go out.'

Miller, whom I met at a cafe in Chicago's Hyde Park, not far from where the Obamas used to live, explained that black parents in low-income neighbourhoods go to extreme lengths to keep their children safe. It is not simply a matter of setting boundaries, establishing curfews, and making sure they get their homework done. It is about hermetically sealing them from their immediate environment, where the risks are too great to leave anything to chance. 'For him, it was that cocoon world,' says Miller, referring to the young intern. 'I have a lot of parents and also grandparents who create cocoons for these young people. They transport them everywhere. They don't get on public transportation. They don't go out and hang out in the parks. Because it's just too dangerous.'

Raising children in America either in or around poverty is very hard. In his 2007 book, *Come On, People*, entertainer Bill Cosby, whose reputation had not yet been damaged by widespread allegations of sexual misconduct, exhorts black parents to step up and provide the kind of nurturing conditions for their children to thrive. His recommendations are detailed and plentiful: 'As soon as a young woman in your care misses a period, remind her to check with a doctor to see if she is pregnant,' he writes. 'If you are a substance abuser, think of the children and get help'; 'Get the kids out for a walk or a bike ride. Play catch with them. Take them to the playground'; 'As the children get older, introduce them to healthy meals with non-fried food, whole grains, lean meat, fish, chicken, and lots of fruits and vegetables'; 'If you suspect that your child has ADHD, get that boy or girl to see a mental health professional pronto.' And, 'For some kids today, the "great outdoors" is that small space between the car door and the front door. It shouldn't be that way. The beautiful thing about nature is that it doesn't care what colour you are. Fish don't discriminate – they don't want to be caught by anyone.'[15]

But these children are not being raised in a society with free medical care, adequate social services, accessible supermarkets selling cheap organic produce, and parents with the time, energy and wherewithal to make all that happen. It's hard work being poor, whether you have a job or not. The African proverb 'It takes a village to raise a child' became very popular in the United States in the nineties. But most African Americans don't live in villages. Many live in impoverished, isolated urban communities, and few Americans, it seems, really want to talk honestly and practically about what it takes to 'raise a child' in those conditions.

After a sixteen-year-old was shot dead in Dallas on the day profiled in this book, the first comment at the bottom of an online story came from Marg Bargas, who said, 'I have two adult kiddos and there's no way they would've been out walking streets after dark, AND I always knew where they were. I do not blame the victims but all parents could do better.' The boy in question was accompanying his friend on the short walk home to his grandmother's house after a family night of drinking cocoa, playing Uno, and watching a film with his mom, friend and sister. His mother, a loving and attentive parent we'll meet later in the book, knew exactly where he was; she just couldn't save him.

Parks, youth clubs and other facilities in these areas are either of poor quality or non-existent. Schools are often of a low standard and either unsafe or policed like prisons – neither of which are conducive to good learning. If a family doesn't have a car, the museums and other facilities located in town centres or in the suburbs are difficult to get to. And even if a family does have a car, such attractions are expensive. On top of all that, parents are often stressed by trying to keep it together in a low-wage economy. I once interviewed a family in Los Angeles with three sons, each of whom had spent time in jail and two of whom were in for life. When I asked the mother where she thought it all went wrong, she said she'd had no idea they'd been involved in crime from an early age because she was holding down two jobs just to feed them.

Toshiba was not entirely on her own. Mario did his best with Stanley, as did another elementary school teacher she remembered, Ms Hepfinger. 'She would come get him and take him places,' she said. 'She really came through.' Toshiba felt she had done everything in her power to keep Stanley out of trouble since he was very young. 'Stanley was a handful,' she says. 'He just always kept me going. Always kept me busy. I'm always in school. Always everywhere.' Her task sounded like a blend of the Sisyphean and the Herculean: a relentless, uphill battle of overwhelming scale. 'I tried,' she says, her eyes welling and voice cracking.

'Youth', according to a saying attributed to the German playwright Bertolt Brecht, 'is when you blame your troubles on your parents; maturity is when you learn that everything is the fault of the younger generation.' It is a rare generation, of any race or era, that believes their children are more moral, respectful or diligent than themselves. Legendary anchor Tom Brokaw hailed those who grew up during the Depression and then went on to fight the Second World War as 'The Greatest Generation'.[16] But I doubt their parents, who were raised at the turn of the century, regarded their offspring as such.

In this respect, African Americans are no different from anyone else. On 17 May 2004, to commemorate the fiftieth anniversary of *Brown v. Board of Education*, the Supreme Court ruling that banned segregation, Bill Cosby delivered a speech at an award ceremony for the nation's oldest civil rights organisation, the National Association for the Advancement of Colored People. Cosby used his address to berate working-class black Americans for their fecklessness in the face of the opportunities made available by the civil rights movement. 'Ladies and gentlemen, these people, they opened the doors, they gave us the right, and today . . . in our cities and public schools we have 50 per cent drop out . . . Ladies and gentlemen, the lower economic and lower middle economic people are not holding their end in this deal.'[17]

To great applause, he lambasted poor parenting. 'I'm talking about these people who cry when their son is standing there in an orange suit. Where were you when he was two? Where were you when he was twelve? Where were you when he was eighteen, and how come you don't know he had a pistol? . . . These people are not parenting. They're buying things for the kid. $500 sneakers, for what? They won't buy or spend $250 on *Hooked on Phonics*.'[18]

In what became known as the 'pound cake speech' he ridiculed a victim mentality that slams police brutality without first addressing personal responsibility. 'Looking at the incarcerated, these are not political criminals . . . People getting shot in the back of the head over a piece of pound cake! Then we all run out and are outraged, "The cops shouldn't have shot him." What the hell was he doing with the pound cake in his hand?'[19]

His speech was greeted with a standing ovation by his immediate audience but sparked controversy elsewhere. Some praised him for his candour and for using his platform to pry open a conversation that either was not taking place or was taking place behind closed doors. Others condemned him for pouring scorn and ridicule on society's poorest and most embattled.

His most strident critic was academic Michael Eric Dyson, who responded with a book, *Is Bill Cosby Right? Or Has the Black Middle Class Lost Its Mind?*, in which he slammed Cosby for spinning a 'thin descriptive web' of 'flawed logic'.[20] As part of his breathless polemic, Dyson unearthed a study, *Morals and Manners Among Negro Americans in 1914*, that illustrates how the thrust of Cosby's observations has remained consistent over time even as the generations have changed. One respondent from Arkansas, almost a century earlier, was quoted in the study as saying, 'There is a tendency to permit children to have too many liberties before they are really able to see for themselves or really know what are the consequences that result from too early taking upon themselves the responsibility which belongs to mature years and I believe the parent is wholly in error.' Another from Georgia claims, 'I do not think that parents are quite as strict with their children as they were when I was a child.' During the interwar years, a columnist in the *Amsterdam News*, New York's principal black newspaper, opined that young blacks who insisted that racism gave them no chance to get ahead should 'deport [themselves] with greater decorum and decency on street cars' and stop behaving 'like so many jungle apes'.

Dyson concludes, 'The themes that occupy black life now – how well we're attending to our children, how much of pop culture they should consume, the role of religion in their values education, the training that poor parents need to succeed, the economic and social barriers that prevent their flourishing – have been a consistent worry of black life for at least a couple of centuries.'[21]

Toshiba certainly believes that opportunities for youth have declined since she was young. 'When we were coming up, even though I stayed in the projects, we always had something to do,' she says. 'We had a centre to go to. We went to parties. Everybody got home safe. This generation has changed.' Most generations do. But statistics suggest that many such recollections owe more to nostalgia for the past or despair about the present than to what actually happened then or is happening now. The murder rate in Charlotte today, for example, is close to half of what it was when Mario was Stanley's age. Rapes, robberies, assaults, burglaries and car thefts have nosedived by a similar rate.[22] In other words, it's likely that fewer partygoers were getting home safe in Toshiba's day than they are now.

According to the Adolescent Pregnancy Prevention Campaign of North Carolina, when Mario was Stanley's age, the pregnancy rate for teens aged fifteen to nineteen in Mecklenburg County, which includes Charlotte, was more than double what it is now.[23] Meanwhile, the rate of teenage black pregnancies in the county fell by 39 per cent between 2007 and 2012 and continues to drop each year.[24] Most of the ills associated with the most acute and calamitous moral declines – shootings, crime, teen pregnancy – are actually improving.

It's not difficult to see where people get the impression that trends are heading in the opposite direction. Many of the assumptions that inform public commentary about black life are, in fact, misinformed. Take just two examples. It's widely assumed that African Americans are more likely to take drugs than any other racial group. That's not true. According to the Inter-university Consortium for Political and Social Research, whites are considerably more likely than blacks to have ever used cocaine, hallucinogens, marijuana, LSD, stimulants such as crystal meth, and pain relievers including oxycontin. While African Americans were more likely to have used some of those drugs in the last thirty days, the only drug African Americans were more likely to have ever tried was crack.[25]

It's also widely assumed that black men routinely abandon their children. That's also not true. Black people are less likely to marry than whites, and black men are less likely to live with their partners. But according to the National Center for Health Statistics, when children are under the age of five, black fathers are more likely to feed or eat meals with them, bathe, change their nappies, dress them and read to them daily than fathers in any other racial group, whether they live with their kids or not. As their children get older, black fathers are more likely to take children to and from activities daily, talk to them about their day, and help them with their homework. Black men are also disproportionately more likely to be single parents than dads from other racial groups.[26]

The one aspect of black life that has changed dramatically since Toshiba and Mario were Stanley's age is incarceration rates. But that has less to do with a change in behaviour – over a generation crime is going down – than a change in policy; during that same time span prison numbers have shot up.[27]

These faulty assumptions matter because they feed into the notion that it is deficiencies in black culture in general and black parenting in particular that are responsible for the shootings, that on some level the shootings reflect the collective death wish of a community incapable of and unwilling to care for its young. So pervasive and ingrained are these views that the truth ceases to matter – they become scripts that many Americans repeat reflexively, and often uncritically, with all the confidence endowed by fact. The scripts are so ingrained that the very people denigrated by them recite them as if by rote.

Of the ten children covered in this book, seven were black, two were Hispanic, and one was white. All were working class and male. For now, if only to lighten the load on Toshiba's shoulders, let us focus on two key facets of American society.

First, America is not a meritocracy. 'Belief in America's essential fairness, that we live in a land of equal opportunity, helps bind us together,' writes Joseph Stiglitz in *The Price of Inequality: How Today's Divided Society Endangers Our Future*. 'That, at least, is the American myth, powerful and enduring. Increasingly, it is just that – a myth. Of course, there are exceptions, but for economists and sociologists what matters are not the few success stories but what happens to most of those at the bottom and in the middle.'[28]

Indeed, with each passing year, America is becoming more class-ridden and plutocratic. The gap between rich and poor grows, and the likelihood that the poor will become rich diminishes. Those who do move up expend great energy and money, and don't get very far. Poor kids who work hard and go to college still fare worse than rich kids who did badly in school.

Second, America is racist. Not all Americans. But America – its judiciary, economy and social fabric. How could it not be? It's only been fifty years since it ascended from an essentially apartheid state and African Americans secured the vote and their civil rights. Much has changed since then. Mixed-race relationships are at an all-time high,[29] black voter turnout is at least on a par with white,[30] and, of course, there is a black president.

But racism is a hardy virus that mutates to adapt to the body politic in which it is embedded. For all the ways in which America imagines itself colour-blind, the statistics suggest otherwise. African Americans are six times more likely to be incarcerated, twice as likely to be unemployed, and almost three times more likely to live in poverty than whites. The discrepancy between black and white wealth and income is greater now than it was at the time of the March on Washington in 1963,[31] and schools in the South are more segregated now than they have been for forty years.[32]

Michael Harrington, author of *The Other America*, argues that once the poor are born to the wrong parents, in the wrong part of the country, and in the wrong racial group, all but a few are doomed. 'Once that mistake has been made,' he writes, 'they could be paragons of will and morality, but most of them would never even have had a chance to get out of the other America.'[33]

America is not unique in this regard. Virtually every Western nation has racial and class hierarchies, and in much of the world inequalities are widening. But there are few countries where class distinctions are regarded as anathema to the nation's core belief system and where racial disparities are simultaneously so brazenly displayed and denied.

Before continuing, it is necessary to stop and frisk one last straw man who inevitably prowls any argument about structural inequality: personal responsibility. I have never heard anyone claim that individuals should not take responsibility for what they do. But lest there be any confusion: we all have free will. We all have agency. We all must take responsibility for what we do. Our life trajectories are not predetermined. These are essential tenets of our basic humanity. The fact that someone is poor or black or both does not give free licence to behave in a certain way or avoid the consequences of actions. I was raised black and poor (though in England, where race and class interact differently), and I have two black American children. I was raised to take responsibility for what I do, and that's the way I raise my kids.

This book is full of people who made bad decisions; as a result, some put themselves in the line of fire, while others pulled the trigger. Not all bad decisions are equal. Some of the people who populate these pages are dead; others are in prison; some are still walking the streets. In all likelihood, Demontre Rice was born black and working class just like Stanley, Judy and Mario. So race and class excuse nothing. They are not the crutches with which the misanthropic and morally ambivalent can prop themselves up as though standing tall.

But they can explain a great deal. The circumstances into which people are born and the range of opportunities to which they are exposed shape both the choices available to them and the process by which they make those choices even if they, ultimately, still make the choice. I have yet to meet anyone who denies that individuals have free will. But I also have yet to meet anyone who makes a convincing argument that circumstances don't shape what you can do with that will.

A paper presented to the Federal Reserve Bank of Boston's annual conference in October 2014 revealed that, by the time they get to the age of forty, high school dropouts born to rich families are as likely to be earning high salaries as college graduates from poor families.[34] Or as the *Washington Post* put it, 'Poor kids who do everything right don't do better than rich kids who do everything wrong.'[35]

Some beat the odds. In his career as a behaviour specialist, Mario can recall those who made it. 'I will say it's possible,' he concedes. There was a boy at Stanley's elementary school they called 'the runner'. 'He would get mad and start running. We ended up on [Interstate] 77 chasing this boy in and out of traffic,' says Mario with a smile. That boy managed to work his way out of behaviour class and into the mainstream. 'Now he's in his junior year in college,' says Mario. But the fact that he can even remember this particular case suggests that 'the runner' wasn't running with the pack. He was the one who got away.

Such stories don't change the odds. They just illustrate them. Failing to understand that seems like a chronic lack of imagination and empathy. 'Take a bunch of teenage boys from the whitest, safest suburb in America and plunk them down in a place where their friends are murdered and they are constantly attacked and threatened,' writes Leovy in *Ghettoside*. 'Signal that no one cares, and fail to solve murders. Limit their options for escape. Then see what happens.'[36]

Trey, Stanley's friend, made it out. He left Charlotte to study at Benedict College, a historically black college in Columbia, South Carolina. 'Before I left, I was in the same predicament as everybody. I weren't too focused. I was always in trouble. With the wrong crowd and the police.' When I asked him what had steered him from the path that had taken both Stanley's and Ajewan's lives, he answered with one word. 'School. Once I got that acceptance letter . . . Oh snap. God let me try to change my life.' How he managed to apply himself, to separate himself from the bad influences, wasn't clear. Trey did not even know himself.

*

For all that, it is not difficult to see why so many critics – like Cosby, Mario and Williams – focus on parenting, albeit in different ways. It's not an inverted sense of racism that leads them there so much as a lack of alternative framings for what they can see and influence. The structural roots of this crisis are deep and horribly knotted. They include, among other things, race, class, geography, poverty, history, education, health, politics – a panoply of endemic issues over which people feel they have little control and for which the polity offers few solutions. Racism and poverty are not going away any time soon, so anyone interested in saving the lives of the young people they are working with right now might understandably see little benefit in utopian thinking and concentrate, instead, on what they feel they have some control over.

On no issue is this more evident than guns. When I asked an open-ended question to all the parents who lost children that day about why they thought these tragedies keep happening, firearms never came up. Guns are ever present. They're part of the reason why I'm meeting the families. But the connection between the prevalence of guns and the families' bereaved state is not initially acknowledged.

But it is there. When I asked them specifically, 'What do you think about guns?', all who had an opinion, which was most, would bemoan the fact that they are so freely available. But given that their children were killed less than a year after Sandy Hook and that, despite serious efforts from the White House, gun control legislation could not even make it out of the Democratic-controlled Senate, none of them expected anything to happen about it. Instead, most lamented the way in which adolescent arguments have now become deadly and reminisce about the good old days when disagreements between youths were settled by the ancient art of pugilism.

A father whose son died from a gunshot in Newark in the early hours of the following morning, and who will be featured later in this book, echoed the sentiments of many when he said, 'Back in the day, when we grew up, you get in a fight, somebody might jump you, you know, but the next day you speak to the person and you keep going. But now you get in an argument with somebody, they come back and shoot you.'

Most of the family members I spoke to evidently see the ubiquity of guns as a problem. But it does not necessarily follow that they see getting rid of guns as a viable solution. So child gun deaths, indeed any gun deaths, have become generally understood in the same way as car accidents. They are the unfortunate, if heavy, price one pays for living in twenty-first-century America. Even those at the roughest end of the problem can no more imagine ridding the country of guns, or limiting their distribution, than they can imagine getting rid of cars if their loved one were run over. It just would not be a feasible thing to consider. Indeed, with a car death there might be a local campaign to put up a stop sign or change the speed limit. At least no one would claim that was unconstitutional. But in virtually every case, on the day on which this book is set, the deaths prompted no broader question about the role of guns, let alone an engagement with the issue.

Even for those living with and combatting the consequences of gun violence, such as Mario, who organised the Million Youth March of Charlotte, challenging this element of the status quo is scarcely understood as a priority. When I explained the premise of the book, Mario understood it immediately. Why wouldn't he? The Million Youth March of Charlotte was founded in response to a shooting. Nonetheless, it's as though imagining a world without guns on this scale, like imagining a world without poverty or segregation, is the kind of utopian indulgence that serves no obvious purpose.

When I asked him whether gun control is part of MYMOC's agenda, he pauses. 'We haven't discussed that yet,' he says. 'I'm not for guns, to be honest. They have laws and regulations here. But you look at Facebook, and it's nothing to see a teenager holding a gun. And that bothers me. They can get it just like that.'

In 2010, when the NRA held its annual convention in Charlotte, Judy Williams protested. They staged a mock funeral with all the names of those who had died by gun violence taped to the casket. 'I don't think the Second Amendment means what they think it means,' she says. 'You can dress it up and take it to church, but that don't make it right that there should be no control.' If the NRA were coming back next year, would she do it again? I ask. She pauses. 'The reality of it is they are not going to do away with guns in this country . . . The fact is that they are so plentiful on the streets and people have them . . . It's ludicrous to think you can take guns out of people's homes in this country . . . It ain't gonna happen.'

But would she protest or not? Another pause. 'I would, because I don't think they should be as easy to access as they are, and they could change the laws. I think a lot of murders wouldn't occur if people didn't have access to a gun.' But even she, who has dedicated so much of her life to supporting families whose loved ones were slain by guns and who believes such laws are necessary, also, deep down, believes they would be ineffective. 'Most of the guns used in crime are illegal guns. So even if you change the law, felons don't care nothing about the law.'

By the time the anniversary of Stanley's death had come around, the graffiti at the Marathon petrol station had been painted over. His former girlfriend had had a baby by another man, which had seriously upset Trey. Ms Hepfinger, with whom Toshiba had lost contact, wrote on the online register, 'I will always have great memories of Stanley. He touched my life and many others. He was a student of mine at Walter G. Byers and I will miss him. I am thinking of you and your family.'

In August 2014 Mario was honoured at the Trailblazers 100 event for his service to the community. On the anniversary of Stanley's death, Mario posted on Facebook, 'I have had a lot going on the last few weeks, that I honestly thought I would wake up and be alright today. Who was I kidding, I woke up in tears, it hit me so hard as if it just happened. It's so hard to believe that a whole 365 days have gone by and today marks one year since your life was cut so short . . . So I say continue to Rest Easy Stanley N. Taylor, Rest In Paradise.'

When we met the first time, in early March 2014, he'd been planning to hold a demonstration in late May to raise the issues confronting the city's youth. 'We're going to make it a family day,' he said, before going on to list a couple of the key elements. 'There'll be giveaways, marching bands preferably.'

Even back then, he was disappointed by the lack of support his initiative was receiving from community leaders. 'When I first started, my goal was to get the city to embrace it and churches to embrace it,' he said. 'But it hasn't happened like that. It's like pulling teeth. You'd think that with doing something positive for the youth that more would get involved. But I'm having a hard time getting the city leaders involved. The same people who are talking about it won't do anything about it. Having a hard time getting donations. We need donations. Everything we're doing is coming out of our pockets. All churches have youth groups, and you'd think they'd want to be involved in something positive like that. We're at a standstill because we don't have donations.' He was worried they might not make their goal of a march on 31 May. 'Time is steadily ticking.'

When I caught up with him for a second interview in December 2014 at MYMOC's second Community Give Back Day, the clock was still running. The march had not taken place, but nationally the #BlackLivesMatter movement had taken off. Eric Garner's killer had just escaped indictment by a grand jury. Darren Wilson, the policeman who shot Michael Brown, had also walked free from a grand jury, and the embers in Ferguson still glowed dimly. After lighting a candle for Ajewan, those assembled held a minute's silence for the Garner and Brown families. The march had first been postponed until late July and was now on hold indefinitely until they could summon the funds and political support. As he picked up icing from the carpet and pleaded with the children to take their sticky cakes into the hall, I asked him what he thought the problem was. He sighed. 'I wish I knew. We've *tried*. We've *really tried*.'

4

Pedro Cortez
(aged eighteen)

San Jose, California
23 November, 4.22 p.m. PST

Capitol Park, in East San Jose, sits at the foot of the Diablo mountain range, ensconced in childhood fantasy. It's a vast patch of green with a playground, fenced-off basketball courts and soccer fields, picnic tables, barbecue grills, a baseball diamond, and a school. It's bordered by Bambi Lane, Van Winkle Lane, Peter Pan Avenue, and Galahad Avenue. From here you can either wander off on the Lower Silver Creek Trail – a 6.5-mile walk that will, once developed, take you from Lake Cunningham Park to the Coyote Creek Trail – or leave the area on Cinderella Lane. The yards of the modestly sized bungalows that surround the park in this mostly Latino area boast lush greenery, including palm trees and the occasional fountain. It was by far the most scenic place where any child lost his life to gunfire that day and had the most expensive property (you could sell a house here and use the proceeds to buy seven houses where Stanley Taylor was shot). At sixty-four degrees with a light wind, it was also the warmest.

In the late eighteenth century, San Jose belonged to the Spanish, which made it the first civilian town in their colony of Nueva California. It passed to the Mexicans in 1821, only to join the United States in 1850. Today the turf is claimed by the Norteños, a constellation of gangs loosely affiliated with the Nuestra Familia, a Chicano prison gang. *Norteños* means Northerners – more precisely, Northern Californians. They wear red, often have tattoos with four dots on their hands or at the corner of their eyes, and may sport the number 14 – *N* is the fourteenth letter in the alphabet. More Americanised than other Latino gangs, some of their members may not even speak Spanish. They also lay claim to the imagery of and nostalgia for the Latino American labour movement in general, and labour leader Cesar Chavez in particular, who came into contact with many Norteños while he was imprisoned for his union work.

Their principal rival gang, the Sureños (Southerners), is larger but less well organised and has its base in Southern California; they wear blue and sport tattoos with three dots. The widely recognised border between North and South is 240 miles south of San Jose in Bakersfield. 'It is true that this is marked territory,' Arturo Dado told the *San Jose Mercury* a few days after he lost his grandson. 'It is marked red.'[1]

On 23 November 2013, Arturo's grandson, eighteen-year-old Pedro Dado Cortez, wore black. His family insists he was not a gang member, although they feared he might be attracted to gang life. 'I used to take away his red clothing,' said Silvia Dado, his grandmother.[2] 'He would always say he would be fine, to not worry about him or his friends, but I would worry anyway and still get rid of his red shirts.' Pedro lived with his grandparents, who described him as 'popular but naive'. 'They just like to hang out the way young men do,' said Arturo. 'And they didn't carry guns, shoot at people or rob them – none of that.'[3]

To friends and family, Pedro went by Junior or Moko. In most pictures he wears a wide-peaked baseball cap and a relaxed smile crowned with peach fuzz. In memorial videos he's nearly always got his arm around someone – his sister or an assortment of young women – often with a bottle of Hennessy in the other hand. In one YouTube video he lip syncs to *Beautiful Girls*, dancing his way in and out of self-consciousness as his friends, entangled in a pile on a mattress, laugh in encouragement. Pedro was legally blind – with a condition that had deteriorated considerably since he was thirteen – but managed to get by with what sight he had. He wore powerful contact lenses that he said were painful. He had dropped out of school and worked for his stepfather in a moving company. He was still hopeful that he could save up enough money to learn to drive and get a car.

Although he and one of his friends were wearing black that afternoon, it's believed that another in their group might have been wearing red. They were walking up Van Winkle Lane at around four – in broad daylight and a very public place. This, it turns out, is the most dangerous time to be out in a gang-ridden area.

In several studies of gang homicides in Los Angeles, researchers uncovered a range of characteristics that distinguish gang killings from other killings. They are more likely to take place on the street, involve guns and cars, take place in the late afternoon and have more participants of younger ages, usually men.[4]

To that extent, Pedro's assassination was a textbook case. Before dusk could roll over the Diablo mountains, a black Camaro convertible pulled up alongside him and his friends, and a gunman wearing a bandanna over his face started shooting. The car then 'took off burning rubber', most likely down Galahad or Peter Pan, leaving Pedro with a bullet in the heart. He died right there. According to one local website, over the next twenty-four hours East San Jose crackled with gunfire in apparent retaliation, with some homes being shot at.[5] That morning, Pedro had called his sister, Miranda Brianna, with whom he was close, just for a chat. That evening she downed some Hennessy – his favourite drink – in his memory: Pedro was on the 'Heeeeeen Team'.

'Blue, red, orange, none of that is going to save you,' his stepfather told youngsters at a candlelit vigil in the park a few days later, listing the gang colours as his face flickered in the flames. 'That didn't save my Junior. I was supposed to be working with him today. Instead I went to work alone,' he said, his voice cracking and eyes welling. 'I cried in the elevator.' One of Pedro's memorial videos, showing pictures of him in everything from a tux to three-quarter-length shorts, scrolled to the sound of Philthy Rich's 'Thinking of You', a rap ballad with a sampling of Diana Ross:

> Shit is all the same, niggas die, mommas cry
> Bitches turn sour now she fucking on that other guy . . .
> Nothing to live for, my niggas doing life sentences
> Either dead or in jail we doing life sentences.

Finding money to bury Pedro was a problem. A fundraising site went up. 'Please help with anything,' asked his aunt. On the Wednesday after his death, they held a car wash. At the vigil people collected coins and bills. It was more than two weeks before Pedro was finally laid to rest. According to her Facebook postings, by that time Miranda was struggling to get out of bed in the morning; by the New Year she was worried about her drinking. Requests went out for people not to wear gang colours to Pedro's funeral. 'No colours, no drama,' Miranda wrote on Facebook, 'we are trying to have a good time saying our last goodbyes to Junior.'

In most US cities where children got shot on the day profiled in this book, such a murder would have barely made it through a twenty-four-hour media cycle. A few seconds on the television, maybe. A few hundred words in the paper with a quote from a family member, maybe – and that's it. If the perpetrator was caught, that too would merit a couple of hundred words. An event of note, but of precious little import. Pedro's murder was different. His death appeared not only on the evening news in San Jose and in the next day's paper but also in follow-up TV bulletins from the family vigil in the park a few days later and in a feature by *San Jose Mercury* columnist Joe Rodriguez subtitled 'Teen Slain on Streets Named for Kids' Tales'. 'In a neighbourhood inspired by imagination and fantasy,' he wrote, 'a starkness had set in, and there is a fear over what may come next.'[6]

Much was made of the fact that Pedro was the city's forty-fourth homicide victim of the year.[7] That's forty-four too many. But still, for a city of San Jose's size, by American standards it's not that high. Most bother to count only if the homicide rate reaches a round number or a significant milestone, like exceeding the previous record or last year's figure. Compared to other cities and towns featured in this book, only Grove City, where Jaiden Dixon was shot the day before, had a lower homicide rate. The deadliest city of all, Newark, had a rate more than ten times as high.[8]

But San Jose is different. It has grown exponentially since the Second World War to become the nation's tenth largest city. Between 1950 and 1970 its population grew fivefold[9] as large numbers of people relocated there after the war; between 1990 and 2010 it leapt another 20 per cent[10] thanks to the tech boom and immigration. 'It used to be a cow town,' a friend from Oakland told me. 'And then Silicon Valley happened, and it just blew up.' The consequent low-rise sprawl gives the city a distinctly suburban feel; it seems you are rarely more than fifteen minutes from anywhere but will probably have to take the interstate or the freeway to get there. It's a city dwarfed in reputation by its two closest neighbours, San Francisco and Oakland, even as it continues to outgrow them.

Expansion brought its problems. San Jose once prided itself on the sobriquet 'Safest Big City in America'. By the beginning of 2013, it was the fifth safest. It had a higher crime rate than the rest of America, and yet police were catching half as many criminals as they had a few years earlier.[11] 'San Jose never compared itself to places like Newark or Chicago,' explains Rodriguez, the newspaper columnist. We met one night for drinks while I was in town trying to find Pedro's family. 'It compares itself to how it used to be. Things went downhill pretty fast. When you're doing really well and then suddenly you're not, then you take the fall badly. It's like *Paradise Lost*. So at the paper we followed up on all the deaths, because in San Jose these kind of shootings are still news.'

Four days after Pedro was shot, at around 8.30 p.m., San Jose Police Department's Covert Response Unit, along with patrol officers, dogs and officers from the Gang Suppression Unit, arrested twenty-year-old Balam Eugenio Gonzalez. He had bushy black eyebrows and thick black hair, compensating for what might one day pass for a moustache. They booked him immediately for Pedro's murder but did not release his name for another few days, citing the sensitivity of the investigation. They believed the murder was gang-related, making it the tenth such homicide that year.[12]

After two and a half years in prison, Balam was also charged with the fatal shooting of Armondo Miguel Heredia on 23 August 2012 as well as the attempted murder, on 18 August, in another drive-by shooting that left one person wounded.[13]

I'm a linguist by training. I studied to be an interpreter and translator in French and Russian, and hoped to be a Moscow correspondent one day. Then I did a placement at the *Washington Post*, fell in love with an American, and ended up there instead. From the time I was first posted in New York, I intended to learn Spanish but never did. For the most part, I could get away with it. When I went out west there were translators, and sometimes down south people would translate for me and I would muddle through. It wasn't ideal. But, thanks to my linguistic privilege, as an English speaker, I could function. However, in stories as sensitive as this, in communities that can be hard to reach, my inability to speak Spanish could have been a problem.

From everything I could tell from their Facebook pages, most of Pedro's family spoke English, although his grandparents, with whom he lived, spoke Spanish. I left notes and messages for them everywhere I could on social media. I sent letters (some translated into Spanish) everywhere I thought they might be in San Jose. I flew to San Jose and knocked on the doors for which I had addresses. I received no response. At this point I just started asking around. Elsewhere in the country, while pursuing stories for this book, that has worked. Here it didn't. Not because nobody spoke English. I'm sure lots of people did. But in a gang-rife area that is 90 per cent Latino, a black man with an English accent asking if anyone knew the family of a Latino teenager who'd been shot just couldn't win the confidence of those who had come to the park to watch their children play and to have a stroll. It was one variable too many. Aside from Kenneth, Pedro was the only other child who was killed that day with whose family or friends I did not make a connection.

On the first day I walked around Capitol Park, where Pedro was shot, I saw a small shrine to his death next to the entrance sign. Some synthetic roses and a candle with a picture of the Virgin Mary on it – the kind that adorns so many sites of gun shootings – had been placed under it. Had I just stood there for twenty-four hours, rather than racing around to different addresses, I would certainly have met someone, for the next afternoon I came back, and the shrine was still there with one addition: an empty bottle of Hennessy – Pedro's favourite tipple.

5

Tyler Dunn
(aged eleven)

Marlette, Michigan
23 November, 8.19 p.m. EST

As clouds glowered over rural Michigan, three long, sharp, discordant beeps sounded in slow, even succession over my car radio, followed by a dispassionate voice warning of extreme weather on every available station. In measured, urgent, intrusive tones, it promised conditions that were not just extreme – thunderstorms, lightning, flash flooding – but almost biblical in their impact. Hail was coming, the voice said, that might ruin your roof, lightning that could kill, weather so ferocious one should stay away from windows. These calamities, I was warned, would be moving through counties I had never heard of, which meant I had no idea whether I was heading towards the storm or away from it.

But there was little reason to worry. Unlike in the city, where weather creeps up on your built environment and then mugs you unawares, here it made its presence and intentions clear long before it approached. The horizon is so broad, the landscape so sparse, and the sky so huge that the weather declares itself with great ceremony. Long streaks of lightning cracked at the early-morning sky to the west like a huge cosmic whip. The clouds brooding in the distance were drifting south and west and clearing on their journey. Despite the dire warnings from my car radio as I headed northeast, towards Michigan's thumb, I could see that the storm was skirting around me.

Sanilac County, where I was heading, has a lower population density than Finland[1] and is slightly less racially diverse than Norway (it is over 95 per cent white).[2] According to Michigan's Department of Agriculture, Sanilac leads the state in its acreage devoted to soy, corn, wheat, dairy farms and general cattle operations, and is third in its acreage dedicated to sugar beets.[3] Straight roads lead past silos, Dutch barns, rows of corn, grazing livestock and fallow fields interspersed with the occasional township and homestead as you head towards Lake Huron (one of the Greats), which serves as its eastern border.

Marlette, population 1,879, lies on Sanilac's southwest flank, the third-biggest town and a twenty-five-minute drive to the county seat of Sandusky. The shiny blue watertower bearing the town's name announces itself from afar to the left while McDonald's golden arches peer over the trees to the right. From the south, the first sign welcoming you into town bears the motto 'MARLETTE, THE HEART OF THE THUMB'. Underneath the second sign, which simply states 'MARLETTE CITY LIMIT', is a footnote of sorts boasting, 'HOME OF THE BOYS' CROSS COUNTRY DIV 3 STATE CHAMPION RUNNER UP'. The nearest cinema is in Sandusky; you're about a half-hour drive from the nearest Starbucks and non-Christian bookshop.

Long ago, writes Kate McGill, one of the town's early settlers, in *The Beginnings of Marlette,* this 'had been the home of the Sauk Indians, later of the Chippewas. But the settlements at Detroit had driven them back until in 1854 only a few scattering bands remained. Through the primeval forests, guided only by the blazed trail of the woodsman surveyor, came the hardy pioneer, to hew out for himself a home and fortune in the new land.'[4]

The Irish and Scots in Ontario, Canada, 'loaded their guns, sharpened their axes and came to investigate', floating over the Huron. Rumours had swirled of 'tall timber and fertile soil that was almost free for the asking',[5] and gradually the immigrants made the area their own. A century and a half later it feels like the town that ate Gilbert Grape by day; driving through by night, particularly during the winter, you feel like an extra in the movie *Fargo*.

Brittany Dunn, aged twenty, wouldn't be anywhere else. 'I'd rather live here than in the city,' she says. 'It's more laid back,' says her grandmother, Janet Allen, who moved the 70 miles from White Lake for the 'peace and quiet'. 'You've got your own space,' continues Brittany. 'In the city you're, like, on top of each other, neighbour to neighbour.' I was sitting in a pizzeria opposite Marlette's only Chinese restaurant, with four generations of the Dunn family: Janet, Lora Dunn Bartz (Janet's daughter), Brittany (Lora's daughter), and Ciannah (Brittany's very well-behaved seven-month-old baby), as well as Thomas Bartz, Lora's husband. 'Doesn't it get boring?' I ask.

'No,' says Lora. 'It doesn't get boring. It's like a journey if you have to go to the mall or something. It's like a day's worth of travelling.' She says this as though it's a good thing, allowing her poker face to give way to a wry smile.

This vast expanse of land, both fertile and fallow, wild and tamed, was her son's playground. To a city dweller like me, Tyler's outdoor hobbies make him sound like a character from a Mark Twain novel. Tyler Dunn, who was eleven when he died, loved trapping critters, hunting, catching fish in the creek behind the house, four-wheeling and dirt-biking in the summer, and sledding in the winter. 'When children are demonised by the newspapers, they are often described as feral,' wrote George Monbiot in the *Guardian*.[6] 'But feral is what children should be: it means released from captivity or domestication. Those who live in crowded flats, surrounded by concrete, mown grass and other people's property, cannot escape their captivity without breaking the law. Games and explorations that are seen as healthy in the countryside are criminalised in the cities. Children who have never visited the countryside live under constant restraint.'

By this definition, Tyler was semi-feral. He was free to roam and explore and engage with the natural world, and was trusted to do so with precious few constraints. The Dunns lived three miles down a dirt road off Highway 53, which runs straight from the interstate into Marlette. Several miles from the nearest traffic light – or even streetlight – and surrounded by fields, he was safe to do 'his own thing' and have his parents check in on him occasionally.

Yet the call to the wild was always competing with the call to the screen. Like Jaiden, his favourite TV show was *Duck Dynasty*, with *Spongebob* and *Family Guy* close runners-up. But it was gaming that really had him hooked. When he accompanied his parents on errands, he'd take a computer game with him. At home, he'd keep to himself, texting friends on his mother's phone. And he loved video games. Particularly Call of Duty, which morphs modern warfare into entertainment. Mark Twain never had these distractions; if he had, *Huckleberry Finn* would, no doubt, have turned out quite differently, if Twain had got around to writing it at all.

'Whenever he came to my house, it was just a weekend of Call of Duty,' says Brittany. 'That's all I heard on the TV.'

'Then he came over to our house and he just raced cars,' says Janet, referring to a different video game.

'That's because you didn't have Call of Duty,' explained Lora.

Tyler had a round, almost perfectly spherical face, crowned with a crew cut. To look at his pictures from infancy, it's as though he never really lost his puppy fat – he simply grew into it and developed a character that suited it, with a slight dimple in his chin, a button for his nose, and full cheeks that an overly familiar adult might just lose their fingers in. He was, by all accounts, a happy kid. When he was in fifth grade, his class was across the hall from sixth-grade teacher Luke Reynolds. Whenever Luke saw Tyler they would fist-bump. 'I don't know how it started or why,' says Luke. 'But that's what we always did. We wouldn't even say anything. Just bump, smile, and keep walking.' The next year, Luke was his class teacher. 'He was just a very easy kid. There were never any discipline problems. He always seemed pretty content.'

With a willing audience at home, Tyler was happy to be both the jester and the butt of the jokes. Brittany moved away to live with her boyfriend, leaving Tyler with his mother, two other sisters, and Thomas, who was technically his stepfather, although he'd always been present in Tyler's life. Janet tells how he'd 'wiggle his butt like a worm' to the 'girly songs' when he was smaller. Another time, at Brittany's graduation, he allowed his sisters Ashley, fifteen, and Tiffany, seventeen, to duct-tape him to a tree. 'He was only there for a few minutes,' insists Brittany. In one picture that regularly resurfaces on Facebook, he stands bare-chested with a big smile and a bra made out of two coconut halves that Ashley had worn to a Hawaiian-themed birthday party a year or so earlier.

Tyler came by those full, fleshy cheeks honestly. Lora, his mother, bears a resemblance to Roseanne Barr, and Brittany shares his features. When I asked them what he liked doing, their first response, as a chorus, was 'eating'.

'He loved food,' said Lora. 'Junk food.'

'Grandma used to make these little crabbie patties,' recalls Brittany. 'And those hamburgers. He'd eat those. Nobody else could get one.'

'Actually, he did take a bunch one day,' Janet says, recalling Tyler in the act of a flattering transgression. 'There was a bunch in his pockets.'

'Saving them for later, probably,' said Brittany.

One of the rare moments of disagreement between them came when I asked if he was spoiled. 'Yes,' said Brittany and Janet, as one and without hesitation.

'No,' said Lora, somewhat unconvincingly.

'Yes, he was,' repeated grandmother and granddaughter in disbelief.

Brittany took up the case and ran with it. 'He was the only boy out of three girls, he's the youngest, he's the baby; yes, he was spoiled,' she said, with an air of resignation rather than resentment. "Mom, so-and-so's picking on me,"' she said, imitating Tyler. 'And then the girls would get in trouble. Tyler never did anything. Never had to do his own laundry. He was spoiled.'

Lora looks down at her pizza with half a smile, refusing to admit an indulgence that she is pleased others have noticed. 'He wasn't spoiled,' she mutters.

But he could be sedentary. When he was doing something with a clear goal, like fishing or hunting, he was engaged. But exercise for its own sake – competitive sports, for example – was of little interest. 'I don't know if he was so into the gym thing,' said Lora, when I asked what he liked doing at school. 'He'd rather sit than move.' If there was work to be done, he'd find a way to avoid it. When the men in the family went to fetch wood one winter, Tyler was found in a ditch, making snow angels.

Because all the other children who died that day lived in cities, towns or suburbs, they were almost certainly oblivious to the fact that hunting season had just begun. In this part of Michigan, around 23 November, you couldn't avoid it. Deer hunting had started only a week earlier, on 15 November; pheasant shooting had started on Wednesday, 20 November. In late autumn, churches in Marlette advertise evenings for 'deer widows', and men bond in search of prey and tall tales.

'Tradition here in the Thumb is that the opening day of pheasant-hunting season and deer-hunting season, you can just about close all the schools because the kids are going hunting,' the Sanilac County sheriff, Garry Biniecki, told me. 'You go and try and get a seat at the downtown restaurant in Sandusky, and you'll probably have a hard time because there'll be this mass army of orange.' Orange is the colour of hunting uniforms worn to identify people so they're less likely to get shot. 'It's an exciting time.'

With the exception of Tyler, hunting season didn't particularly excite the Dunns. Apart from his paternal uncles, none of his immediate family hunted. And although Tyler enjoyed field sports, there is little evidence he was particularly good at them. He had never, to anyone's knowledge, successfully shot a living thing. He had only a pellet gun and an airsoft gun of his own. He loved to fish in the creek behind the house, but he didn't have an awful lot to show for it. 'Sometimes he'd catch something about this big,' says Brittany, bringing her thumb and forefinger close together to indicate the trifling size of his haul.

One winter, Darren, her boyfriend, took Tyler trapping. 'They trapped for muskrat and things like that,' explains Brittany, barely concealing her disgust. 'You put a trap in the ditches. You catch 'em and then you skin 'em and then you cook 'em . . . Yeah. Nasty. It's gross. Real nasty . . . He liked that.' But for more regular hunting trips, Tyler turned to his friend Brandon (not his real name). Brandon lived about a mile away (which in these parts qualifies as 'round the corner'), towards town, on a dirt road off Tyler's dirt road. Brandon, aged twelve, would sometimes come down and pick up Tyler on his pre-teen hybrid – a go-cart with a monster truck body and a motor – and they would roam the neighbourhood on it together. They'd been friends since kindergarten. They weren't inseparable; both had other friends they liked to hang out with, and they occasionally fell out. Once, Lora told Tyler he could no longer play with Brandon after Brandon abandoned him in town and went off with another friend, leaving Tyler crying as he called his mom to come and pick him up. Their friendship also had a brief hiatus when Brandon moved to Colorado with his mother, Connie, who went there to care for her sister, who, according to the police report, was 'possibly dying of terminal cancer'.

But they were close. Rifle through Tyler's school pictures and Brandon will appear episodically. Connie brought Brandon back to Marlette to stay with his father, Jerry, for the 2013 school year. Jerry, who was separated from Connie, owned a trucking company. He had always played an active role in Brandon's life, and Connie encouraged that. Not long after Brandon returned, the two boys were having play dates again.

Jerry often took Brandon hunting and occasionally trucking, too. And if Tyler was over – he spent more time at Brandon's place than Brandon ever did at his – Jerry would take both of them. Jerry's truck runs, ferrying milk and topsoil around the Midwest, usually took him away for eleven hours at a time. When the boys went with him, he'd give them some money to help him out. Tyler loved it. Sometimes Jerry would have them sit up front in the truck with him; at other times they'd be in the back playing video games.

On Thursday, 21 November, Jerry had taken the boys hunting. Tyler had slept over at Brandon's on Friday night, and on Saturday the boys were scheduled to accompany Jerry in the truck down to Springfield, Ohio – a more or less straight run 260 miles south and back – to drop off a load from Michigan Peat. When Lora checked in with Tyler on Saturday afternoon, he asked her to bring his bike to Brandon's on her way to town. She dropped it off around 2 p.m., but the boys never did go biking because it was too cold: 18°F, with winds gusting at over twenty-five miles an hour.

Shortly before Jerry was about to leave for Ohio, the boys said they wanted to stay home and play on the computer. Jerry left them to it. He made this trip as often as three times a week, and Brandon took care of himself fine. Jerry would leave at 1 p.m., while Brandon was in school, and be back by 1 a.m. the following morning, when Brandon was in bed.

Evidently, the prospect of Jerry's leaving the boys unattended had been a concern to Lora. Usually, when she dropped Tyler off at Brandon's, she would check to see that Jerry was home. But this time, unbeknownst to her, when she dropped the bike off, Jerry was already on his way to Ohio. 'Tyler knew he wasn't allowed there unless there was supervision,' says Lora. But Tyler didn't call. Nor did Jerry. And Lora went out with Thomas to celebrate a girlfriend's birthday ninety minutes away in Union Lake.

Jerry checked in with the boys a few times throughout the afternoon while they played Xbox. The last time Brandon called Jerry was around 6.30 p.m., when Brandon asked if he could order pizza from Treve's in town.

Almost two hours later, Brandon walked out of the house with his hands up, wearing red shorts with no shirt or socks, the police telling him to keep his hands where they could see them. He had just called 911 and told them he had shot Tyler.

'Do you have any weapons?' the policeman yelled.

'No,' said Brandon. 'It's on the kitchen floor.'

Another police car arrived. A policeman walked Brandon to his car as Brandon pleaded, 'It was an accident. I didn't know the gun was loaded.'

According to the police report, a police officer went inside the house, where he found a lever-action rifle on the kitchen floor and Tyler lying on the dining-room floor, in a Mountain Dew T-shirt and sweatpants, with a large pool of blood surrounding his head. He wasn't breathing or moving. There was a huge wound on the left side of his head. The policeman checked for a pulse but found none, called dispatch, and told them Tyler was dead. As he got up to leave the house, he saw a shotgun lying on the living room couch and four holes in the dining-room window.

Nobody but Brandon will ever know for sure what happened that night, says Sheriff Biniecki. Brandon claims they were playing Xbox when he got a rifle out of Jerry's closet to show to Tyler in the dining room. He didn't know it was loaded when he asked Tyler to take hold of it while he went to get his milkshake from his bedroom. He came back with the milkshake, put it on the table, and took the rifle from Tyler, who passed it to him butt first with the muzzle pointing in Tyler's direction. They had finished looking at it, and Brandon was resting it against the wall when the gun got caught on his shorts pocket and went off. He called 911. '[I called them] to bring an ambulance because my friend was hurt,' he later told the detective in Sandusky. 'All they sent were cops, and when the cops showed up they put me in a car, and now I am here.'

Biniecki considers Brandon's account, which he re-enacted several times at the police station with a broomstick for a gun, as basically credible. 'But we believe either the gun was getting passed back to the boy, or the boy took the gun and was standing it up in a corner, and as he was doing so it went off. Obviously there had to have been one in the chamber, and obviously, with that kind of weapon, it had to have the hammer back and ready to fire.'

Back at the scene, Brandon sat in the car, apparently in shock and distress, while police combed the house. He'd been crying and was visibly shaken. When they searched him, they found in his shorts pocket two 12-gauge Remington buckshot shells and a mobile phone. There was blood on his hands and on the phone. As he was placed in the back of the car, he repeated, 'We were just messing around. I didn't know the gun was loaded.' In an indication of quite how feral the day had been, when asked how he'd come by the shells in his pocket, Brandon explained that he'd found them in his bedroom earlier that day when looking for sparklers and had stuck them in his pocket for safekeeping.

Outside the house, tape went up and more cars arrived, bringing officers, detectives and crime scene investigators. The officer who arrived first checked on Brandon occasionally to find him either distressed or bored: you get the impression of a frightened boy struggling to make a connection between the irreversible tragedy he has just caused, the horror he has just witnessed and the enormity of the trouble he is now in as a result. Asked how he was doing, he replied, 'Not good. I just shot my best friend.' Throughout the night he kept asking for his phone so he could at least play games on it while he waited, worrying about where he would be sleeping that night, and saying he wished he'd stayed in Colorado with his mom. He eventually fell asleep for about half an hour before being woken by an officer and told he was being taken to Sandusky for questioning.

Inside, they searched the property to discover a veritable arsenal. In Brandon's room was a Remington 1100 shotgun, loaded and perched against the dresser with one round in the chamber and four in the pipe. Brandon says his father had originally left the gun in the kitchen but then moved it to his room when he had company over. There were also two other single-shot shotguns (a New England

Firearms and a Winchester 370) near the closet. In the top dresser drawer were some marijuana in tin foil and two rolled joints.

When asked later how many guns he had in the house, Jerry couldn't quite remember. First he said seven or eight, only to recant, broaden the margin of error, and up the potential number, correcting himself to admit to between five and ten.

Brandon didn't know Tyler's address, but he could describe where his house was. The police went there to find only Tiffany and Ashley at home, who told them if they wanted an adult they should call their grandmother, Janet, who lived nearby. Janet came over shortly after midnight and was told the news. She called Lora. There was no reply. She kept calling for well over an hour and took Ashley and Tiffany back to her place for the night. Lora's mobile was dead. She'd left it in the car to charge. When she came out, she saw several missed calls from her mother and knew something was up. She dialled Janet. '

Are you on your way home?' her mom asked.

'No. Why?' said Lora.

'I think you need to come home,' said Janet.

Lora's mother wouldn't give an explanation over the phone, but that didn't unduly concern Lora. She assumed Ashley and Tiffany had thrown a party and been caught by their grandmother. She cut the night short and headed back to Marlette. Night falls heavy here, cloaking the land in uncluttered darkness. On dirt roads in the middle of fields with no street lamps for miles, the flashing lights of stationary police vehicles announce themselves with the force of a lighthouse.

Because Brandon's street was en route to her mother's house, Lora saw the lights flashing where she had last seen her son and drove towards them.

'I turned down there and called my mom. I got right in front of Brandon's house when she picked up.'

'Mom, do you have Tyler?' she asked.

'I think you'd better just come here,' said Janet.

'And then she put the sheriff lady on the phone,' recalls Lora.

'Don't go there. Just come here,' said the 'sheriff lady', and Lora obliged.

'There's been an accident,' the policewoman said.

'OK', said Lora, matter-of-factly.

'Your son's in Lapeer County Hospital.'

'OK,' said Lora. 'Why didn't you tell me that, because I just came through Lapeer?'

'No, Lora,' said the policewoman. 'Lora, he's been shot and killed.'

A year later, Lora is still upset at how the news was broken to her. 'So she made me think one thing, like that he was injured, and then turned around and changed it to another story, like he was dead.'

When Lora was halfway home from Union Lake, Jerry was in the lobby of the Sanilac County sheriff's office in Sandusky. It was 2 a.m. He had been called on his way back from his truck run. It had been a long day. He'd been asked to come and pick up Brandon, but he had no idea why. They asked him whether there were any custody issues between him and Connie, whether he often left his son alone, his opinion about Tyler, and whether he thought the two of them were responsible. Asked if any of his weapons were loaded, he said they might have been. Finally they asked if Brandon had taken hunter safety classes. Jerry said he hadn't because he was doing the apprenticeship programme, in which a child ten or older can hunt for two years without the safety certificate if he or she is in the company of an adult. Beyond that, he'd given Brandon only basic instructions. 'I told him to hold the gun with the barrel pointing in the air. Never to point the gun at anyone, and never put any shells in the gun unless you are outside.'

How that gun had got into Brandon's bedroom was a mystery to Jerry. He thought it had originally been in the living room and didn't remember moving it. All the guns in the house were his, he said, apart from the 20-gauge, which he'd bought Brandon for hunting. He said the .30-30 rifle that killed Tyler had been in his closet the whole time, and that he'd put three rounds in the tube roughly a year earlier and had not touched it since then.

Only then, when these preliminary questions were over, was Jerry told why Brandon was at the sheriff's office. On hearing the news, according to the police report, 'Jerry became quite emotional and acted normally for a person receiving the information that was provided to him.'

Jerry and Brandon were reunited so Brandon could be read his Miranda rights in Jerry's presence. Before the interview, the detective 'went over the truth/lie scenario' with Brandon to make sure he knew the difference. He also impressed on Brandon that if he didn't know the answer to any question the police asked him, he shouldn't guess, and it was OK to change his mind. Connie later told the police she'd never caught Brandon in a lie, though when he got in trouble in school he would occasionally offer only partial truths.

It was 2.30 a.m. when Brandon repeated his story. 'The gun fired when it was being lowered in a diagonal manner. It caught on a piece of my shorts by the pocket. I was lowering the gun to set it against the wall because me and Tyler were done looking at it.' He didn't rack the lever, he said. He didn't know it was loaded. He was unfamiliar with the rifle.

It is relatively easy, with hindsight, to establish a pattern that would otherwise not have been obvious. Had Brandon not shot Tyler, a handful of minor episodes, nagging doubts, and odd moments relating to his behaviour would probably never have amounted to anything. But he did shoot Tyler, and over the next few days police interviews with a range of people connected to one or both of them provided hints that, even if this was not an expected or even likely turn of events, it was always a possibility.

In her police interview, Connie said that the entire time she was with Jerry, she had always been nervous about the number of guns he had in the house and always assumed they were loaded. Once, Tyler had come back from Brandon's house with knives. Lora had taken them away from him but had never thought to raise the matter with Jerry.

And then there were the incidents at school, which emerged in the wake of the shooting, when the children were receiving grief counselling. According to the police report, on Wednesday, the day before hunting season began, Brandon had boasted during class that he had pointed a 20-gauge at a boy's stomach while it was cocked and loaded without the safety on. Brandon also joked that because he hadn't seen any deer yet, he'd told the boy that he should put antlers on his head and run around the garden like a big buck so Brandon could shoot at him. The child who'd overheard them couldn't say for sure but thought they were 'goofing around' about the antler story; he also thought that 'they were serious' about aiming the 20-gauge at the boy's stomach. Brandon first denied any knowledge of this exchange and then said he couldn't remember.

In early September 1881, wrote Kate McGill in her account as an early settler in Marlette, 'A cyclone of fire swept across the county and in four hours' time had laid the entire Thumb of Michigan a desolate waste . . . A change in wind saved the village but the next day, not a farm building or a fence was left between the village and Cass River except the house of James Keys. Cattle, horses, sheep, hogs and chickens lay in the fields roasted to death. Apples hung, baked to a turn.'[7]

The emotional fallout from Tyler's shooting wrought an analogous toll on Marlette. 'We're a small rural county,' says Biniecki. 'When you have a tragic accident like this, it does affect everybody. Right from the families involved at the epicentre of this all the way out. Everybody knew the victim's family. Everybody knew the shooter's family. As you'll find out weaving through this, both sides were devastated.'

The question of how to weigh those two experiences – grief for the dead and sympathy for those who must live with their mistakes – is not easy. In Marlette it tore at the very fabric of this tight-knit community.

Within four days of the shooting, Brittany put up a 'community' page on Facebook called 'Justice for Tyler Dunn'.[8] The words 'your amazing' were emblazoned in bright green over three pictures of Tyler: one of him on the go-cart, one close-up, and one of him with his shirt off wearing nothing but a big smile and that coconut bra of Ashley's. Another photo shows Tyler sitting in a rocking chair in a T-shirt, appearing to be holding court. In the 'About' section it simply states, 'March 5th 2002–November 23rd 2013. Tyler Dunn was only 11 years old when his life was cut short. Please Help support his family and friends.' The last posting from the family was less than two months after Tyler's death; they were selling T-shirts and hoodies for $25 and $30 respectively. Both say 'Justice for Tyler' on the front; the T-shirts have a picture of Tyler on the back. A year after Tyler's death, the page had 792 likes.

Erica Bartz posted the following on the page a week after the shooting:

> I do not wish or pray for blood in return for the death of my cousins son. I pray for comfort for their loss, healing for their broken hearts, and strength to carry on. I do not wish bad upon anyone, especially a 12 year old boy. I do expect there be justice, yes justice for Tyler Dunn who's life has been ended way to suddenly because of irresponsible parents who have no concern or safety for children. As for the kid who was at the other end, I pray for him to tell the truth. So anyone offended by 'Justice for Tyler Dunn.' Its none of your concern an your two sense is not needed unless it's words to remember Tyler or to be sympathetic for the family. If this was your son, grandson, brother, your family member, or close friend you would

> want to know the truth and have justice put on those responsible for their short life that could have and should have been prevented from ending so horribly.

But the tension inherent in that posting – compassion for Brandon alongside a preemptive swipe at those who equated seeking justice for Tyler with retribution against Brandon – gave a hint of a bitter divide. Five days after the shooting, Tyler's own Facebook page was still up. On it, Rikki Mangone posted:

> Yes what happened to Tyler was a horrible thing. But blaming the friend is not right! Brandon did not do it on purpose! It was an accident when two young boys were messing with a gun. Tyler AND Brandon need to be in your prayers! Tyler lost a life and now Brandon will have a shitty one. So for everyone saying shit about Brandon needs to stop.

Twenty-six people liked the post. At least one did not. Janet, Tyler's grandmother, responded shortly after four in the morning, sparking the following exchange:

JANET: HOW DARE YOU RIKKI, YOU NEED REMOVE THIS POST OFF OF TYLER'S WALL, WE HAVE NO SORROW FOR BRANDON.

THERESA CONQUEST-WILLIS: Wow no sorrow for a boy that made a mistake. No sorrow for a child that now has to go through the rest of his life with the guilt of what has happened. How dare you ma'am.

ZACK PALLADENO: Word.^

JANET: HOW DARE I!!!!! NO I HAVE NO SORRROW FOR HIM, NOW, HOW WOULD U FEEL IF IT WAS THE OTHERWAY AROUND, I'M TYLER'S GRANDMOTHER, AND YES I DARE!!!!!!!!!!!!!!!!!!!!,!!!!!

THERESA CONQUEST-WILLIS: Ma'am the tragedy is on both sides.

JANET: THAT'S YOUR, OPINION, NOT MINE, SOMEBODY COCKED

THAT GUN, SOMEBODY PULLED THAT TRIGGER, AND IT SURE WASN'T TYLER CAUSE HE'S NOT HERE TO TELL HIS SIDE

JANET: AND IF YOU THINK I'M GOING TO HAVE SORROW FOR HIM, YOUR OUT OF YOUR FUCKING MIND

THERESA CONQUEST-WILLIS: Wow that's all I have . . .

TINA FUHR: All I have to say to Rikki . . . This was not an appropriate place to post this message. If you've haven't noticed, nobody on Tyler's wall has ever mentioned Brandon's name. Nor has anyone on here saying shit about him. This is not the place to discuss Brandon and what he did. This is a place for family and friends to find comfort with each other in the loss of my dear nephew. Also, in my opinion (whether you agree or not, I don't care) he was old enough to know not to touch/play with guns, yet he did. It has caused a ripple in our family that will never be forgotten, nor forgiven. Friendly reminder: When it comes to your life and life of others, there are no accidents, only choices.

RIKKI MANGONE: I am very sorry to the people who will be living with this angry towards a 12 year old boy. I pray that one day both sides will be seen. Are the people saying bad things willing to have another innocent child's life taken by suicide because he hears and sees other people with the negativity? This was a tragedy for both sides and I am very sorry for everyone involved.

(Lora joins the fray.)

LORA: I think Rikki (and anyone) needs to remove them selfs from Tyler Dunn wall . . . and u too don't know so butt ur nose and ur opinions out of it and I don't really care what Brandon does with his life now

THERESA CONQUEST-WILLIS: Ma'am I'm not on his wall I'm on Rikkis and the last I checked it was a free country if you don't like what's being said then take yourself out of the conversation there are two families suffering in this tragedy and the last thing anyone needs is someone's bullshit.

JANET: SHE DON'T HAVE TO, SHE'S TYLER'S MOTHER SO YOU CAN SHUT THE FUCK UP!!!!!!!!

And so it went on.

Guns were more readily available and accepted in Brandon's world than in that of pretty much any of the day's other victims. In much of rural America, guns are an everyday part of life, for both recreational and practical reasons. 'Being a rural community, we have problems with everything from skunks to critters,' explains Sheriff Biniecki. 'We even have coyotes that will chase newborn calves. And it's not uncommon for a farmer to have a firearm handy to dispose of them. They're always ready for action.'

In Marlette, gun ownership was, if not normal, then certainly not deviant. 'My mom has guns in her house,' says Lora after a moment's reflection. 'They're her husband's. He don't hunt too often. So he just has 'em. And Tyler used to go over there. They weren't visible where you can see 'em. But they're there.'

With so many guns around, the potential for calamity is ever present. A few weeks earlier, two men in an airboat in Saginaw Bay, an hour from Marlette, said they were shot at by a duck hunter.[9] Only five days after Tyler was shot, a sixteen-year-old shot himself in the foot while hunting; the incident took place twenty minutes away, in Snover.[10] Six months later, a twelve-year-old was shot in the hand after a fourteen-year-old removed a gun from a gun safe and dropped it.[11]

Although Sheriff Biniecki treats each gun death as its own discrete tragedy, one nonetheless detects in his voice a weary, if compassionate, familiarity about cases like Tyler's. He has been in law enforcement in Sanilac County for almost forty years, starting as a deputy and working his way up. He has creases in his shirt so sharp you could cut your finger on them. The star on his shoulder and the model ship in his window give the impression more of a military man than of a rural sheriff.

'Unfortunately, every few years history starts to repeat itself,' he says. 'We've had other shootings. Not always fatal. But these things do happen. We've had other adults, who, while hunting, shoot other adults. It's still personal. It's still human error. And you have to take some personal responsibility for what happened. Part of my being sheriff is sometimes I try to comment on things in such a way that maybe it'll have a lasting effect. It might keep a tragedy like this from ever happening again.'

Biniecki didn't grow up around guns. He was raised in Detroit and came to the area when he was ten. When his dad won a gun in a raffle, not long after they'd arrived, he gave it to one of his friends. 'He wasn't against them. He just wasn't ever really exposed to them so he thought, "Why have 'em around?"' Among the first questions one of Biniecki's friends asked him when he arrived in the area was whether he had a gun. When he was twelve he worked all summer to buy his first gun – a single-barrel shotgun for hunting pheasant.

Immediately following Tyler's death, Biniecki sounded sympathetic. 'It's just a tragedy,' he told the local press. 'We believe it was an accident, unintentional. It's tragic. Two lives were affected. One boy won't be with us, and one will have to deal with this for the rest of his life. Everyone needs to remember that every gun is loaded. Even if it's unloaded, point it in a safe direction, and no one will ever be shot unless it's intentional. The weapon didn't go off by itself.'[12]

The key to preventing accidents like this, he insists, is education and parental responsibility. 'I think that we as community leaders need to make sure that we use the opportunity to further educate parents that if you do have a gun, unload it and put it away. Teach your kids how to make sure it's unloaded, and put it away. Teach your kids the safety rules. And then over time don't get lax with it, because sometimes', he insists during our interview, 'parents get lax, and children are always curious. Put those two things together and bad things can happen. I believe in this day and age with the Internet and everything that's in these smartphones and all the things that's connected to it, all the information's there. You can even take classes online.'

Shortly after the shooting, Biniecki gave the local newspaper a basic course in how gun safety protocols were not followed in this case. Trigger locks and similar devices can disable weapons from firing, he said, and gun owners should keep safety locks on guns and keep them in a locked safe. Either way, they should be in a different place from the ammo box. 'They do not have an updated safety feature,' he pointed out. 'It's a ratchet lever-action, when the hammer comes back, it's cocked and ready to fire.'[13]

'All of us know human nature,' he told me. 'Children are curious. They're at an age in their life where they're like a sponge from the time they're old enough to talk to start thinking and acting for themselves. And if they don't know and they're not taught at that young age that that's a weapon and it's dangerous, then bad things can happen. We tell 'em the knife is sharp. We tell 'em the stove is hot. We need to tell them at a young age what a firearm is and what can occur with it.'

This makes sense. And it is worth noting that neither Brandon nor Tyler had been to safety classes, though Brittany says she was looking into them for Tyler. And Sheriff Biniecki walks the walk. The weekend before we met, he told me, he'd helped run a youth day for the Wild Turkey Federation, a conservation organisation, which provided safety instruction (among other things) for youngsters. His two daughters grew up around his handgun and he would occasionally take them to the gun range and was always insistent on them observing safety protocol.

The trouble, say researchers, is that the emphasis on safety education alone doesn't really work. Even when children – especially boys

– have been taught the risks, the lure of an actual firearm trumps the warnings about its potential danger.

In one study, pairs of boys aged eight to twelve were left alone in an examination room at an Atlanta clinic, where they were observed by researchers through a one-way mirror. Researchers didn't tell them there was a .38-calibre handgun concealed in a cabinet drawer. But within fifteen minutes, three-quarters of the children found it, two-thirds handled it, and one-third pulled the trigger. Only one, out of almost ninety, told an adult about the gun, and for that he was teased by the others. More than 90 per cent of the boys had received some gun safety tuition.[14]

A 2013 *New York Times* article on 'accidental' shootings cited the case of eleven-year-old Joshua Skorczewski in western Minnesota. The boy was so excited about going to a gun safety class one evening that he took an unloaded 20-gauge shotgun from the family gun cabinet beforehand, loaded it, and pulled the hammer back to practise. He realised he should put it back, but his finger slipped, and he shot his twelve-year-old sister, Natasha, dead.[15]

Any moral panic about 'accidental' child shootings must be kept in perspective – not because there are so few but because, relative to other accidental deaths, there are greater dangers to children that spark less anxiety. A *New York Times* investigation in 2013 predicted that because of misclassification, the number of gun-related deaths of children recorded as 'accidental' is double the official number.[16] However, even accepting the higher figure proposed by the *New York Times*, accidental gun deaths would still rank fifth among fatal injuries for children, after car crashes, drowning, fire, suffocation and accidents to pedestrians.

Nonetheless, so long as you have a society with a lot of guns – and America has more guns per capita than any other country in the world[17] – children will be at risk of being shot. The questions are how much risk, and what, if anything, is being done to minimise it? If one thinks of the various ways in which commonplace items, from car seats to medicine bottletops, have been childproofed, it's clear that society's general desire has been to eliminate as many potential dangers from children as possible, even when the number of those who might be harmed is relatively small. If one child's death is preventable, then the proper question isn't 'Why should we do this?' but rather 'Why shouldn't we?' It would be strange for that principle to apply to everything but guns.

But the kind of research that might show what works where gun safety is concerned is in short supply. That is no accident. At one time, guns, the primary source of death of black youth and second-leading source for all youth, were considered a public health concern. The Centers for Disease Control and Prevention produced findings and reports on how to limit gun deaths in the same way that they produce reports on healthy eating and how to prevent sudden infant death syndrome. They found, among other things, that the presence of guns in the home increased the likelihood of death rather than reduced it.[18] The National Rifle Association was not pleased with this particular conclusion or the research in general. 'Our concern is not with legitimate medical science,' Chris Cox, the NRA's chief lobbyist, told the *New York Times*. 'Our concern is they were promoting the idea that gun ownership was a disease that needed to be eradicated.'[19]

So the NRA used their immense lobbying power to effectively put a stop to the government's finding out how to make people safer around guns. In 1996, Arkansas Republican Congressman Jay Dickey, who later described himself as the NRA's 'point person in Congress', successfully removed $2.6 million – the precise amount spent on gun research the previous year – from the CDC's budget.[20] The law now reads, 'None of the funds made available for injury prevention and control at the Centers for Disease Control and Prevention may be used to advocate or promote gun control.'[21]

Because legislation already in place prohibited the CDC from lobbying for or against legislation, the ruling was redundant. But it had the effect of keeping both resources and researchers away from that area of study for fear that their findings would prove politically inconvenient and attract the wrath of pro-gun legislators. 'We've been stopped from answering the basic questions,' Mark Rosenberg, former director of the National Center for Injury Prevention and Control, told the *New York Times* in 2011.[22]

In January 2013, in the wake of the Sandy Hook shootings, President Barack Obama started a second term that became increasingly strident in its advocacy for gun control. One of his executive actions sought to shift the climate of caution by issuing 'a Presidential Memorandum directing the Centers for Disease Control to research the causes and prevention of gun violence'.

The problem has, however, been ongoing. On 14 November 2013, nine days before Tyler was shot, President Barack Obama nominated Vivek Murthy for surgeon general. But the process most assumed would be routine – Murthy was well qualified and bore not a whiff of personal scandal – became mired in controversy. Republican legislators focused on his support for an assault-weapons ban and on a tweet he'd sent out in 2012, a few months after the shootings by James Holmes in an Aurora, Colorado, cinema that killed twelve and injured seventy others. 'Tired of politicians playing politics w/ guns, putting lives at risk b/c they're scared of NRA. Guns are a health care issue. #DebateHealth,' he tweeted.[23] It took more than a year for him to be confirmed by the narrowest of margins, after the NRA rallied its members against 'the most politically active surgeon general [nominee]'[24] in living memory.

Research that does exist shows that children face substantial risk in the presence of guns. In more than half of American homes where there are both children and firearms, according to a 2000 study, the weapons are in an unlocked place, and in more than 40 per cent of homes, guns without a trigger lock are in an unlocked place.[25] Almost three-quarters of children under the age of ten who live in homes with guns say they know where the guns are.[26] A

2005 study showed that more than 1.69 million children and young people under eighteen live in homes with weapons that are loaded and unlocked.[27] According to a Department of Education study, 68 per cent of school shootings between 1974 and 2000 were carried out with a gun from the attacker's home or the home of a relative.[28]

And the laws, it seems, are effective. One study indicated that in the twelve states where child-access prevention laws were on the books for at least one year, unintentional gun deaths fell by 23 per cent.[29] Another, from 2005, revealed a link between the presence of such laws and the prevention of youth suicides.[30]

Twenty-eight states and the District of Columbia have child-access prevention laws, which range in severity from imposing criminal liability when a minor gains access to a negligently stored weapon to forbidding adults from providing children with firearms.[31] Michigan, where Tyler died, is not one of them. But that's not for want of trying. A bill to create a safe-storage law, which would criminalise those who fail to lock up their firearms so that children can't get at them, was introduced in every session of the Michigan state legislature for fifteen years. It made it out of the committee stage only once.

The NRA vigorously opposes such laws, in Michigan and elsewhere, for two reasons. First, they argue that the number of children who die in accidental gun deaths is minuscule and decreasing. Second, because forcing gun owners to keep guns under lock and key makes it virtually impossible for them to defend themselves effectively in the home. (I imagine the 'Home Defense Concepts' seminar at the NRA convention would have sounded very different if you had to find the key to your gun safe first.) But research shows that people are most likely to be shot not by strangers but by people they know or by themselves. A study in 1998 showed that for every gun in the house that was used for self-defence in a 'legally justifiable shooting', there were four unintentional shootings, seven criminal assaults or homicides, and eleven attempted or completed suicides.[32] According to Sheriff Biniecki, most of the gun fatalities in Sanilac County are 'domestic-related' – a former husband shooting an ex-wife, or 'a convicted sex offender who took out his stepdad and uncle . . . It's about every three years it seems to rear its ugly head.'

Laws, of course, do not guarantee good outcomes. They only punish bad ones and set the standard for what the socially acceptable behaviour should be. 'There were a lot of things went into play that set this up for failure,' says Biniecki, referring to Tyler's death. 'The boys were deer hunting before. They're around [firearms]. Now, one step didn't take place. Could the father have locked 'em up and the boys have broken into it? Sure. But in this particular incident that's not what happened. We know the gun was out. We know the boys had access to it, and we know the tragic results. I think a lot of it is our personal responsibility.' And with personal responsibility, he insisted shortly after the shooting, come personal consequences. 'We're going to seek charges,' he told the local paper. 'Someone has to answer for it. The kids should not have been home alone.'[33]

On 20 February 2014, Jerry and Brandon appeared in District Court. According to a circuit court clerk, Jerry was a three-time felon. Over the past couple of decades, he had been convicted, at different times, of dealing drugs, 'manufacturing marijuana and a schedule 4 drug', resisting and obstructing a police officer, 'operating a vehicle while impaired', and 'operating a vehicle with an open container'.

Felons in the United States are not allowed to have guns. So Jerry was charged with weapons-firearms possession by a felon, which is itself a felony carrying a maximum of five years in prison. For leaving two boys alone with loaded guns that ended in the death of one of them, he was charged with contributing to the delinquency of a minor, a ninety-day misdemeanour. He was released on $2,500 bail.[34]

Brandon was arraigned in juvenile court and charged with careless discharge of a firearm, causing death, which carries a maximum two-year sentence. On 10 April, Brandon pleaded guilty; on 5 May,

Jerry pleaded no contest, telling the prosecutor he felt bad about the shooting and had told Brandon to plead guilty because 'he had made a mistake'.

At a hearing on 1 May, Lora told me, Connie wept as Brandon stood in grey sweatpants and a hoodie, and the judge placed him in 'intense probation' at her home. The next day he was sentenced. There were twenty-nine terms to his probation. He was sent to a junior detention facility for ten days, with a further twenty days 'held in abeyance', to be enforced if he failed to comply with the other twenty-eight restrictions on his liberty. The probation would be reviewed by the court every thirty days, said Sanilac County Prosecutor James Young, who anticipated it would last until Brandon was eighteen or nineteen, or 'until such time that he no longer needs services and demonstrates he needs no more probation'.[35]

The terms for probation included electronic tagging, a 7 p.m. to 7 a.m. curfew, participation in anger-management classes, counselling, thirty hours of community service, random drug and alcohol testing, paying for Tyler's cremation services, and a minimum of ten written assignments provided by his probation officer.

Point 4 says he must stay with Connie in Michigan; point 7 that he should not leave the state without the prior consent of his probation officer; and point 19 that he have no contact, direct or indirect, with Tyler's family. Among them, those three points proved difficult to adhere to. These rural communities are small; the social networks are tight. Though Brandon hasn't sought contact with Tyler's family members, they are difficult to avoid. Connie moved less than half an hour's drive away. Tiffany was on a shift at McDonald's in Marlette one day when they came through; other family members occasionally see him around.

Six weeks after Brandon was sentenced, it was Jerry's turn. Citing his previous convictions, the judge sentenced him to a year in Sanilac County Jail for the first count of weapons-firearms possession by a felon and ninety days to run concurrently for the second count of contributing to the delinquency of a minor. He also had to cover certain costs, including for the court-appointed attorney.[36]

The law had spoken. But it declared its values without any moral consistency. Jerry got a year because he'd once committed 'serious crimes' that precluded him from having a gun. He got three months for leaving several guns, at least one of which was loaded, unattended in the house and then leaving his son and a friend unsupervised with them. That crime, contributing to the delinquency of a minor, would have been the same if Tyler and Brandon had found his porn stash. Not only did the punishments not fit the crimes; the crime in no way fitted the transgression. His negligence had arguably left Brandon corrupted, but it had certainly left Tyler dead.

Tyler's family believes that both Brandon and Jerry got off too lightly. Particularly Brandon, who they are convinced shot Tyler on purpose. They think there has been a cover-up. Something fishy. They can't say precisely what. But to them the story doesn't hang together. Lora doesn't buy the idea that Tyler was trying to put the gun down and the latch got caught on his shorts pocket. 'To me I think he was lying. I don't believe that even happened. I already knew from the get-go that I didn't think it was an accident. I believe his finger was on the trigger.'

Over pizza with Brittany, her mother, her stepfather, and her grandmother, I asked what would constitute justice for Tyler. Brittany paused. 'I would want eye for eye,' she said. I paused.

'You mean you want Brandon executed?' I asked.

She nodded. 'Brandon needs to be gone. I don't think he should be able to live his life. That's just my personal opinion.'

I paused again and looked around the table. 'Does everyone agree?'

They all nodded.

'And Jerry?'

'He should have time for what he did,' said Lora.

'He should probably sit inside for the rest of his life,' added Brittany. 'He had a role in it, but he technically didn't pull the trigger.'

In her capacity as the personal representative of Tyler's estate Lora has since filed suit against both Brandon and Jerry, seeking more than $25,000, according to the *Sanilac County News*.[37]

I asked Lora if Jerry or Connie had ever reached out to them since Tyler was killed. She said they'd had no contact since Jerry's girlfriend had come over, a few days after the shooting, to return Tyler's effects. Would they have liked to hear from them? 'It would have been nice for them to say something. Put a card in my mailbox or something. But no. Never heard a word from them.'

'Even at the court they could have turned around and said something,' said Janet.

'Yeah, when he stood up in front of the judge and said it wasn't his fault,' recalls Lora.

'Well,' says Janet, 'it wasn't his fault because he wasn't home.'

When it comes to protecting children around guns, parents are flawed and laws are clearly inadequate. But with occasional encouragement from government, technology has become more reliable. For well over a century, gun manufacturers have been working on weapons that would be difficult for children to misuse.

In 1887, Smith & Wesson produced the .38-calibre Safety Hammerless, followed two years later by the .32-calibre model. It had a metal lever at the back that the shooter had to push down with the base of the thumb as the forefinger pulled the trigger. This 'New Departure' safety grip was designed specifically so that a young child's hands would be too small to perform both functions at the same time. 'One very important feature of this arrangement', explained the catalogue, 'is the safety of the arm in the hands of children, as no ordinary child under eight years of age can possibly discharge it.'[38]

But more recent, sophisticated initiatives have attracted the wrath of the gun lobby. In 2000, after Bill Clinton announced a deal with Smith & Wesson that would include putting locks on handguns and implementing 'smart-gun' technology, the NRA branded the company 'the first gun maker to run up the white flag of surrender and duck behind the Clinton–Gore lines'.[39] They called for a boycott of the company. Smith & Wesson eventually backed out of the deal.

The technology developed anyhow. There are now loading indicators that show whether a weapon is loaded and whether a round remains in the chamber. And smart guns have come a long way. The Armatix iP1 – a stubby-looking black handgun with a matt finish – doesn't work without a watch, which is less a device for timekeeping than one for safety. Both watch and gun have electronic chips that communicate with each other. When the gun is less than ten inches from the watch, which needs a five-digit PIN before it can be activated, a light on the grip turns green, and it can fire. When it's further away from the watch, there's no light and the gun can't fire. In other words, the only person who can fire it is the person who has the watch and knows the PIN – which is likely to be the owner.[40]

In a tear-stained press conference, standing next to one of the fathers who'd lost a child at Sandy Hook, President Obama expressed his frustration that technology commercially available and acceptable for more mundane purposes couldn't be put to use to ensure safety. 'If we can develop technology that you can't unlock your phone unless you've got the right fingerprint, why can't we do it for guns?' he said. 'If a child can't open a bottle of aspirin, we should make sure that they can't pull the trigger on a gun.'[41]

A range of versions of this kind of gun have been tested, including those that use voice recognition, grip recognition, fingerprints, and remote apps (through which you could disable the gun remotely). The benefits – in terms of making accidental shootings, suicides and illegal gun transfers more difficult, and rendering gun theft useless – are self-evident. So much so that in 2002, New Jersey passed a law stating that only smart guns would be allowed to be sold in the state within three years of a smart gun hitting the market anywhere in the country.[42]

The Armatix was the first to make it to the United States commercially. For a short while, it looked like that 'anywhere' would be the Oak Tree Gun Club, one of California's largest gun stores, located just outside Los Angeles. Briefly, it was the only outlet in America to stock them. 'It could revolutionise the gun industry,' James Mitchell, the store's owner, told the *Washington Post*.[43]

While nobody was claiming it would cure gun violence, it was difficult to see how smart guns could make anything worse. 'If you have two cars, and one has an air bag and one doesn't, are you going to buy the one without the air bag?' Belinda Padilla, president of Armatix's US operation, told the *Post*. 'It's your choice, but why would you do that?'[44]

One reason would be if that choice didn't exist. The NRA is extremely hostile to smart guns. They see them not as part of the safety agenda but as part of the anti-gun agenda. They oppose 'government mandates that require the use of expensive, unreliable features, such as grips that would read your fingerprints before the gun will fire'. They '[recognise] that the "smart guns" issue clearly has the potential to mesh with the anti-gunner's agenda, opening the door to a ban on all guns that do not possess the government-required technology.'[45] They are particularly keen to prevent New Jersey from leading the way in government's demanding such technology.

Once news came out that Oak Tree would be stocking the Armatix iP1 gun, activists threatened a boycott of the store. Padilla was personally targeted. She received threatening messages after someone posted her mobile number online. Someone else posted pictures of the address where she has a PO box, drew an arrow towards an image of a woman in the frame, and wrote, 'Belinda? Is that you?' On Calguns.net, a California gun owner's site, one person wrote, 'I have no qualms with the idea of personally and professionally leveling the life of someone who has attempted to profit from disarming me and my fellow Americans.'[46]

The pressure was so intense that the store eventually eradicated all evidence it ever had a deal with Armatix. Advertising signs were taken down, clothes with logos were removed, the stall at the shooting range disappeared. There was no suggestion that the NRA was behind any of the threats.

Nonetheless, the New Jersey state senator who originally sponsored the bill to make smart guns the norm in her state offered a truce. She would drop the mandate if the NRA refused to stand in the way of the development and sale of smart guns. 'I'm willing to do this because eventually these are the kinds of guns people will want to buy,' she said. The NRA was having none of it. 'The NRA is interested in a full repeal of New Jersey's misguided law,' Chris Cox replied.[47]

Whether any of these laws and technological developments would have saved Tyler's life we will never know. The US General Accounting Office has estimated that 31 per cent of accidental deaths caused by firearms might be prevented by adding child-proof safety locks and loading indicators.[48] People are flawed, and only so much can be expected from children in terms of personal responsibility. It is also important in these cases to make a distinction between an accident and negligence. What is clear is that none of these things would have done any harm, and almost all of them would have limited the odds of its happening.

Tyler's family arrived at Sanilac County Courthouse for Jerry's sentencing dressed for the occasion. Brittany wore a green hoodie with four different pictures of Tyler on the front and 'Justice for Tyler' on the back. Lora wore a grey version without the pictures on the front. In the corridor outside the court, some sat and others stood. When they weren't breaking the silence with chat and banter they paced aimless and sombre circles across the marble floor.

Jerry arrived five minutes late, wearing a blue shirt with white stripes, blue jeans, cowboy boots, and a black baseball cap for 'Hercules Pumping and Concrete', beneath which his lank grey hair hung down past his shoulderblades. He had brought a friend, dressed similarly, who took Jerry's hat as Circuit Court Judge Donald Teeple called him forward. 'Do you understand why you are here?' Teeple asked, explaining the charges. 'Yes,' said Jerry. The judge asked his lawyer if she had anything to say. Acknowledging the 'terrible incident' that had taken place, his lawyer explained, 'There was no intent on Mr Northrup's part. It was an act of omission.' The judge then asked Jerry if he had anything to say.

'It was a very bad, tragic accident,' he said. 'I wasn't there. I didn't do it. I was working.'

'But you did have guns in the house,' insisted the judge.

'Yes,' said Jerry.

'Well, that's how it happens . . . This family has to live without their child for the rest of their lives.'

'I understand that,' said Jerry, his voice becoming less audible with each response.

'That's about as bad as it gets.'

'Yes,' said so faintly now it was more a murmur than a word.

The judge handed down the sentence – a year in jail – and as the room cleared Jerry was directed to sit in the jury area while an officer of the court collected the paperwork. Then, after Jerry had put one more signature to his incarceration, the infantilisation of his new life began. He was no longer a free man. He stood and shook his head as the policeman asked if there was anything in his pockets, only to find some change in one of them. He took it out, reached over to his friend, and handed it to him. The patting down continued as he raised his arms. Then he stood with his hands in front as the cuffs went on. Right hand first. Click. Then left. Click. Then back to the jury chair while other paperwork was completed. It was 9.20 a.m. when he was escorted out of the empty courtroom into the hallway, hands cuffed before him and his friend, carrying two hats, his face wet with tears, walking behind. Jerry stepped into the elevator and was gone.

6

Edwin Rajo
(aged sixteen)

Houston, Texas
23 November, 7.15 p.m. CST

Next to the administrative office in Lee high school, located in southwest Houston, hangs a banner announcing, 'ALL DOORS. ALL HALLWAYS. LEAD TO COLLEGE'. But for a handful of students, they are more likely to lead to room 143 – the special-education centre run by Jennisha Thomas, a driven, African-American woman in her thirties. Any student who needs particular academic support passes through here. Ordinarily, that might be only once or twice for registration and review. But, each year, one or two end up camping out in her room because they struggle behaviourally in a formal classroom setting and keep getting sent there. In his first year at Lee, Edwin Rajo, aged sixteen, was referred there at the beginning of the year but scarcely ever went back. 'We would hardly have known he was here,' says Jennisha. 'We never heard about him.' But in his second year, he and his friend Gabriel (not his real name) were there virtually every day. 'I don't know what happened,' she says. 'It was like he'd had some go-go juice.'

Lee is a tough school, serving a student body that struggles with a range of challenges. Seven out of ten students failed the State of Texas Assessments of Academic Readiness English test; 96 per cent are economically disadvantaged.[1] The school runs a backpack programme, which provides students with two days of meals on weekends. Lee draws much of its intake from refugee communities from all over the world – wherever there's a war going on, there's a good chance students from that region will end up at Lee.

If that were not enough, there is also a significant gang presence in the school – not from one gang but from the whole gamut of black and Latino gangs that are rife in the area. While I was interviewing Ms Thomas, her administrator rushed in to tell her she was needed urgently outside, where a fight had broken out. Ms Thomas excused herself and went to slip on her shoes. 'Faster,' urged her administrator, and Ms Thomas was off to try to mediate. Within a week of my being there, several pupils would be arrested onsite after a huge fight.

Gabriel was like a don in the school. He was a quiet, unflashy presence whose word carried as much weight as that of many teachers, if not more. He's a cool customer with a commanding aura. Edwin was his wisecracking sidekick: taller, skinnier, sillier, barely in control of himself let alone others. Gabriel and Edwin did a lot of 'chilling'. Whereas Stanley Taylor's friend Trey could not quite describe what that involved, Gabriel was more forthcoming – for Edwin and him it meant playing soccer, smoking weed, playing Grand Theft Auto, drinking and talking. 'Edwin wasn't *bad*,' says Ms Thomas. 'He was immature. He was acting in high school how he should have been acting in middle school. In middle school he was still quiet and in his little shell. When he got here, he started being playful. He'd do things like take kids' ID badges, run down the hallway, slap boys between their legs – boy stuff. But he wasn't *bad*; he was *busy*. So almost every day he would get sent here because they couldn't handle him. He was all over the place.'

Impulsive and childlike, if Edwin sensed he could provoke a teacher, he would not only 'go there' but stay there until the job was done. 'He got a kick out of seeing teachers get to that boiling point,' says Ms Thomas. He also lacked any kind of filter. If he thought your hairstyle sucked, your dress didn't fit, or your nose ring looked daft, he'd tell you, apparently not realising he might be causing offence. For the most part, his misbehaviour manifested itself in episodic acts of senseless defiance, particularly with regard to one teacher.

For example, students were not allowed to wear black undershirts since they were identified with the Southwest Cholo gang. Edwin wore one anyway. When that teacher told him to take it off, Ms

Thomas said, Edwin acted up. 'I'm not giving you this shirt,' he said. Over the PA the call went out for Ms Thomas to assist in talking Edwin down.

'Edwin, what's the problem?' she said.

'He want me to take off my shirt,' Edwin said. 'He gay. He just wants to look at my body. I don't want him looking at me.'

'Edwin take off that shirt,' said Ms Thomas, through gritted teeth.

'I ain't gonna give it to him. I'm gonna give it to her,' said Edwin, gesturing towards Ms Thomas.

'I don't care who you give it to, just take it off,' said Ms Thomas. Edwin took the shirt off and threw it on the floor.

Most teachers in the special education department didn't have a problem with him. 'You always knew what you were getting,' said one. 'He was straightforward,' said another. Most did not indulge him, but they picked their battles. But others found him frustrating and disruptive. 'There were particular teachers he knew he could get a rise out of,' says Ms Thomas. 'Full throttle. "You at school today?"' she said, imitating Edwin's thought process. '"Let me see if I can make you mad."'

He'd never been diagnosed, but Ms Thomas guessed he was more likely to have attention-deficit hyperactivity disorder than oppositional defiant disorder. 'If you're oppositional defiant you're like that with everybody. We never had that problem with Edwin here because we always shut it down. He was never disrespectful to us. But he would be referred here almost every day for something. There wasn't a day when I didn't have to fuss at him.'

Edwin liked school, says Gabriel, because he saw it as a great venue for horsing around. 'I think he liked it because there are lots of people here and he could be distracted and mess about,' he explains. The actual schoolwork Edwin found both boring and pointless. When his childhood friend Camilla (not her real name) would ask him what he wanted to do with his life, he'd say, 'Nothing.' 'I don't like school,' he told her. 'I just want to work at High Times' – a local tobacco shop that sells pot paraphernalia.

A number of times over the few months since school had started that semester, Ms Thomas had called Edwin's mother, Marlyn, to discuss his behaviour and to try to make plans to set him back on track. Marlyn, age thirty-nine, was eight months pregnant when I met her more than a year after the shooting. She speaks almost no English, relying on her children to interpret for her, so we spoke through a translator, Miriam Garcia. Marlyn came to the United States via the border town of Laredo in 1985, hiding in the driver's cabin of an eighteen-wheeler with eight other people. She was nineteen, and she wanted something better than what she felt the future held in her native Honduras. One of seven children from El Progreso, an impoverished farming town at the foot of the Mico Quemado mountain chain, her future there appeared bleak. She paid coyotes eighteen hundred dollars – half up front and half on the Mexican side of the border – and travelled for a month, through Guatemala and Mexico. 'I always wanted to have a family and give them more than we had, but I knew that doing that would be very difficult. I wanted to come to America because I thought I could make decent money and send it back to my parents to help them out.'

It didn't quite work out like that. She did raise a family. Edwin was her oldest, followed by Sandra, fourteen; Victor, twelve; and Giovanni, nine. But she never learned English and never got the kind of training that would pull her out of the most basic, vulnerable manual labour. She cleans apartments and sometimes cooks for people. 'The gold fell from very high in the sky,' wrote John Berger in his book about the immigrant experience, *A Seventh Man: Migrant Workers in Europe*. 'And so when it hit the earth it went down very, very deep.'[2] She barely has enough money to support her own family; it's unlikely she's sending much home.

Marlyn had come a long way at great risk and effort to give her children a better life. Now her eldest was playing the fool at school. She could not fathom what had got into him. He had been a sickly infant, hospitalised for seven days when he was eight months old for pneumonia. Marlyn was terrified back then. 'He was my first child. He was my life. I was very worried. They are all my life,' she said, casting her hand in the direction of her other children. 'But he was my first, so he was very special in that way.' While he was in the hospital, he was also diagnosed with asthma. His father had asthma. The doctors told them it was hereditary. It was the reason why they could never have a pet. But as the years went on, Edwin's asthma became less pronounced before effectively dissipating into a range of less serious allergies. As a child, he had always been very calm and obedient, and sought to set an example for his three younger siblings. He'd never done brilliantly in school academically, but up until this point he had not caused any trouble either. Now Ms Thomas kept calling her in.

Each time they told Edwin they were calling his mother, his demeanour would change markedly. His mother was not familiar with the clowning and defiant behaviour of his school world. Having her hear about it would not get him in serious trouble – Marlyn doesn't appear to be a big disciplinarian. But, more devastatingly to him, it would disappoint her and diminish her impression of him as the responsible eldest son.

Holding her hands together palm to palm, as though in prayer, she would say to him in front of his teachers, 'I can't believe you're doing this to me. Promise me you'll stop. You're supposed to be an example for your brothers and sisters.' Edwin would give his word. He said he was just playing and put the trouble down to a bad relationship with just one teacher. 'I promise you they're not going to call any more,' he'd tell her. And that promise would be as good as the next call. 'By December I promise you my grades are going to go up,' he told her. 'That's what I was looking forward to,' she says.

Ms Thomas had a plan for Edwin. She'd decided to move him into her behaviour class, which had fewer students and two teachers. She called a meeting for 8 a.m. on Monday, 25 November, to talk about it with her superiors, and was getting the paperwork together the previous week. On Friday, 22 November, as Jaiden lay on life support over a thousand miles away, Ms Thomas came back to school from a meeting elsewhere to find that Edwin had been sent to her again. 'Why are you down here?' she asked him, somewhat wearily. He wouldn't say exactly, beyond saying that his teacher had sent him to wait for her. She entered her office, and he followed her in, placed a chair against the wall, and sat in front of her desk playing Fruit Ninja on his phone. 'Miss, do you like playing Fruit Ninja?' he asked, swiping away at the produce with his finger. 'No, Edwin,' she said. 'I don't play those stupid games.' She asked him what he'd done this time. Once again he'd been joking around and refused to stop when he was told. 'Edwin, I'm gonna choke you if you don't stop,' she said, repeating the threat she jokingly made to all her students whose behaviour wore out her last nerve. Edwin carried on playing Fruit Ninja. He stayed in her office for the remainder of the day, and when the bell rang he got up. 'See you later, miss,' he said. 'See you Monday,' said Ms Thomas, who starts to cry as she recalls saying goodbye for the last time.

That weekend, Ms Thomas collated the paperwork for the Monday morning meeting. 'I'd already pretty much completed it, but I'm, like, a perfectionist, and everyone has to put their eyes on it,' she says. 'So after I cleaned up the house on Saturday morning I took another look, made sure everything was laid out in his folder correctly, and put it in my little backpack so it'd be ready.'

At five feet ten, Edwin was a fairly tall, slender, handsome boy with tight black hair like wire wool and bushy eyebrows to match. He looked young, even for sixteen; he had a smooth-looking face not yet ravaged by acne or stubble, with the complexion of watered-down milk. Depending on where you are, he could have been mistaken for many races and ethnicities, including white. Marlyn has darker, Amerindian features one would associate with South or Central America. But Edwin was more of a shape-shifter. In France people would assume he was from the Maghrib; in Germany he might be Turkish; in Spain or Portugal some locals might claim him as their own. In Houston, he was Latino.

It was perhaps a mark of his immaturity that he'd not found a way to capitalise on his good looks. He never had a romantic relationship. He'd had plenty of crushes, says Gabriel, but he was always too shy to talk to girls. No matter how many times Gabriel told him to lighten up, Edwin could never get the courage up to ask a girl out. He'd laugh it off. 'Your girl will be my girl too,' he'd tell Gabriel. When Gabriel told him he'd have to get his own girlfriend, Edwin would plead for help. 'I can't, but that's because you don't help me, man,' he said. Gabriel would tease him relentlessly, approaching 'random girls' and telling them Edwin liked them. 'He'd turn completely red,' says Gabriel, who would then tease him some more. 'Hey, what's up with you, Mr Tomato Head?' 'He was shy,' says Marlyn. 'But the girls were after him.'

One girl he was particularly close to was Camilla. Camilla came from a rough family. Her mother, it is claimed, was a Cholo gang member. Her apartment is defended by a ferocious pit bull. Camilla openly and proudly identifies as a gang member. Her Facebook page carries the letters SWC (Southwest Cholo) after her gang name. She has not only bought into the gang culture; she literally wears it. Her hair sits high atop her head in a supertight ponytail, her eyebrows are drawn on in black, string rosaries hang around her neck. Big black shirt, big black pants, a black belt so long one end hangs lank close to the ground, black and white bandanna around her neck, and a pair of black Chuck Taylors on her feet. Butch and dark, black on brown – it's the *chola* style.

'He was always playing with her, but she had a tough attitude,' says Marlyn. 'They loved each other very much. She protected him a lot.' 'I knew him since third grade,' says Camilla. 'He was my best friend. We went to school together in the morning, and then we'd come home together after school. We were like brother and sister.'

Once, Gabriel asked him why he didn't date Camilla. 'You're always with her. You might as well go out with her.' 'Nah, man, she's like my sister,' said Edwin. 'Are you sure? Because you're always with her,' said Gabriel. 'Nah,' insisted Edwin. 'She's my home girl.'

For the last few years, Edwin and Camilla had been living in Bellaire Gardens, a low-rise apartment complex on a busy road of commercial and residential properties in southwest Houston in an area called Gulfton. A greenfield site until shortly after the Second World War, Gulfton was rapidly developed during the seventies, at the height of Houston's oil boom. Ambitious energy workers flocked to Texas from the Rust Belt and abroad, prompting opportunistic developers to hastily build 'luxury' apartment complexes for young professionals. In the absence of zoning laws, these new complexes sprouted up all around Gulfton and boasted fancy names like Chateaux Carmel and Napoleon Square, with amenities such as swimming pools, hot tubs, laundry rooms, and even discos, while offering free gifts including VCRs to new tenants. These gated communities, strewn along roads with dense traffic in between commercial outlets, were often built like small fortresses, with many stipulating that no children were allowed. Precious little in the way of social infrastructure – parks, libraries, even schools – followed.[3]

When the oil bust came, this new clientele moved on, and the speculators were suddenly left with vast property portfolios and no tenants to fill them. They found new customers by slashing rents, eliminating the 'no children' rules, and forgoing background checks to draw in low-income migrants, primarily from Mexico and Central America. Within a decade, Gulfton had been transformed in Houston's imagination from trendy 'Swingersville' to the 'Gulfton Ghetto', and soon became notorious for gang crime.

Bellaire Gardens is one of those complexes. It sits between a store selling bridal wear and highly flammable-looking dresses for *quinceañera* – the celebration of a girl's fifteenth birthday – and the back of a Fiesta supermarket, a Texas-based Hispanic-oriented chain with garish neon lighting that makes you feel as though you're shopping for groceries in Vegas. Opposite are a pawn shop, beauty salon, Mexican taqueria, and Salvadorean restaurant.

The complex comprises two two-storey apartment buildings and is laid out in a square with a swimming pool and laundry room at the heart of a larger courtyard. The apartments are brick and in a poor state of repair. Each one has a porch, where plants, bicycles, and barbecue grills wait for warmer weather. Marlyn was always happy there. 'It was very nice,' she says. 'He loved that place. We knew the neighbours. Nothing bad ever happened. They all grew up there so they all loved it.' She lived there for eight years. They moved once, incidentally to a complex where Camilla's family was also living at the time. But she missed Bellaire Gardens so much she soon returned.

They lived in an apartment overlooking the swimming pool in the central courtyard; Camilla's unit lay on the periphery, closer to the entrance past the laundry room and just a minute away. Marlyn didn't approve of Camilla's family. She knew them well enough to say hello to them but had never visited their apartment and was none too keen on Edwin's spending so much time there. She heard they dealt drugs and feared that Camilla might lead Edwin astray. 'She's my best friend, she won't do anything to me,' Edwin told her. But Marlyn was not convinced. Camilla had a sense that Marlyn was not a fan. 'Your mom keeps looking at me weird,' she told Edwin. 'She doesn't like me.'

But although Camilla came from more difficult circumstances, she was also much more focused at school and aspirational than Edwin. He went to school to mess around, but she had goals. She wanted to be a pharmacist. She played snare drum in the school band. She was getting good grades. None of her siblings had done well in school. 'She was a bright girl,' said one of her teachers. 'She could have been the one.' When she felt down because she had performed badly academically, she would get upset and Edwin would try to cheer her up. 'Let's go chill with some home boys and smoke some weed,' he'd suggest. 'I can't because I have to stay for band practice,' she'd tell him. Her nickname for him was McLovin, after the hapless character in the teenage movie *Superbad*.

The Southwest Cholos run this neighbourhood, complex by complex. There is no avoiding them. 'They start them really, really young,' a teacher at Lee High told me. 'In elementary. Third grade, fourth grade. And that's just how it is for kids.'

What defines gang membership are extremely subjective and loose criteria. Gang leaders don't hand out membership cards. Sometimes there is initiation. However, since gang affiliation can be a guide to criminal activity and allegiance, with at least semiformal codes and boundaries, authorities are constantly trying to demarcate a more definite way to identify them.

Almost inevitably, such proscription falls back on stereotypes. In a 1999 article in *Colorlines*, it was pointed out that 'In at least five states, wearing baggy FUBU jeans and being related to a gang suspect is enough to meet the "gang member" definition. In Arizona, a tattoo and blue Adidas sneakers are sufficient.' In suburban Aurora, Colorado, local police decided that any two of the following constituted gang membership: 'slang', 'clothing of a particular colour', 'pagers', 'hairstyles', 'jewellery'. Black people comprised 11 per cent of Aurora and 80 per cent of the gang database. The local head of the ACLU was heard to say, 'They might as well call it a black list.'[4]

'You join for protection,' explains one of Edwin's teachers. 'Even if you're not cliqued in, so long as you're associated with them, you're good. You have to claim a clique to be safe. If you're not, if you're by yourself, you're gonna get jumped.' This is what makes the term *gang-infested* so loaded and so unhelpful. Many young people in certain areas are gang members in the same way that Soviet citizens were members of the Communist Party and Iraqis under Saddam Hussein were in the Baath Party – there was precious little choice. In and of itself their gang affiliation doesn't tell you much. To treat all affiliation as complicity is to write off children in entire communities for being born in the wrong place at the wrong time.

When it came to the Southwest Cholos, Camilla was a devoted member; Edwin was not. Though nobody said it, one gets the impression that his immaturity would have been a liability. He was a wannabe. 'They accepted him,' says Ms Thomas. 'He hung with them. But he wasn't in yet.' His mother knew nothing of this. But then parents rarely do.

When I was sixteen, I went on a camping holiday to Germany with a friend. On the way back to England we stopped in a small Dutch border town called Nijmegen. The first thing we did was go to a 'coffee shop' and buy as much marijuana as we could. It might have potentially lasted us for a couple of weeks, but my friend and I stuffed it all into two huge joints. We went for a walk, bought packets of cookies, bags of potato crisps and pastries, sat in a clearing behind a housing estate, and smoked them both. We laughed uproariously and lay down for what seemed like hours, either rambling like fools or in total silence. Eventually the police came. They asked us questions in Dutch. We thought their accents hilarious and kept on laughing. They told us to go back to the campsite, but when they saw us head off in completely the wrong direction – we had no idea where we were – they circled their van around and picked us up.

At the site, they made us show them our passports and train tickets. 'There's a train that leaves here this afternoon that will get you to the Hook of Holland in time for the night boat,' they told us. 'You should be on it.' By this time, even though we weren't quite thinking straight, we knew we were in trouble. We scrambled to pack our things – not easy when you're as stoned as we were – and sheepishly, still not fully sober, we went home. My mother was pleased to see me, but surprised because I had come back a day early. On the mantelpiece was an unopened envelope with the results of two O levels that I'd taken in politics and economics. I'd received As on both tests. If anyone had asked her how my summer went, she'd have told them I'd had a lovely holiday and did well at school. She had no idea I'd ever smoked marijuana, let alone about my brush with the law in the Netherlands. As far as she was concerned, her A-grade son couldn't wait to get home, and so he returned from his adventure prematurely.

Parents might have perfectly loving, functional relationships with their children but still, particularly in the children's teenage years, have precious little idea what they're getting up to. Of course, there might be signs that an adolescent is having sex, taking drugs or drinking. But they might not be obvious, the parents might miss them, the child might be incredibly good at covering his or her tracks or the parents might avert their gaze in a mixture of discretion and denial. It is possible to transgress any number of boundaries and still keep curfew, achieve acceptable grades and be civil at home. Parents might have known their children longer than anyone else and understand their impulses better than anyone else. But that's not the same as actually knowing what they're doing at a given moment.

Marlyn, like most parents, had a very different understanding of what Edwin was doing from what he was actually doing. She knew he was messing around in school. How could she not, given the number of times she'd been called in? But beyond that, she was less aware of what he was getting up to. When I asked one school friend, Diego (not his real name), what he did when he hung out with Edwin, his response was brief and to the point. 'Play soccer and smoke blunts,' he said. Gabriel said that, among other things, they liked to smoke. On his Facebook page Edwin refers to smoking quite a bit. 'Man just snook out of ma house and went to go smoke a joint with ma homegirl Camilla-fukkin-high-B).' There are several posts declaring things like 'Everything's better when you're high'; one post displays a picture of a woman with smoke pouring from her mouth and the words 'Blaze it up.' For a few months in July, his

Facebook cover photo was a marijuana leaf surrounded by smoke. There were signs.

So when Marlyn, looking for evidence of why he was behaving badly at school, brought his hands to her nose and smelled marijuana, it was a surprise only to her. She says Edwin cried and asked for forgiveness. He told her his hands smelled like that because he was helping Camilla roll a joint. It's the kind of story a mother believes because she wants to. But then there were other stories few mothers could reasonably imagine. That summer, Edwin and Camilla had become embroiled in a feud with a boy called Stevie G. (not his real name), who was affiliated with a rival gang, La Primera (LP). His girlfriend had moved into the Bellaire Gardens apartments to live with her aunt and tried to befriend Edwin and Camilla. But they neither liked nor trusted her. She was in LP, and they figured she was feeding information back to her boyfriend. 'We talked a lot of mess about her on the Internet,' says Camilla. When Stevie G. heard about their insults, he was livid. Earlier in the autumn he'd come to Camilla's apartment, had threatened her and had trash-talked Edwin. Not long before that, he'd shot at Camilla's brother when he was hanging out on Bissonnet Street. Camilla and Edwin thought they needed to protect themselves if Stevie G. ever came back. So they pooled what little cash they had and bought a gun, which they stashed at Camilla's house. 'But we were thinking like little kids,' says Camilla. 'I didn't really know anything about guns. I just know you shoot with it and that's it.'

On Saturday morning, 23 November, as Kenneth's and Stanley's deaths lit up social media, Edwin slept in. Marlyn had made flour tortillas, which were his favourite, but he said he didn't feel like eating them and asked for sausages and a couple of eggs instead. He was a picky eater, and Marlyn wasn't interested in wasting food. 'You'd better eat them both,' she told him. He said he would, and as he ate he took some sausage from his plate and put it in her mouth. They chatted about school and his friends. He'd just met a new girl and claimed he was going to ask her out on Monday. He asked Marlyn for ten dollars so he could buy the girl a burger. 'What about Joanna?' his mother asked, referring to another girl he was interested in. 'She's with somebody else,' he said.

For the rest of the afternoon, he lazed around the apartment, going upstairs to play PlayStation and then returning to his mother's room, where he lay with his legs over hers, while his phone charged and Marlyn watched television. It was unseasonably chilly that night for Houston – overcast and breezy with winds gusting at 27 mph. Edwin was cold and snuggled with Marlyn, coaxing her phone from her so he could check his Facebook page.

Around 5.30 p.m., just as Brandon was calling for a pizza in Marlette, Edwin put on his socks and asked if he could go to hang out with Kevin on Bissonnet Avenue. Marlyn said no, it was too cold and it was getting dark. Then his younger siblings had another idea. At the back of the Bellaire Gardens complex were some abandoned apartments where they'd recently found some puppies. Edwin hadn't seen the puppies yet, and the kids asked Marlyn if they could go and feed them. Marlyn agreed, so long as they all went together. She prepared some rice and shredded meat to feed to the dogs. They all left together, and she stood at the door watching them as they turned the corner. 'Be careful, and don't go anywhere else,' she shouted after them. But as soon as the door was closed, Edwin peeled off, telling his siblings he was going back to get his coat but instead doubling back to visit Camilla. 'He knew if he'd asked me I'd have said no,' says Marlyn.

When he arrived at Camilla's he looked as if he'd just woken up. 'I've come to see my best friend,' he told her. 'Your best friend's on Bissonnet,' she told him, teasing him in the knowledge that his first choice had been to hang with Kevin.

They chatted for a while, and then Edwin asked where the gun was. She thought her brother had taken it because of Stevie G., but when she checked it was still there. She gave it to him. Neither was remotely familiar with guns. He cocked it and then took the clip out. For a lark he pointed it at her and made out like he was going to shoot her. Then he gave it to her. 'Make out like you're gonna shoot me,' he said.

Although Ms Thomas cannot speak to the veracity of anything that happened that night, from what she knows of Edwin this scenario rings true. She refers to Edwin as a '*what if?* kid', chasing hypotheticals as a dog would chase a car. 'He'd say, "Miss, what if I drop out of school?"' Ms Thomas recalled. 'And I'd say, "What if you live under a bridge?" "Hey miss, what if I walk out this door right now?" "What if you get suspended?" That was where his mind was at.'

But Camilla obliged. She held the gun at an angle, as though it were an extension of her arm, gangster-style. They assumed that because the clip was out the gun was empty. They didn't realise that when he'd cocked it he'd put a bullet in the chamber. 'I didn't really know how to clear out the chamber,' says Camilla. 'I didn't really know it would go in there. Because it was my first gun.' She pressed it against his chest and pulled the trigger. Pop. Then silence. Edwin's eyes widened in shock and pain; Camilla's eyes widened in disbelief as she felt the gun recoil. 'Oh shit, you shot me,' he said. 'Oh, sorry,' said Camilla. They stared at each other in a suspended moment, each realising they could not turn the clock back and that Edwin had little time left. 'I picked him up to carry him downstairs. But when I looked at him his eyes were rolling back already,' says Camilla. 'Basically he was already dying.'

Camilla panicked. 'I didn't know what to tell my mom or anybody,' she said. 'Because nobody knew that we had a gun. Not even my mom. We hadn't had it for even a month. I didn't know how to tell them.' She hid the clip in the bed and the gun elsewhere and told her mom that Stevie G. had shot Edwin through the window.

Across the courtyard, Marlyn was getting anxious. It was close to 7 p.m., and the kids had been away for close to half an hour. 'If they don't come back in ten minutes, I'm going to find them,' she told herself. She went to get some shoes and a sweater, but before she could get herself ready she heard them climbing the stairs. Trouble was, there were only three of them. 'Where's Edwin?' she asked. 'We don't know,' the children said. 'He never came with us.'

Marlyn knew he'd gone to Camilla's. She told Victor to go fetch him, but Victor refused, saying he hated going to Camilla's house because it was gross. Giovanni volunteered. 'Tell him if he doesn't come now I'll go over there and bring him back by the ear,' she told Giovanni. Giovanni left, only to come back alone, breathless and with, as Marlyn recalls, 'terror in his face'. 'Mom, come quickly, Edwin is dying at Camilla's house.'

Sandra was the first to get there. She found Camilla crying on the stairs while her mother tried to revive Edwin at the top of the stairs, just outside Camilla's room. Camilla kept to her story – Edwin had been looking out the window when she'd heard gunfire and saw him fall back. Marlyn was fast on Sandra's heels, springing into life and sprinting across the courtyard, after briefly being paralysed by shock. She flew up the stairs and pushed Camilla's mom out of the way. Thinking he had reacted badly to some kind of drug, she yelled at Camilla's mom, 'What did you give him? He has asthma.' 'No,' Camilla's mom said. 'He has a bullet wound.'

Marlyn searched in vain but could see no blood. Camilla had shot him at such close range it was not immediately obvious where the wound was. Then Marlyn opened his jacket and there was the hole. She heard a noise in his chest, like a gurgling – the same kind of noise Nicole had heard as she held Jaiden. When Marlyn pushed, some blood spurted out. She held him in her arms, the whole time screaming, 'Edwin, what did they do to you? What did they do to you? Answer me!'

He'd been there for about half an hour, and no one had called emergency services. She knew he was dead. His skin was purple, his eyes were rolled back high under his lids. But she hoped for a miracle. She called 911. When the paramedics arrived, they told everyone to clear out. When they finally carried him down on the stretcher, they told her it was too late. He was gone.

Camilla told Marlyn the story about Stevie G. and the bullet through the window. Marlyn didn't buy it, but at first the media did. The local ABC news affiliate ran a piece on its website later that night stating, 'The shooter is still at large and the case remains under investigation.' In the early hours of the next morning the local ABC news anchor, Foti Kallergis, was tweeting that police thought the shooting was gang-related.[5]

Meanwhile, Camilla's story was unravelling fast. The police found the clip on the bed and the shell in the room. And it didn't take a ballistics expert to realise that Edwin was shot close up rather than from a distance. 'I knew I had to tell them the truth,' says Camilla. 'They found the clip and they found the shell. So they knew the shooting happened inside the house.' She eventually confessed all at the police station. She didn't get back home until 5 a.m. on Sunday morning.

Ms Thomas was getting ready for church when she got a call from her former secretary saying Edwin was on the news. She wouldn't tell her why. Ms Thomas assumed he had done something stupid. But when she turned on the television, there was no mention of it. News of his death had not lasted all the way through the overnight news cycle on local network television. So she went online and saw that he'd been involved in a deadly shooting. Even then it took her a while to figure out what had happened. He'd just been in her office two days before; his paperwork was in her briefcase. Now she had to call her superiors and cancel Monday morning's meeting. Edwin would not be transitioning to behaviour class. He was dead. It just didn't make sense.

On Monday morning, Gabriel arrived at school still refusing to believe the rumours. All through the weekend he'd heard people talking about it, but he thought Edwin was involved in an almighty, sick hoax. He was in Edwin's class for the first period, and he planned to confront him about playing such a tasteless prank. Usually he would come in late to see Edwin sitting at the same desk with his head resting on his folded arms as though he were asleep. But the desk was empty, and he could deny it no longer. He sat in Edwin's empty chair and started to weep.

By that time, Ms Thomas had managed to get in touch with most of the special-ed. teachers who knew Edwin. A small convoy of educators and counsellors from school took the eight-minute drive to Bellaire Gardens to see how they could help. It was a crazy scene, with detectives and police swarming throughout, a family mourning in one apartment, and a young girl in shock across the courtyard.

As they walked up the stairs to Edwin's apartment, they met his sister, Sandra, who sat zoned out on the front porch, listening to the songs kids were posting on Facebook to memorialise her brother. Inside, Marlyn sat clutching a small five-by-seven-inch framed photo of Edwin, muttering tender words in Spanish to herself. Up the narrow staircase, in the room Edwin shared with his two younger brothers, Giovanni and Victor played video games, avoiding the eyes of yet more visitors. On Edwin's bed lay his school uniform – trousers, shirt, and socks on the bed, along with his inhaler, and shoes on the floor. Ready to go.

'Who did this?' asked Ms Thomas. 'Mama,' the younger brothers said, and went back to their gaming. Across the courtyard, Camilla stared at a huge flat-screen television, which was on mute, while a pitbull barked in its cage. One of the counsellors sat with her for a while. Eventually Camilla spoke. 'I can't talk right now,' she said and then continued to sit in silence. She was more communicative on Facebook, where she grieved openly. Solipsistic, raw, desperate for affirmation, her first posting – the day after she'd shot Edwin – reads, 'Whyy!!?? Why does shit like dis allways have to happen to me :,,(I'm soo sorry Edwin Martinez [Edwin's Facebook name] :'''(I love you homie RIP:((I hope I see you soon . . .'

The second post, written on the same day, reads, 'Listening to Bob Marley reminds me of you Edwin Martinez [*cry emoticon*] homie goodnight I love you you'll allways be on my mind <\3 I'm sorry it end like dis :"(:'"(Rest In Paradise ! [*heart emoticon*].' She tagged his brother Victor and his sister Sandra.

A couple of days later, on 26 November, she reached out in one posting to the Rajo family:

> I just wanna say thanks to everybody whos been here for me all my family & Edwin Martinez family [*heart emoticon*] thank yall and all my freinds thanks yall really help me a lot [*cry emoticon*] [*cry emoticon*] even the people that bearly know me thanks [*cry emoticon*]
>
> I miss you my Mclovin my best friend . . . [*cry emoticon*] I'm sorry [*cry emoticon*] [*cry emoticon*] REST IN PEACE I love you even doe I never told you I know you knew <\3 [*cry emoticon*].

Marlyn, meanwhile, was struggling with the practicalities. Ms Thomas had offered to raise money to help bury Edwin, but Marlyn said they would be OK. They sold T-shirts and applied for public funds for funeral costs, but when you speak no English, are grieving, and have to rely on traumatised children to translate for you, these things take time. She says she was told that because his shooting was accidental, he was not eligible for public assistance. She was stumped. Over a week later she called Ms Thomas to take her up on her offer of help. Ms Thomas put out an e-mail. There is money in Houston, an oil-rich city; it's just not immediately accessible to the likes of the Rajos. But before the day was out, Ms Thomas and her colleagues had collected $1,800, which was enough to lay Edwin to rest. His body would lie in the morgue for more than two weeks. Marlyn was also struggling emotionally. When Ms Thomas arrived at the wake at the family's apartment, she wondered if Marlyn was going to make it. She walked in to find her leaning over the coffin, holding onto Edwin as a slideshow beamed pictures of him on the wall. She pried Ms Rajo gently away and led her to the nearest seat, where the mother put her head on Ms Thomas's lap and wept, asking, 'Why?' over and over again. Someone who'd recently undergone a root canal slipped her a Vicodin. It was the first night she'd slept in weeks.

They finally buried Edwin on 13 December. The funeral, held at the Santana funeral home, was almost exactly the same: Ms Rajo leaning over the coffin, Ms Thomas acting as her emotional caretaker. 'When I saw him in the coffin,' says Marlyn, 'I wanted to go with him. But I know my other kids needed me.' No preacher showed up. So there was no service. No prayer. No scripture was read. A couple of family members said a few words, but otherwise nothing. 'We just sat there staring at the body for two hours. It was just like another wake,' said Ms Thomas. Finally they closed the casket. As people left the funeral home to make their way to the burial site, Marlyn asked if she could travel in the hearse with the coffin. 'No,' said Ms Thomas, and with the help of her assistant they bundled her into the first car they saw. When they got to the burial site the funeral directors opened the coffin again. It was like the torment was never going to end.

For a while afterwards, Marlyn thought she was going crazy. She imagined that maybe Edwin was hidden somewhere and would come back. The doctor gave her sleeping pills, but in the end she fell back on her religion. Raised Catholic, she is now Evangelical. 'Church has helped me get through the pain. It's made me more religious. But even though I say that, sometimes I still feel the pain, and every day there is more pain. Then I start praying.' When I met her, fifteen months after Edwin's death, she started crying before I'd asked a single question.

As happened in the tiny hamlet of Marlette, Michigan, where Tyler Dunn was shot by a friend, Edwin's death divided families and friends. So long as Marlyn remained in the Bellaire Gardens apartments, she would bump into Camilla's family all the time. When she did, she yelled at them, 'Why? Why did you kill my son?' They responded with insults. They told her she was going crazy and even blamed her. 'You should have let him smoke weed in your house, then he wouldn't have had to come here,' they said. They accused Edwin of bringing the weapon into the house and asking them to hide it for him. 'But that's not true,' says Marlyn. 'I know that Edwin did not have a weapon. Only God knows the truth, and Edwin's not here to deny it . . . I told her mother it's her fault. She the one selling drugs and having weapons in her house.'

At one point, she and Camilla came to blows. 'I was on drugs,' explains Camilla, 'and she was shouting at me, "You killed my son." You know, that really hurts me,' Camilla continues, 'because he was my friend.' 'Hey, that was an accident, man,' Camilla told her. 'You can't say that kind of shit to me every time I pass by.' According to Camilla, Marlyn threw a can at her, and so Camilla tried to beat her up. 'She kept calling me "devil" or "murderer" and shit like that.'

Camilla was also struggling. She wanted to kill herself. 'I wish Edwin had shot me or I'd shot myself or something. Edwin's resting in peace right now, and I've still got to do everything. I still got to deal with people looking at me wrong because they know what happened. I wanted to kill myself, but I didn't have the guts to do it, so I thought, man, I'm just gonna be in the gang and I'm just gonna come out for Edwin because Edwin was a Cholo. That's how I was planning on dying. I was lost in my mind. I just messed up my whole life. I only smoked weed with Edwin. But after he died I got really into the bars [Xanax, prescription painkillers]. I started drinking beer and taking coke.'

More than a year after the shootings, she is acutely aware of her fragile emotional state, even if she is unable to do much about it. 'I was a mess. I tried almost everything. Just to be high and forget about all my problems. But the next day, I wake up and they're still there. The only reason I didn't shoot myself is because I started reading the Bible and stuff. I used to be an atheist, but that's the only thing that gave me hope. Because it's hard to live with something like that. Because everybody throws it in your face once in a while. "You know what you did." Sometimes when my mom gets mad she says, "It's because of you that we have all these fucking problems."'

Camilla had some counselling and was even committed to a psychiatric ward for a while. 'I've never been to the hospital for more than two weeks. Because they made me feel like I'm crazy. And I'm not crazy. They made me take off my shoelaces. They made me take off my headband. And I don't like that.' Her promise in school evaporated. When she wasn't high, she was belligerent, and sometimes both simultaneously. 'I just thought, fuck school. I didn't care about it no more. They kicked me out because I'm in a gang and I saw someone in school who was repping for someone else and so I tried to fight them. But I didn't care. I thought any of these days I could die. One my friends could die. One of my family members could die. Just like Edwin died out of nowhere. That day, I didn't know that was going to happen. Your friends die every year. I don't know when it's my last day with the people I love. I don't care about the future because it's not here yet.'

But there were also significant differences between the fallout from Edwin's death and that following Tyler Dunn's. First of all, unlike with Tyler's death, after which two people were punished by the courts, nobody has been held accountable for Edwin's death. The case was referred to a grand jury,[6] but there's no evidence that it ever met, and no one was ever charged. Less than two weeks after we spoke Camilla had been arrested for 'retaliation' in what appears to be an unrelated matter. She was later sentenced to two years in prison.

Marlyn's principal grievance is that more than a year after that fatal day, no charges have been brought and no price has been paid. 'They never called me when it happened,' she says, referring to

Camilla and her mother. 'They had him there, and they didn't do anything. Perhaps if they'd called me when it happened I could have done something. By the time I got there he'd already been there for half an hour. She wasn't imprisoned. She faced no charges. I called the police to find out why she wasn't imprisoned. She's free. She wasn't even reprimanded. They said there will be justice. There will be a process. But it's been more than a year. Somebody should be held responsible for this. She sells drugs. They should go to prison. If a pet was killed like that, there would be justice. They showed no remorse or guilt, and in the end nothing happened to them.'

Paradoxically, given that there has been no punishment, there has also been more forgiveness. Camilla went to Edwin's funeral. Her Facebook cover photo shows her sitting next to Edwin's grave, all in black, surrounded by flowers and balloons, smoking what looks like a joint. Her previous photo shows a large crowd standing around the grave. She says she's still in contact with Sandra and Victor. (Sandra said she wasn't.) 'His sister and brother are cool,' she says. 'But every time I'm with them I know what happened. I feel bad because they don't have a brother no more. The only person I'm not cool with is his mom. And I understand that. Because sometimes I even get mad at myself. He was my best friend.'

There was a moment on Facebook when it looked as if tensions might flare, as they did in Marlette. The day after the shooting, Adan Castaneda posted, 'Fucked up Knowing Who Killed Him!' At that stage, most didn't know what had happened or who was involved. A rumour that it was suicide was quickly quashed. But Adan's friends demanded to know what he knew. Yasmine stepped in and said, 'Don't say her name.' Then Camilla joined the fray.

CAMILLA: Adan, don't be saying he got killed nigga. It was an accident.

ADAN: I know it was an accident.

CAMILLA: I sorry doe nigga.

ADAN: Is alight.

EMJAY: we know it was an accident and accidents happens to everybody.

CAMILLA: life's a bitch I don't wanted to end like this.

Within the gang, it was debated whether she should be kicked out, killed for killing one of their own, or given a pass. She talked to her OG (Original Gangster, or gang leader) about it. They decided it was an accident and she had suffered enough. 'They said we were young and stupid and it was just an accident, and if someone messes with me about that then it's them who's gonna die or whatever,' she told me. Even Marlyn, despite their altercations, believes it was a genuine accident – most of the time. 'I don't think she would have killed him on purpose,' she says. 'I think she loved him. But sometimes my pain as a mother makes me feel otherwise.'

The Rajos moved away from Bellaire Gardens. Marlyn couldn't stand the memories. When I met them they had just settled into a new housing complex ten minutes away. They'd moved in a week earlier and were not yet unpacked. There was no furniture, and though she was heavily pregnant Marlyn insisted that the translator and I sit on two tables. She stood, running her hand over the curve of her extended belly. Shortly before the interview was over I asked if, given everything that had happened, she regretted coming to America. Honduras has a far, far higher rate of homicide in general and gun deaths in particular. But she'd come looking for a better life for a family that did not yet exist; now her eldest son was dead. 'No,' she says. 'It's hard here. It's very hard. It's hard work just to stay alive. But I don't regret leaving. I don't regret coming. Sometimes I think God must know what happened to my son and why. But I don't blame the country. It could have happened anywhere. Knowing the situation in Honduras I think my children are better off here.'

A month after I spoke to her she gave birth to a boy weighing five pounds twelve ounces. She named him Edwin.

7

Samuel Brightmon
(aged sixteen)

Dallas, Texas

23 November, approx. 11.00 p.m. CST

In her biography of Harlem Renaissance writer Zora Neale Hurston, *Wrapped in Rainbows*, Valerie Boyd explains why it was so difficult to track Hurston's whereabouts during her early twenties: 'In 1911 it was relatively easy for someone, particularly a black woman, to evade history's recording gaze.' She continues, 'If not legally linked to a man, as daughter or wife, black women did not count in some ways – at least to the people who did the official counting.'[1]

The question of who counts and who is counted is not simply an issue of numbers. It's also about power. Collecting information, particularly about people, demands both the authority to gather data and the capacity to keep and transmit it. Those who have both the authority and the capacity need to feel that those they are keeping tabs on matter. In the aftermath of Hurricane Katrina, as the dead floated in the streets of New Orleans and the living were stranded on highways and rooftops, a huge crowd of mostly black and poor people descended on the city's convention centre. When asked why relief organisations had been caught off guard, Michael Brown, the hapless director of the Federal Emergency Management Agency, responded, 'We're seeing people that we didn't know exist.'[2]

In short, not everybody counts, and therefore not everybody is counted. We know, for example, how many American soldiers died during the Iraq invasion, because the US government had to keep record. One can only imagine the outcry if they hadn't. But we can only guess how many Iraqi civilians or insurgents have died, because there was no Iraqi state to count them and it was not in US interests to keep a tally, let alone learn their names. We know how many US police officers are killed in the line of duty in any given year, but there is no national tally for how many people are killed by police officers.

During the early nineties, when child and teen gun deaths ran at more than twice the rate they do now,[3] many a child's death went unreported in the media. The deaths were deemed so frequent and predictable, and they occurred in places so foreign to those who had the power to cover them, that they might as well have been in Iraq. So back then, a young life could be extinguished without trace. The police would barely be interested. The circumstances, the names, the ages of the dead were not considered of sufficient public interest to log each one as a matter of course. Dan Kois, who ran the Gun-Death Tally for the online magazine *Slate,* says that would not happen today.

'I think by this stage, pretty much every homicide and accident that take place are reported,' Kois told me. The development of social media, citizen journalism and new technology have made it more difficult for the established media to simply ignore gun deaths in certain areas. 'In most cities, there are separate blogs recording gun deaths, and this keeps the newspapers and other local media outlets honest. The numbers we got chimed with the statistical projections [for gun homicides and accidents].' Kois, a senior editor for *Slate,* acknowledged that the numbers it collected fell well short (by more than half) of all the gun deaths that occurred, because, as I pointed out in the Introduction, suicides are generally not reported.

The Gun-Death Tally, set up in the wake of the Newtown shootings, sought to record every gun death in the country.[4] The website, which ran for a year, compiled its data through basic Internet searches and crowdsourcing; anybody could send in news of a gun death, and site managers would add it to the tally. The site represented each death using a stick figure in one of three sizes – large for adults, medium for teens, and small for children – with web links to news reports of what happened.

'The feature was meant to be a provocation of sorts,' Kois wrote, when the site was closing. 'We knew that those rows of figures, each one attached to a name, piling atop one another every day, made for an arresting visual, one that might trouble even the most ardent gun-rights supporter.'[5]

Five weeks after the Gun-Death Tally was launched, Joe Nocera wrote a column for the *New York Times* titled 'And in Last Week's Gun News . . .', in which he provided brief descriptions of a handful of those who had died from gun violence in the previous week.[6]

'There were nine or ten items,' Nocera told me. 'There was no editorialising by me whatsoever. Just these clips. I thought it was powerful and very effective. If you live in Lexington, Kentucky, or Providence, Rhode Island, you don't have a sense of all the gun violence there is out there.' From this emerged 'The Gun Report', a daily digest on the *New York Times* website relating to all things gun-related, including fatalities. It ran from Monday to Friday; the one on Monday compiled the events of the preceding weekend. 'It's simply a Google search every day of gun deaths,' says Nocera. 'It's the only thing I've ever done that got reviewed by the *New York Review of Books*,' he adds with some pride.

Both *Slate*'s Gun-Death Tally and the *New York Times*'s 'Gun Report' were comprehensive and provided useful starting points. Neither was definitive. Four of the young people featured in this book did not appear on one of the two sites; one death appeared on neither.

Slate wound down its efforts after a year and directed followers to the Gun Violence Archive, which conducted a similar but more extensive effort on a website bound to attract less traffic since it was not part of a general news outlet. The *New York Times* held out for a little longer before a dispute over overtime pay for the editorial assistant compiling the data allegedly triggered its demise.[7] In the paper, Nocera offered a different explanation. 'A few months ago,' he wrote, 'I began to feel that we had made the point already. Day after day, week after week, there was a numbing sameness to the shootings.'[8]

But if the fact of a gun death is now generally reported, it is often done so in the most summary, almost dismissive, fashion. Such was the case for Samuel Brightmon's death, whose shooting appeared in the *Dallas Morning News* under the headline 'Teen Fatally Shot While Walking Down Street'. 'Police are investigating after a teenager was fatally shot Saturday night when walking down the street in Southeast Dallas,' the article read. 'Police say Samuel Brightmon, 16, and another 16-year-old were walking in the 7300 block of Schepps Parkway around 11 p.m. when they heard gunshots. As the teens tried to run away, Brightmon was shot and collapsed in the street, according to police. Brightmon was taken to Baylor University Medical Center of Dallas where he was pronounced dead. No suspect has been identified.'[9]

The following day the *Dallas Morning News* filed another brief report by Claire Z. Cardona, adding that 'Crime Stoppers is offering a $5,000 reward for information that leads to the arrest and indictment for the felony offense', and giving readers the number of the tip line to call.

The local Fox News affiliate ran a picture of Samuel bearing a wide, bright, toothy smile and wearing a blue-and-white shirt. He has clear skin, a strong jaw, and bright eyes – a face too young for life to put lines on it. The Fox website had almost identical information (since deleted), under the headline 'Dallas Teen Killed By Random Gunfire': 'Dallas police are asking for help to find the person who killed a teen who was walking down a street. It happened just after 11 p.m. Saturday along Schepps Parkway in Pleasant Grove. Sixteen-year-old Samuel Brightmon was with a friend when they heard gunshots. They tried to run, but Brightmon was hit. He died at the hospital.'[10] They did manage to get a quote from his mother. '"It's so unreal right now. It's a million and one things going through my head, but then I just can't focus on anything. The only image I see is the last image I have of me holding him," said Audry Smith, the victim's mother. Brightmon's friend was not hurt. Crime Stoppers is offering a $5,000 reward for information leading to an indictment.'

That was it. They didn't have an awful lot to go on. The police report is similarly minimal, adding only that it believed the shooting was not gang-related. There was no profile, no testimony from his school friends or teachers. No sense of who he was, let alone why he was killed. His death was counted. It just didn't count for much.

Samuel Courde-Bernard Brightmon, known to his family as 'DaDa' (a nickname based on his middle name), died less than a week short of his seventeenth birthday. He was the second of three children of Audry Smith and the third of seven children by Willie Brightmon. Willie and Audry were long separated, but Willie was a constant presence in Samuel's life. They were two of a number of parental figures, including his Aunt Debra (Audry's sister), and Claudia, Willie's second wife, who remained a good friend of Audry.

Samuel's best friend was his sister Whitney, a tall, reedy girl only eleven months his junior, who paid close attention as I twice interviewed her mother but said little. When they were younger, they'd sleep together because Whitney didn't like sleeping by herself. When they were older, Samuel would often climb into bed with Whitney after he woke up. They would finish each other's thoughts and sentences. 'Them two, they were like Bonnie and Clyde,' says Audry. 'Everyone used to think they were twins because they were so close in age and did everything together.'

Whitney was Samuel's fiercest defender. 'I acted like a big sister to him,' she told me. Once, when they were at their Aunt Debra's house, Samuel told his aunt that some boys had jumped him. 'Before I could even get my shoes on, my middle daughter and Whitney took out running to fight the boys for him,' Debra recalls. 'By the time I got there they had already found the boys and cornered them down. They were hot.'

Samuel was a prankster. His friends recall his japes the way teenagers do – laughing so hard that you're still struggling to follow the story when it becomes clear that they've already delivered the punchline. The kind of anecdotes you really had to be there for. Once, he brought in a rubber duck and chased students around while making voices like Ernie from *Sesame Street*. Another time, he put on Whitney's pink, fluffy boots and scarf and made like he was on a catwalk. He put a cornball on someone's desk. His mother has a video clip of him doing a daft dance in school – all spidery legs and flapping arms. 'That's him,' she said. 'Just goofy. Always.'

The fact that he rarely made anybody else the butt of his jokes was consistent with his personality. He was conflict averse. And from an early age he was always eager to please. 'He wanted to fit in,' says Claudia, who met me at Soulman's Bar-B-Que, a Texas chain, next to the freeway. 'He was like the peacekeeper. So when the other sisters and brothers would get to fighting, he would always say, "Let's stick together."' She continued, 'Whatever he did he just smiled his way out of it. He didn't want to get in trouble. So he would just put a smile on ya so you'd be like, "OK, I'll give you a second chance", because of his smile. He was sweet.'

'DaDa was like the son I never had,' says Debra. 'Whenever I needed something done, like taking out the trash or something a son would do, he would do it. If I just got home from the grocery store, I didn't have to worry about my groceries being taken out of the car. He was just a helpful kid. A happy kid. Full of jokes. He wasn't a fighter. He wasn't a troublemaker.'

There was a worry that his trusting nature would get him in trouble. 'My most fear for him was because he'll befriend anybody,' says Willie. 'He ain't never met no stranger. That's his type of mentality. He's so naive.' Willie grew up in Marshall, Texas, a small town a couple of hours' drive away, not far from the Louisiana state line, where everybody knew everybody else. He felt Samuel's manner was better suited to his own rural upbringing than to an urban environment. 'Back home, ain't no such thing as a stranger. But in the city, some people will take your kindness for a weakness. For him it was like, "Oh Daddy, no, it won't be like that." And I said, "Yes, son, it will."'

Debra also worried that his desire to please might lead him into bad company. Once, when Audry and the children were staying with her, Samuel started hanging around with a group of kids, including a girl he'd taken a fancy to, whom Debra didn't like and of whom both her daughters had given poor accounts. 'I think he just wanted to make everybody happy,' she said. 'But these kids could have got him in trouble.' Debra told him to stay away from them. She was worried that he was so anxious to please others that he risked losing all sense of who he was and what he wanted. 'I broke it down for him. I used to try to get him to understand that it's OK to be different. I'd tell him, "Be true to you. Be who you are."'

Samuel took it badly. He huffed and sulked for a while. 'He was upset about it that night,' Debra recalls. 'But the very next day he wrote me a letter apologising for his behaviour and saying he understood. That meant a lot.'

Audry had worried for some time that what at first sight might have looked like an easygoing manner masked a deeper fragility. Samuel was dyslexic, and the early years of school had not been easy. 'The handwriting,' she says, listing the basics he'd struggled with. 'Not catching on with the other kids. He was tired of going to summer school every year. The teacher always calling and saying, "He needs help, he needs help, he needs help."

'That took a toll on him emotionally and gave him low self-esteem,' she says. 'He was quiet and reserved. He didn't make friends easily. When he was younger he didn't like the sports. He didn't like the touching and the hitting. He was so sensitive he would always cry. He seemed desperate to please everybody.' When he was around ten he told a counsellor that he sometimes thought of hurting himself. The counsellor recommended an evaluation, and after a few tests doctors suggested admitting him to a psychiatric ward.

That proved too big a step for Samuel. 'He cried,' says Audry. 'Whitney cried. She didn't want him to go, and he didn't want to stay [at the hospital]. He didn't want to be away from Whitney or me. They felt like it was jail because of course they take your belt, your shoelaces, all of that. So they let him do the outpatient thing, where he would come in the morning and stay all day.'

As he grew into his teens, he became more confident. He wanted to be a policeman. 'From a young age, that had been his obsession,' says Audry. 'He loved cop shows – *Criminal Minds*, *Cops*, whatever was on. He even had a police app on his phone so he could track their activities.' When Samuel was fifteen, Audry moved Whitney and him from a big school with more than three thousand students to a new, smaller school in the northeastern suburb of Richardson, near her work, in the hope that he would get more hands-on attention. He campaigned for the vice-presidency of the student council, an elected position that demanded going to each class to canvass for votes. He pledged to get a basketball team off the ground, and he won. A team duly followed, although, because the school was so small, it played in a city league rather than against other local schools.

The first response in the comments section after the *Dallas Morning News* piece ran online came from one of Samuel's schoolmates. He called himself Parker Moore and identified himself as the student council president of Samuel's school. He wrote, 'He's a great kid and a go-getter. He was definitely going places in life. I last talked with him just on Monday about our ideas for a student council fundraiser. I can hardly believe this is really happening. Rest in peace, friend.'

Samuel didn't have much of a social life beyond school and family, though he did have a girlfriend. He was basically a homebody. 'He loved playing his video games,' says Audry. 'He wasn't an outdoor person. He loved his BB gun. He loved something to shoot at. But he never went anywhere. And if he went anywhere it was with me or Whitney.' For most of Samuel's life, it seems, those closest to him did their best to protect him from both the tenderest parts of himself and the toughest elements of the outside world.

*

Such was the brief life whose death received such short shrift in the Dallas media. The woman who wrote the 81-word account of Samuel's death for the *Dallas Morning News* is Melissa Repko, a young, engaging reporter whom I met at a hipster coffee shop in a gentrifying part of town. Melissa occasionally worked Sundays on the crime blog. It's a shift with a macabre but predictable routine and a busy start. 'If something's going to happen then it will usually happen between the hours of midnight and 4 a.m.,' she says. 'The kind of time when your mother tells you nothing good happens.' Shootings, drunk drivers and domestic violence are the staples from the Saturday night before. 'There's a police database that I go to, and then I make calls. I search for murders, sudden deaths, aggravated assaults,' she says. 'It's pretty common to have at least one shooting, although they're not always fatal.'

Two months after Samuel's murder she still remembered the case as much for what was not in the report as what was. 'I did remember it only because he was so young and it's quite rare they have no indication of there being criminal activity.' It was her task to record it, not to follow it up. So when the day was done, she'd hand the story over to the regular crime team, who take up the weekend stories they think are worth running with. Samuel's death didn't make the cut.

That didn't surprise Repko. Indeed it would surprise very few. Pleasant Grove, the area where Samuel was shot, is poor, black and located on the south side of Dallas; it is disparagingly known as 'Unpleasant Grove'. As one of Samuel's teachers said, 'If it had happened in Richardson [the location of his school], people would have been in shock. But in real far south in Dallas, that's not unusual.' Had she ever been there? 'I don't go down that way,' the teacher said. 'That's not a safe area for a white woman.' Evidently, it was not a safe area for a young black man either.

Shootings were common there, confirmed Repko. 'People are desensitised to it. They reason that's just where bad things happen.' I heard this refrain often when talking to the journalists who'd covered that day's shootings. Clearly, I was the only one who had called them to follow up on the story. They would kindly rifle through their notes and tell me what they knew and, if they'd been to the crime scene, what they had seen. Invariably, when I asked if they had any contact details for family members, or if there had been any developments in the investigation, they would explain, somewhat matter-of-factly, why they had moved on. 'Unfortunately, homicides are not uncommon in that area,' said one. 'Unless something unexpected happened it just wouldn't be the kind of story we'd follow up on,' said another.

As a journalist myself I understand this. I have no idea what happened to Jesus Josef, an eight-year-old Haitian boy whom I met in the Dominican Republic in 2005. He turned up at a refugee centre with his neck twisted from carrying heavy loads and his shoulders bearing welts from mistreatment by the family who had bought him and used him as a domestic slave. Nor do I know the fate of Kulo Korban, whom I met in Sierra Leone in 1998, and who'd had both his ears and three fingers amputated by rebels in the conflict there. After a week spent reporting from each place, I moved on.

I write this with neither pride nor guilt. There is a level of detachment inherent, and arguably necessary, in the profession. Without it, one would become emotionally depleted. Moreover, one is constantly gauging what more there is to say and who would be listening if you said it. Outlets have limited resources. Editors have to justify budgets for keeping you in a certain place or sending you back to trace each individual story, which in turn must be balanced against what other new stories you might be missing. Journalism is not social work. And even social workers, to be effective, must move on. That said, these are little more than rationalisations for how I, and other journalists, exercise our relative power. We choose whose stories are told, whom we go back to, and where our resources are deployed. And those choices are not objective. They are made on the basis of what stories we subjectively consider are worthy of being told at any given time. The fact that most media outlets are commercial enterprises is of course a factor. The more a story costs and the less likely it is to bring in readers (and therefore revenue), the less likely institutions are to invest resources in it. But it is not the only factor and generally not the most important.

Even without the profit motive, news values are not human values. If they were, the front-page story of every newspaper and the leading item on every bulletin would be 'Child Dies of Hunger'. But since we know that millions in the world don't have enough to eat and that at any given time a child somewhere might perish from malnourishment, it is not deemed news. In all likelihood a newspaper that decided to run that headline every day would sell precious few copies.

'We've got compassion fatigue, we say, as if we have involuntarily contracted some kind of disease that we're stuck with no matter what we do,' says Susan Moeller in her study of responses to the reporting of atrocities. She argues that it is avoidance, not fatigue, that averts our gaze.[11]

In *States of Denial: Knowing About Atrocities and Suffering*, Stanley Cohen contends that the avoidance comes from a lack of empathy:

> The problem with multiple images of distant suffering is not their multiplicity, but their psychological and moral *distance.* Repetition just increases the sense of their remoteness from our lives. These are not our children; we have no bond with them; we can never experience their presence; all we know about them is that they exist for that dislocated thirty seconds during which the camera focused on them.[12]

The fact that sections of the public don't want to know about certain kinds of repetitive suffering does not make the fact that the media does not report on it less problematic. First, it is to some degree a self-fulfilling prophecy. By failing to report child hunger consistently we cease to think about it and come to accept it as an unfortunate, intractable fact of life. Since it's unlikely to be reported, it's less likely to be discussed. The less we talk about children starving, the less we talk about why they starve and what we might do to feed them, and the less public pressure there is on politicians to address starvation.

Second, this reasoning comes with a set of assumptions on behalf of those who make editorial decisions about who 'we' are and what 'we' want to know and what 'we' think 'we' know already. This is where the distance comes in. The further you are from experiencing child hunger or from knowing anyone who has experienced it, the less likely you are to see it as a priority or to see its victims as newsworthy. Put bluntly, a child dying of hunger is a far more newsworthy event for those who know the child than for those who don't and are never likely to. That does not negate the ability to empathise, analyse, and engage beyond one's immediate experience. It simply recognises the distance between subject and object.

'The only feeling that anyone can have about an event he does not experience is the feeling aroused by his mental image of that event,' wrote Walter Lippmann in his landmark book, *Public Opinion*. 'That is why until we know what others think they know, we cannot truly understand their acts . . . Our opinions cover a bigger space, a longer reach of time, a greater number of things, than we can directly observe. They have, therefore, to be pieced together out of what others have reported.'[13]

News values are not an objective account of the most important things that have happened in any given time and place. They are the sum total of the priorities and received wisdom of those who provide the news. And those who provide the news are not a representative group. In 2013, the median personal income in the United States was $28,031; 30.4 per cent of people in the nation have degrees; racial minorities comprise 39 per cent of the population and 58 per cent of those who live in poverty.[14] American journalists earn a median salary of $50,028; 8.5 percent of them are from minorities; 92 per cent have degrees.[15] Newsrooms are considerably whiter, wealthier and better educated than the population in general.

So when it comes to covering gun violence, those most likely to frame the news agenda are therefore not the same as those most likely to be affected by the issue. Journalists are less likely to live in the neighbourhoods where such violence takes place. Their opinions about those areas are 'pieced together out of what others (with the same privileges as themselves) have reported' and then further amplified.

When the *Dallas Morning News* won the Pulitzer Prize in 2010 for its series on the divide between North and South Dallas, Tod Robberson, a former foreign correspondent, said he approached reporting from South Dallas as though sending dispatches from overseas. 'The vast disparities we found between northern Dallas and southern Dallas made that possible. I treat it as if readers in North Dallas have no idea what's going on there. I explain it the way I would if I was writing about Lebanon.'[16]

And what is true for reporters may well chime with their perceived audience. Segregation of any kind is a serious barrier to empathy. 'If you're a reader of the *New York Times*, then a child who is shot by a stray bullet during a gang shooting is not easy for you to imagine,' Kois told me. 'Sandy Hook was easy for people to imagine.'

This is as true for class as it is for race. Nicole Fitzpatrick, who lost her son Jaiden in Grove City, Ohio, almost nine hours before Samuel's death, said as much when she explained how his shooting challenged her image of the suburb she had grown up in. 'That doesn't happen here,' she said. 'I'm not living in the 'hood.'

This is less the product of malign neglect than an unconscious omission born from the dead weight of power and privilege that makes the poor and dark in America invisible. In short, there are places in almost every American city where children and teens are expected to get shot – areas where the deaths of young people by gunfire do not contradict a city's general understanding of how the world should work but rather confirm it. To raise children there, whether they are involved in criminal activity or not, is to incorporate those odds into your daily life.

Herein lies one of the most tragic elements to emerge from my research: that every black parent of a teenage child I spoke to had factored in the possibility that this might happen to their kid. Indeed, most of them had channelled their parenting skills into trying to stop precisely that from happening. While others are exerting themselves to get their kids into a decent college, through their SATs, or to excel at sports or music, these parents (who love their offspring no less) are devoting their energies to keeping their kids alive long enough for them to transition either out of the neighbourhood, out of adolescence, or both. It dictates who they think their children should socialise with, where they can go, and when they have to be home. So when you ask them if they imagined that their sons' lives could be so abruptly ended in this way, they give a knowing shrug. 'You wouldn't really be doing your job as a parent here if you didn't think it could happen,' one father in Newark, whose son was shot dead just a couple of hours later, told me.

Friends of the deceased have similarly accommodated the possibility of death into their teenage lives. When I asked Trey, Stanley Taylor's friend, if he ever imagined such a thing could happen to Stanley, he paused for a long time. 'I ain't gonna say it,' he said, suddenly choosing his words very carefully. 'The life we all chose at one point. We were all going down that wrong path.'

It had certainly crossed Audry's mind that she one day might have to bury her son. Only she hadn't imagined it would be Samuel but her eldest, Jeremy. 'Jeremy is the hardhead,' she said. 'The knucklehead. He stays in trouble. When you hear about a fight, it may have Jeremy's name in it. So you have to prepare yourself for Jeremy.' One day that autumn, while chatting with Debra after a report about a local shooting, she discussed taking out an insurance policy on her kids for precisely that reason. She said she'd look into it. But she hadn't got around to it by the time Samuel was killed a month or so later.

So your existence as a working-class African American makes you vulnerable; your presence in areas where working-class African Americans are most likely to live renders you collateral. 'By the numbers,' writes Jesmyn Ward in *Men We Reaped: A Memoir*, which relates how she lost five young men who were close to her in four years, 'by all the official records, here at the confluence of history, of racism, of poverty, and economic power, this is what our lives are worth: nothing.'[17]

This reality was not lost on Samuel's family. 'When it's a black child shot, it's a flash,' says his father, Willie. 'Like a flash of lightning. You see it and you'll be like, "Was that lightning?" That's how it is when a black child gets murdered or gets killed. No big news. But when it comes to other races, oh, well, you know it's going to be on [channels] 1, 2, 3, 4, 5, 6, 7 . . . I hate to say it, but we still live in a racist world. You may have more opportunities. But in the end result you still living in a white world. And we're still thought of as less than. And basically they're saying we don't matter. But if it was their child, they want the world to come to a halt. I'm not speaking out of anger or anything. It's life.'

On 12 March 1963, a man going by the name of Alek Hidell bought a 6.5 mm Carcano Model 91/38 carbine rifle by mail order from Klein's Sporting Goods Store in Chicago at the coupon-clipping price of $19.95 plus postage and handling. His real name was Lee Harvey Oswald, and almost exactly fifty years prior to Samuel's murder, he used that rifle to assassinate President John Kennedy in Dallas.

'Dallas killed Kennedy,' writes Lawrence Wright in *In the New World: Growing Up with America from the Sixties to the Eighties*. He continues, 'We heard it again and again. Dallas as "a city of hate, the only city in which the President could have been shot" . . . It's no wonder Dallasites were defensive and angry. And yet behind our anger was the fear that there must be a whisper of truth in the lies people were telling about our city.'[18]

Dallas is not a pretty city. A sprawling geographic mass tied together by freeways and highways, it has a downtown but no real centre. You can drive around it for days, as I did while interviewing those who knew Samuel, without having a sense of having been anywhere specific beyond the particular destination points to which you were heading.

When the *Dallas Morning News* commissioned a poll in 1983, the assassination was one of three dominant images Americans had of the city; the other two were its pro football team, the Dallas Cowboys, and the TV show *Dallas*.[19] Time has eroded the association between the assassination and the city. But to the extent that the rest of the country thinks of it at all, its carefully cultivated reputation as an all-American modern city – shiny skyline, girl-next-door-cheerleaders, business tycoons, oil money and an impressive string of Super Bowl victories – remains intact.

The late Texas-based journalist Molly Ivins was characteristically damning in her description of the city's social geography. 'There is a black Dallas, there is a Chicano Dallas, there is a Vietnamese Dallas, there is a gay Dallas, there is even a funky Bohemian Dallas,' she wrote. 'But mostly there is North Dallas. A place so materialistic and Republican it makes your teeth hurt to contemplate it . . . The disgrace of Dallas today is that it is probably the most segregated city this side of Johannesburg.'[20]

Indeed, in their 1993 book *American Apartheid: Segregation and the Making of the Underclass*, Douglas Massey and Nancy Denton presented five 'distinct dimensions' by which segregation might be measured. They described the metropolitan areas that scored highly on at least four of them as 'hyper-segregated'. Sixteen cities fit the designation. Dallas was one of them (as were Chicago, Indianapolis, and Newark – three other cities where teens died on the day profiled in this book).[21]

'South Dallas blacks aren't a deprived ethnic group,' wrote Peter Gent in the novel *North Dallas After Forty*. 'They're a different civilisation living in captivity. Just blocks from the phenomenal wealth of Elm and Commerce streets, South Dallas was a hyperbole. A grim joke on those who still believe we are all created equal . . . The blacks seemed to be waiting, watching, knowing they would always be getting fucked. They took solace in the dependability.'[22]

Such is that part of the city where a child's death is barely noteworthy. Broadly speaking, two borders demarcate the north from the south. The first is the Trinity river, which flows 711 miles southeast from north central Texas into an arm of Galveston Bay and then out to the Gulf of Mexico. Three of its four northern tributaries converge just northwest of Dallas, and then it snakes diagonally through the city – a narrow waterway chaperoned through much of the centre by a thick greenbelt – before making more erratic dips and swerves as it heads towards the floodplains and pine forests of East Texas.

The other border is Interstate 30, which is half as long, starting in Fort Worth, Dallas's western twin city, and veering northeast toward the Texas–Oklahoma state line before entering Arkansas and climbing diagonally past Hope – home town of former president Bill Clinton – and ending in Little Rock.

The 7300 block of Schepps Parkway, in Pleasant Grove, where Samuel died, sits in the far southeast corner of the city, considerably south of Interstate 30 but just north of the Trinity, close to one of the river's final meandering kinks before it plunges precipitously towards Galveston. Geographically, Pleasant Grove sits between the two borders; socially, economically and racially it is very much in South Dallas. Driving from the town centre, the imposing, reflective skyscrapers recede from the rearview mirror, making way for the smaller wooden houses and empty lots ahead. Supermarkets and other chain stores become scarce; fast-food franchises, liquor stores, and cheque-cashing outlets mushroom. Even without seeing a single pedestrian, one knows, from having visited any number of American cities, that this is where the black and brown people live. None of this happened by accident.

Democracy came to Dallas at roughly the same time it came to the Eastern bloc – in the early nineties. It's not that people didn't have the vote; first white men and then eventually everybody else got that. But the way votes were counted and the polity was structured meant that regardless of whom you voted for, the oligarchy always got in. All elections to the city council were citywide, which meant that even when minorities got the franchise they struggled to muster the numbers to make any impact. The voices calling for more resources in deprived areas in such a segregated city were as marginalised as the communities who needed those resources.

In a blend of the patrician, civic and venal, a small cabal of wealthy white men ran the city according to what became known as the Dallas Way, with the interests of the local government and local business regarded as both synonymous and symbiotic, each embedded in the other. 'Dallas had always belonged to the men who built it,' wrote Jim Henderson in 1987. 'Men who did not need zoning laws to tell them where to put skyscrapers or which pastures to subdivide . . . They ran their government the way they ran their privately held businesses.'[23]

The consensus for this arrangement did not stretch far beyond North Dallas and finally ended up being judged illegal. It also became increasingly untenable as whites became a minority in the city – today Dallas is 42 per cent Latino, 25 per cent black, and 29 per cent white.[24] But it took a series of federal court rulings before the city finally got a municipal democracy worthy of the name. From the nineties, those who lived in neighbourhoods where poor, non-white people were the majority could elect candidates who would at least ostensibly represent their interests. In 1995 the city elected its first black mayor.[25]

So, for 149 of its 173 years, Dallas was run exclusively and overtly by white, wealthy business interests and often against the interests of African Americans, Latinos and the poor. Dallas is a southern town and Texas was a Confederate state. In *The Dallas Myth: The Making and Unmaking of an American City*, Harvey Graff describes how Dallas revised its city charter in 1907 to allow racial segregation in public schools, housing, amusements and churches; again in 1916 to legitimise residential segregation; and again in 1930 to restrict African Americans' access to office by requiring all candidates to run at large and on a non-partisan basis. 'A second city was built in law as well as social practice,' he argues.[26]

And the separation was vigorously enforced. When African Americans moved into white areas, their homes were sometimes bombed. A granite cornerstone (since removed) in the building housing one of the city's oldest adoption agencies revealed the Ku Klux Klan as a major donor – a sign of the group's respectability during the early part of the century.

In areas such as Pleasant Grove, where poor black people are concentrated, the facts that white women would not feel safe venturing there and Samuel could be shot dead without much media enquiry as to the causes were the direct results of public policy and private practice. Dallas did not simply end up that way; it was made that way.

'It's just another black child and another statistic,' says Claudia. 'Another black child in the ghetto. It wasn't a white child who got killed in University Park or Highland Park, where SMU [Southern Methodist University] is. If it would have been one of them, it would have got a whole column instead of a paragraph. I don't think that's just Dallas. I think it's just America.'

Given how little information was out there, I assumed finding Samuel would be difficult. I found no trace of him on social media, although that, it turned out, is because his Facebook page was under the name Samuel Goodson – a pseudonym conveying his devotion to his mother. When I contacted Melissa at the *Dallas Morning News*, she gave me a primer for the racial dynamics of the city and generously told me what little she could about the shooting, which was not much more than she had written.

With little else to go on, I found the addresses for the funeral director that had handled Samuel's remains and the church where his service had been held. From my headquarters at a Holiday Inn on the side of the motorway, I prepared two envelopes for his mother, both containing letters requesting an interview. I left one at the church and then headed to the funeral home, a large building on the far side of a mall wedged against a freeway.

I told the woman at the front desk my business. She listened only long enough to make sure it was above her pay grade and then fetched someone else. I started again. The next woman listened carefully, smiling throughout, and then, when I was done, told me that she could not understand a word I had said.

This is not as outlandish as it might sound. Language is a relatively small part of communication. The rest we pick up from context. I'd walked in off the street, with a black face and an English accent, to inform her that I was writing a book and needed to pass a package on to the family of someone I'd never met who had died more than two months earlier. On a regular day in a Dallas funeral director's, there isn't really a context for that.

It doesn't help that I cut an unlikely figure in most professional circumstances. Small (five feet six), tubby, black, dishevelled – when Americans think British journalist, which is rarely, I'm not what they think of. Things can get particularly disorienting once they hear the accent. African Americans often think I'm affected – a siddity negro with airs and graces. Sometimes that works to my advantage. People, especially those with a dim view of the mainstream media, might take comfort in what looks like the aesthetic of an outsider.

Others, perhaps seeking somebody authoritative to whom to tell their story, are unimpressed or unconvinced. While I was trying to report on Hurricane Katrina, a white policeman in Mississippi patted his gun and told me to turn my car around as I tried to get to an affected area. I was following the same route as other – white – journalists who all made it through. Whatever people are expecting, they're rarely expecting me. Yet here I am, in a funeral director's in Dallas, waiting.

The woman who could not understand me brought a colleague out. I pared my story and request down to the bare minimum. She went to get Samuel's file, came out a few minutes later, and said, 'His aunt's on the phone. She said she'll speak with you.' I explained myself to the aunt, Debra, trying desperately not to sound too jaded as I went through my lines about the book I was writing for the fourth time in ten minutes. I gave her my number and email address. She said she'd pass on the message to her sister. 'I'll call you back tonight and tell you what she says.'

No call came that night. Nor that week, after I'd returned home to Chicago. I didn't have Debra's number. I was about to call the church and try my luck there. Then, eight days later, as I was picking up my son from his comic-book class, I got a call from a number I didn't recognise with a Dallas area code. As thrown as the woman in the funeral director's, I needed a moment to find the context to make the words make sense. It was Audry Smith. Samuel's mother.

If Pleasant Grove was part of a deliberate effort to corral poor, black people into certain areas of Dallas, then the story Audry told me of how she and her family ended up there owes more to a string of unfortunate events that highlights the precariousness of the American middle class.

Audry, Samuel and Whitney were living together in the suburb of Garland, just outside Dallas. Audry was working as an administrator for a company that provided home help. Her boss was arrested for Medicaid and Medicare fraud. On the advice of her lawyer, she was told to leave the job because, given her role in the company, staying there could be incriminating. In September 2011 she quit. She took the opportunity of an enforced break to undergo a major elective surgical procedure that she needed but had been putting off. She applied for unemployment benefits, was first denied, and then was accepted on appeal.

She had the operation in March 2012 and needed to convalesce for several weeks. That May, she was on the mend and starting to look for work. She picked the children up from school one day. As she headed west on Interstate 30 with Whitney in the back and Samuel in the front, the car ahead of her in the carpool lane (for high-occupancy vehicles) slammed on its brakes. Caught unawares, she bumped into it. 'I bent the hood of my car. But everyone could have driven away at that point,' she says. Just as she unbuckled her seatbelt to check on Whitney, a Chevy Impala slammed into the back of her car. Because she was driving an SUV, which was raised substantially from the ground, the Impala actually ran under her car as it crashed. It was travelling at quite a pace. Her back windshield flew in; her steering wheel went into the motor; her shoes were up on the dashboard; her glasses were in the backseat; her seat collapsed into the back. She blacked out. When she came to, she found her leg jammed under the steering wheel.

The children were fine, but a woman in the Impala had broken some ribs, and Audry was left with a damaged knee. She couldn't walk for about six weeks. Because she couldn't walk, she couldn't work, and because the driver in the Impala didn't have insurance, she couldn't be compensated for loss of potential earnings.

Her unemployment assistance was due to run out in July, and the lease on her rented apartment ran out in August. To qualify for disability she needed to be disabled for a year. She was in a tight spot. She looked for some money to tide her over until she could, literally, get back on her feet. The Dallas Urban League, a longstanding civil rights organisation, agreed to pay her rent for that final month while she looked for somewhere cheaper. But the League's funds fell through at the last minute. She couldn't pay the rent. She was evicted. In less than a year, she'd gone from being housed and employed to homeless and unemployed.

Although the circumstances by which Audry had reached this point were particular to her, the fragility that had allowed her to fall so far so fast are all too familiar in a nation without much of a safety net. One in three Americans either lives in poverty or struggles in the category the census terms the 'near poor'.[27] According to one poll, 80 per cent of American adults have, in the course of their lives, endured a year or more of periodic joblessness, lived in near poverty, or relied on welfare.[28]

'Poverty is no longer an issue of "them", it's an issue of "us",' Mark Rank, a professor at Washington University, in St Louis, who calculated the numbers, told *USA Today*. 'Only when poverty is thought of as a mainstream event, rather than a fringe experience that just affects blacks and Hispanics, can we really begin to build broader support for programmes that lift people in need.'[29]

When such programmes are lacking, it does not take much for those who are barely getting by to find themselves struggling to survive. 'If something goes wrong there is simply no buffer,' writes Joseph Stiglitz in *The Price of Inequality*. 'Even before the crisis, America's poor lived on the precipice; but with the Great Recession, that became increasingly true even of the middle class. The human stories of this crisis are replete with tragedies; one missed mortgage payment escalates into a lost house; homelessness escalates into lost jobs and the eventual destruction of families. For these families, one shock may be manageable; the second is not.'[30]

With her credit shot and no job, Audry could not find another place to live at short notice. She, Whitney and Samuel went to stay with Debra. Debra and Audry are close. The first two times they were pregnant they were pregnant together; they've always lived near each other; they call each other almost every day. Their children were more like brothers and sisters than cousins. Debra is two years older, but her role in the family has always implied a seniority beyond her years. 'Every time something happens I'm the "go to" person,' she says, less with resentment than as a matter of fact. 'That's the way they look at me in the family. Like I can fix everything, and I say, "I really can't."'

But she did what she could to help Audry. 'I don't know why this happened,' she told Audry. 'But everything happens for a reason. Whatever it is, it'll work out. Even though you've been evicted you really can't say that you're homeless. Because if I have somewhere to stay, you have somewhere to stay.'

That was true. But it was also tight. Debra lived in a two-bedroom apartment with her two youngest daughters – her eldest was already off in college. So when Audry, Whitney and Samuel moved in (Jeremy lived with his grandmother), it was a squeeze. 'It was different,' says Debra with a smile. 'But we adjusted. There were no weird issues. It was just annoying that I had additional people. I talked to my girls. I said, "I know it's going to be tight. But we family. This is what we do. We don't have a choice."'

Every day that she was able to, Audry looked for work. She was eager to find her own place. 'I wasn't in a hurry to get away from Debra. But in a way I was in a hurry because it was an inconvenience even though she wasn't saying anything. Of course, who wants to stay in a two-bedroom with six or seven people?'

When Audry found a place in Pleasant Grove five months later that would accept her credit, she borrowed the deposit money from Debra and took it. 'I don't think she really wanted to go to Pleasant Grove,' says Debra. 'But I understood. For her it was like, "OK, this is my opportunity to get my own again." As a grown person with kids, you want your own. I think it was her gaining her independence back. That's perfectly normal.'

Audry knew of Pleasant Grove's reputation, but she wasn't intimidated by it. 'Back when I grew up, the neighbourhood that I grew up in was considered worse then than Pleasant Grove is now,' she says. 'People'd say, "Where you livin'?" And I'd tell 'em, and they'd say, "You don't act like you're from South Dallas." The question that's next is, "Well, how am I supposed to act just because I live in a certain part of town? You tell me how am I supposed to act?" Just because you grow up in a bad area doesn't mean you're a bad person. And that's the stereotype that's put on places like Pleasant Grove and Oak Cliff and South Dallas.'

Though it was not her desire to move there, Audry had no problems living in Pleasant Grove. 'The neighbourhood itself is OK,' she said. 'We used to walk that area where DaDa was killed, just exercising. There's always kids playing basketball at that corner.'

In any case, Audry was thinking long term. She'd found work in Plano, not far from the children's school. 'I had a plan. Move somewhere where the rent wasn't that much. Work on my credit and then buy a house. I was trying to save money. And at the end of the day was it worth it?' she asks. 'No! Did I even get to save money? No.' It was a fifty-mile round-trip commute from Pleasant Grove to work and school. 'The transportation was just eating me up in gas.'

When we met, Audry had moved out of Dallas altogether, to the northwest suburb of Rowlett, half an hour away from Pleasant Grove, just off the George Bush Highway. Though they lived in Pleasant Grove for eleven months, they never really settled in. They knew their neighbours, an elderly pastor and his wife. But otherwise, the long commute to work and school didn't leave much time to make friends. 'That's what makes Samuel's shooting so random,' she says. 'Because my son didn't associate with anyone over there. He didn't hang out, so no one in in his age group there knew him.'

Such were the circumstances that came together to put Samuel in Pleasant Grove that night – an area where his mother had not expected to live but where others, schooled in Dallas's geography of race and class, expected a young man of his age and race to die.

*

Around the corner from where Samuel was shot is Gayglen Drive, where rows of homes resembling army barracks sit back from the street – a community billeted as though prepared for war. This was the only part of the area Audry considered rough. 'Asante, Murdock Villas, Trinity Trails. They kept changing the name of those apartments, but it was always the same problem. It was all contained in those apartments. So we never heard gunfire. It all happened over there.'

The stretch of Schepps Parkway where Samuel fell is literally on the way to nowhere: there is a barrier marking the end of the road, on the other side of which is a huge freeway. It sits wedged between middle-class precariousness and bucolic calm. On one side sprawls the Woodland Springs Park, complete with picnic tables, which is in turn attached to McCommas Bluff Preserve, a 111-acre wooded commons that looks like an unlikely starting point for a leisurely ramble.

On the other side is a rabbit's warren of streets with long, thin, ranch-style houses. The mostly well-tended gardens and impressive cars in the driveways indicate more comfort than affluence; the bars on most of the doors and windows suggest a low-key sense of siege that has insinuated itself into everyday life. On the corner of Neuhoff and Schepps, the precise spot where Samuel fell, a make-shift sign pokes out of the ground offering 'Cash 4 Junk Cars'.

The census tells a story of population growth and white flight. Between 2000 and 2010 the white population of this tract plummeted by 41 per cent while the Latino population grew by 39 per cent and the black population by 25 per cent, leaving it more than half black and more than a third Latino and, like most of America, more populous and less white than it had been.[31]

Samuel didn't have any friends who lived in the neighbourhood. But he did have a schoolmate, Denzel, who used to come to the area every month or so to visit his grandmother and who lived two streets down from Samuel. Denzel talks like molasses pours: slowly, richly, thickly. He tells his stories sparsely – with few embellishments and a Texas twang. He was dating Whitney at the time, so when she invited him over for a night in with the family he came right over.

They made an evening of it, watching *We're the Millers* and drinking cocoa. 'We had a mini family night I guess,' says Denzel. Whitney and Denzel were in the kitchen with Audry when Samuel took a break from his Xbox to suggest that they all play Uno. Audry initially declined. 'We hadn't played Uno in a while,' she said. 'And Samuel used to cheat.'

'I'm not going to cheat this time,' Samuel protested. 'I'm going to play fair.'

So they settled down to play on the floor. Samuel cheated, though not as egregiously as usual. Around eleven, Denzel decided to go home, and Samuel offered to walk him part of the way. It takes around seven minutes to walk from one home to the other. Samuel was just going to walk him to the corner but decided to go a little further. He was on the phone to his girlfriend, Alexis, when he interrupted the conversation to point out to Denzel that they had passed a white Crown Victoria parked at the end of the street, near Gayglen. 'I turned around and looked to see there was a car sitting there,' says Denzel. 'It was all white. But it was black inside so you couldn't see nothing. No bodies. Nothing. The headlights were off. But the brake lights were on. So we turned around and took some more steps. Didn't think nothing of it. I'm thinking they just sitting there to just sit there, I guess. I don't know. So we keep walking, and then two, three steps and I hear a shot fired.'

When I ask Denzel to describe the sound he shrugs. 'It was just like *BLAH*.'

He continued, '[Samuel] said, "Oh, I'm hit." I thought he was playing. I said, "Stop playing." So I rushed over there to him.' Denzel corrects himself. Had he known what had happened he would have rushed. But at that moment he still couldn't believe what was happening. 'I didn't rush over there. I was walking towards him.

And then he's hopping towards the kerb. And he told Alexis over the phone he'd got shot.' Then Denzel called Whitney. 'Whitney. Sam been shot.' 'What happened? What happened?' said Whitney. 'He been shot, you gotta come right away.'

Audry drove straight down with Whitney to find Samuel lying on the ground. She stopped the car in the middle of the street, put it in 'park', and jumped out with the motor still running and the doors open. 'When I did get round the corner Denzel is hollering and screaming and he's upset. But for me I'm more in mama mode. Find the wound. Put pressure to it. When Samuel started regurgitating, turn him over to his side. Not hollering and screaming. I had no time for that. My reaction was more practical.'

Samuel was wearing only one of his shoes; the other was across the street. 'He was moaning when I came out. He said, "Mama." We were trying to find out where he was hit. We called 911. We located the injury site of the wound. I was trying to apply pressure. He started regurgitating from his nose and his mouth, and his eyes started to roll in the back of his head. At that moment I knew that he was dying in my arms, but I was still hopeful.'

The questions from the 911 dispatcher irritated her. 'They were asking, "Is the person still out there with the gun?" I mean, do you think it would even matter to me if he was? When I see my child laying there on the ground. Or, "Are y'all safe?" "Are you in a well-lit area?" None of that makes sense to me. My focus can't be on the crazy questions. Or, "What's the major cross street you at?" when I know you've got GPS and pick up the cell-phone signal. So they're asking all these crazy questions.'

You can hear Audry's frustration increasing during the call. She starts out urgent, clear and panicked. 'My son has been shot right here at Schepps and Parkway,' she yells, with Denzel and Whitney wailing in the background. 'We need an ambulance.' The dispatcher asks her to spell the street name. 'S-C-H-E-P-P-S,' she says, twice. But while Audry is desperate for someone to come and save her son, the dispatcher dispassionately and professionally – if ponderously – gathers a full account of the scene.

'Did he see who did it?'

'No.'

'And he just got shot. You didn't see who did it?'

'No, he was walking with a friend.'

'Is the friend there too?'

'Yes', and then Audry refocuses on Samuel. 'Breathe, breathe, breathe,' she says.

While she is trying to encourage life back into her son, the dispatcher asks, 'Was there a vehicle you saw or anything like that?'

Denzel's voice enters from a short distance and then Audry relays the message. 'It was a black Crown Vic. No. It was a white Crown Vic.'

'Where did he go?' the dispatcher asks, and at this point Audry loses patience and becomes more formal.

'I don't know where it went, sir. I really don't.'

'All right. Where was he shot?'

'In the back.' She asks someone to get a blanket.

'Are you there?'

'Yes.'

'Are you sure you don't know which way the car went?'

'Sir, someone called me on the phone and told me to get around here, so I don't know nothing,' Audry says, finally closing that line of questioning down for good.

'Is he conscious?'

'DaDa, are you conscious?' she asks. A long groan is audible. 'Yes, he's moaning. I can hear him.'

'OK. And no one is around there with a gun or anything like that?'

'No.'

'I'm going to connect you to fire department for arrival instructions, all right?'

'Thank you.'

When the ambulance arrived, it kept its distance for what felt like several minutes, which Audry thought was odd. 'How can you not see my car in the middle of the street with the lights on and doors open?' she wondered. Eventually the paramedics came, but Denzel could make no more sense of what had happened than they could. And he'd been there for the whole thing. 'I know those apartments in that neighbourhood were dangerous,' he told me, indicating the complex on Gayglen. 'My sister used to stay over there, and she said they were dangerous.'

Denzel sat at the crime scene for several hours. When the detective told him Samuel had died, he shrugged. The detective later asked a teacher if he was slow. 'No, he's very bright,' she told her. 'But he's in shock.' Audry looked through the ambulance window and saw them trying to resuscitate Samuel with CPR. She asked them if he was breathing on his own. They said no. She knew he was dead even before she reached the hospital because the ambulance did not turn its lights on.

She called Willie, whose immediate response was dramatic, says Audry. 'The whole night it was him running up and down the hallway of the hospital hollering and screaming,' she recalls, 'sinking to the floor with Whitney, apologising all the time.'

Audry was particularly upset about her last moments with Samuel at the hospital. 'I felt that I didn't get a proper goodbye because at the hospital I wasn't allowed to touch him,' she says. Her son's body was now a crime scene. 'That was really devastating. The only thing I could do was see him from behind the glass. He was laying there like he was asleep, but then I knew he wasn't.' Three months later she showed me a picture she'd taken from the other side of the glass, of Samuel lying on a gurney with his body covered by a white sheet up to his neck.

'How often do you look at that?' I asked.

'Every day,' she said.

*

Audry's coping mechanism from the outset was to try and keep herself busy. Samuel died late Saturday night. On Monday morning she went to work. She went back again on Wednesday. 'It was really just to get away,' she explains. 'I wasn't at peace at the house. There was so many people in and out constantly. I know everyone was there with good intentions. You know, to feed us and check on us. But it wasn't the hug I wanted. It wasn't the laughter or the voice I wanted to hear. So it felt like work was the only place I could go where I knew no one would bother me. When my phone would ring, someone else would answer it. It was like my boss knew and didn't want to say nothing to me if I went in. If I worked a little bit and said, "OK, I'm going to go now", no one said anything. It was my place of peace to go to.'

Her doctor told her she was in denial and moving too fast, and put her on medication for anxiety, to help her sleep and, finally, for depression. The wake, held on 29 November, was on Samuel's birthday. He would have been seventeen. They released balloons at the funeral home and sang 'Happy Birthday'. Samuel always said he wanted his siblings, scattered over different families across the city, to be together. And here they were. 'Well, you got what you wanted,' said Audry. The funeral was on 30 November. Audry was back to work full time by 2 December.

At the funeral, Willie's second wife, Claudia, sat directly behind Audry, in the second row. When it came time to close the casket, Audry reached behind, grabbed Claudia's hand and took her along as she went to see Samuel for the last time. She put Claudia's hand on the casket and her hand on top of Claudia's, and together they closed it for good.

Whitney was in a terrible state. 'I don't think I've seen anybody grieve like Whitney did,' said one friend. 'At the burial I came over and gave her a hug and said, "Are you going back to school?"' Whitney said she didn't know. 'What would Sam want you to do?' asked the friend. 'He'd want me to jump in that grave with him,' she said.

When I first met Audry in February 2014, she fetched a leopard-skin box, roughly the size of a shoebox, and opened it up quite matter-of-factly as we spoke. Inside were keepsakes from the funeral. A couple of papier-mâché doves on thin metal rods, copies of the funeral service bearing the same picture that had appeared on the local news website, testimonies written by friends from school, and pictures of Samuel at various stages of his childhood, from infancy up. Going to the box is a daily routine.

It's one of the many rituals Audry has adopted since her son died. A few months after the shooting, every Saturday night she was still putting on the same clothes she wore the night he died – a pair of pink jogging pants and a T-shirt that says, 'All stressed out and no one to choke.' 'It's not even intentional sometimes,' she says. 'I just find myself with it on. Every Saturday, around the same time, I'm angsty. I don't go to sleep. I never go to sleep until the Sunday morning, only to wake up in tears.'

When I met her again in June, things had improved a little. 'I don't put on the same thing every Saturday. The sleeping I still have an issue with. I don't go to sleep until three or four in the morning. I'm not as angsty and anxious as I used to be. That could be the medication. When I'm with people I try to interact most of the time. When I'm at home I'm quiet.'

Whitney struggles. She says she sees DaDa everywhere. 'Every day. Every little thing reminds me of him,' she says. 'We all had this one particular song. I'd sing and say, like, "DaDa, join in." But he's not there. School? He's not there. Home? He's not there. I hate being in the house without him.'

'One day,' says Audry, 'Whitney just came knocking on the door of my room. She said, "He's not responding." I said, "Who's not responding?" She said, "DaDa. He's not responding to my text messages."'

Whitney left the school in the end. 'Even to look over at his desk and not see him there just made it much harder for her to deal with every single day,' says Audry. 'Samuel was always the one to calm Whitney down in certain situations. He was her voice of reason. Whenever she would get hot about something or mad he calmed her down. I couldn't. I tried to get her to talk to someone. I said it's only a matter of time before she blows up. It's going to happen in school. She's constantly looking over at the desk. And she's mad.'

She didn't get counselling, even though Debra says she needs help. 'More so her because she's a child and doesn't really know how to deal with it. But she doesn't like to open her head.' Denzel says he wasn't offered any counselling and didn't want any. 'I don't open up to nobody,' he says. 'That's just the way it is.'

Counsellors came to the school, where Samuel's desk was left open for the rest of the academic year, with a Bible in it opened to the book of Samuel. One teacher put an angel outside the entrance with a poem on it, to help talk the children through it. But few thought these counsellors were very effective. One of them called Samuel by the wrong name. 'It just instilled in these kids that this is nothing to you,' said another teacher.

Willie has retreated into himself. 'From what I can tell, I think he's grieving hard,' says Claudia. 'He's the life of the party. He'll get you up dancing. Singing. He'd go out at the weekend and have fun with his friends. But now? He's in a shell. It's understandable because you'd never have thought you'd have to bury one of your own children.'

Willie says he's constantly on edge. 'Basically you can't relax no more. There's no ease any more. There's no way I can come in, lay down, and think the kids are OK, nothing's gonna happen. You don't know. You always on guard now. God makes no mistake. So I can't sit up and say, "Why mine?" Because we all gonna die sooner or later. Everybody's name is on the roll. But I question myself: maybe if he was here with me. Well, it can happen out here just the same as it happen anywhere else. As a father you wanna protect them.'

*

Audry still struggles to piece together the precise details of what happened that night. 'I had heard so many different stories in the beginning of how he got shot. At first he was hit in the stomach – in the abdomen. I said, "No, it's not true." I asked, "Did the bullet come out the stomach, because the only wound I seen was in the pelvis?" And no one could tell me anything. Denzel was emotionally distraught, and so his story changed too. He said he didn't hear gun shots. And after a few weeks he said he did.'

Only an eight-year-old girl in the area said she'd heard gunfire. When the police and a journalist knocked on doors, nobody else admitted hearing anything. And despite the arrival of fire engines, ambulances and police cars, despite the screaming and the gunfire, nobody emerged to see what was going on. 'No one came out,' says Audry. 'No one. It's weird. They would have heard the ambulance. Not only the ambulance, but the fire truck and the police. It's like no one was talking.'

And she was reluctant to probe further on her own. When Jeremy, her elder son, started asking questions at the corner store, she asked him to stop. 'I told him when you start drawing attention to yourself, you never know who comes out. I'd rather let me move and then if someone comes forward and says something, that's different. But you've still got a sister you have to worry about.'

Nobody knows why anyone would do this. There was no obvious motivation. The police were convinced it wasn't gang-related; their trail was cold from the get-go. Denzel didn't catch the licence plate number – why would he? And even if he had, the policewoman told Audry she wouldn't believe how many Crown Vics are just stolen and abandoned in the adjacent neighbourhood.

'He had his whole life to live for,' says Claudia, lamenting the senselessness of it all. 'He missed his senior prom. He missed graduation. He missed everything because somebody else wanted to be stupid. And who knows who he is? It coulda been someone he knew. It could have been someone who lived next door. You just shootin' to be shootin'? You just doin' what you want to do? So what do you want to do?'

'One minute we're playing Uno,' says Denzel, reflecting on the capriciousness of his life and Samuel's death. 'Ten, fifteen minutes later. Boom.'

8

Tyshon Anderson
(aged eighteen)

Chicago, Illinois

23 November, 11.05 p.m. CST

Shortly after I moved to Chicago, in 2011, I went to a meeting on traffic awareness at my son's day care. The director advised us that to help children orient themselves, we should try to be consistent with the routes we took when walking to familiar places so the kids would have a fighting chance of finding their way home if lost. To illustrate the point, he outlined the routes the day-care centre took on regular outings. One of the parents asked whether they would continue to pass the site by the subway where there had been a recent shoot-out. The teacher smiled. 'I knew that would come up,' he sighed. 'It's a good point, and we are really going to have to get on top of it. We must talk to the children about how to handle situations like that, because the big problem in those moments is that they panic.'

I thought this was odd. Panic in the presence of gunfire seems a perfectly rational response, whether you're four or forty-four. The problem, it seemed to me, wasn't the panic but the shooting. On the way home that day, I saw posters on the window of the youth club at the end of our street. I passed them every day, but this was the first time I'd really stopped to look at them. 'STOP KILLING PEOPLE' it read. It seemed like the kind of suggestion you shouldn't need a poster for.

Most major cities have, at different times, gained notoriety for their high murder rates. Los Angeles, New York, Washington DC, New Orleans, Detroit, Philadelphia, Baltimore and Miami, to name but a few, have all been there. For the last few years – as it happens, when I was living there – it has been Chicago's turn. These reputations can rarely keep up with their actual statistical ranking. Kansas City, Oakland, Philadelphia, Baltimore, Detroit, and New Orleans all had higher rates of homicide than Chicago in the year this book was set.[1] But none of them were the third-largest city in the country or the home town of the sitting president.

In any case, the infamy was deserved. It is estimated that between 20 per cent and 30 per cent of Chicago children in public schools have witnessed a shooting.[2] In 2012, there were 506 gun murders in the city – an 11 per cent increase over the year before.[3] On Memorial Day weekend of that year, there were 43 shootings, resulting in 10 deaths.[4] In eight of the ten years prior to the day this book was written, the number of murders in Chicago was greater than the number of US fatalities in Afghanistan.[5] The city became disparagingly known as Chiraq, a variation on which (*Chi-Raq*) would later become the title of a Spike Lee film about gun violence in the city. When the snow melted during the spring before my family and I left for England, one gun was found in an alley near our local park and another behind my son's school.

The city became a gory journalistic trove for a slew of stories that were tragic, epic, or brutal – and sometimes all three. By the age of fifty-four, one mother, Shirley Chambers, had lost all four of her children to gun violence in separate incidents. 'I only have one child left,' she said after the third child was shot dead, 'and I'm afraid that [the killing] won't stop until he's gone too.'[6] When the last one was shot, the killing still continued.

On 26 November 2012, almost a year to the day before this book is set, Sherman Miller, twenty-one, attended the funeral of James Holman, thirty-two, at St Columbanus Church. Holman had been shot dead a week earlier. From the pews, Miller texted a friend about how the service was affecting him. 'Dis preacher like he talkin straight to me,' he wrote. 'He talkin bout hurts and pain. I cant run from the pain cause its gone hurt me worse if I'm by myself because I gotta think about everything.' Minutes later, Miller was shot dead on the steps of the church as mourners scattered and wailed.

Whereas Chicago as a whole earned a reputation for gun violence, the shootings were not evenly distributed throughout the city. The overwhelming majority were concentrated in a handful of neighbourhoods in the south and west – predominantly black and Latino areas, respectively.[7] As the response to Samuel Brightmon's shooting in the previous chapter illustrated, the concentration of poor, black and Latino people in American cities happened by design, not default. 'Residential segregation is the principal organisational feature of American society that is responsible for the creation of the urban underclass,' write Massey and Denton in *American Apartheid*.[8] As Dallas did, Chicago perfected that design over the years. By most measures it is, and has long been, the most segregated big city in America.[9] Where shootings were concerned this had two main connected consequences.

First, in the rest of the city, one experienced precious little of this mayhem. Nowhere was completely insulated. I lived on the North Side and still have tales to tell. Yet the episodes were noteworthy where I lived precisely because they happened comparatively rarely. (It's all relative – had a tenth that number of shootings occurred where I now live in London, we would have talked of nothing else.) But occasionally, when reports of particularly murderous weekends in Chicago reached friends in other cities or even abroad, they would contact me to ask if I was OK. If I hadn't watched the local news the previous night or read the paper that morning, I might know nothing about it. It really might as well have happened in another city or even another country.

Second, for those who live on the South and West Sides, there was no escaping it. On the tenth floor of the University of Illinois's School of Public Health, Dr Gary Slutkin points to a map of Chicago with round stickers showing where murders have taken place. Lake Michigan lies to the east, the north is mostly clear, but you can't see some of the South Side for dots. 'It's the same pattern on a map showing the incidence of cholera in Bangladesh. It's an infective process,' he says.

I was interviewing Dr Slutkin after a spate of shootings in the city had once again piqued the attention of my editors. Dr Slutkin, the executive director of Cure Violence, specialises in infectious-disease control and reversing epidemics. He used to work for the World Health Organization. He thinks violence behaves like tuberculosis or AIDS, and sees it as an infectious disease that can be stamped out by challenging and changing behavioural norms. Across the room, a graph shows fatal shootings in Chicago over several years – a roller-coaster of peaks and troughs. 'It's the same curve for almost every city,' he explains. 'It's an epidemic curve.'

The most blighted communities existed as though in a state of siege. In Lawndale, on the South Side, one local woman told the *Chicago Tribune* that even some of the dogs had ceased barking at the sound of gunfire.[10] Charles Brown, a retired police officer in the neighbouring area of Englewood, told me he'd tuned out the deadly crackling and popping that echoed around his house. 'I don't even hear it any more,' he said. 'It's just part of your existence here.'

When I started this book, I assumed that whatever day I picked there was a reasonable chance that one of the children slain would be in my home town, that he would be a young man of colour, and that he would be killed on the South or West Side. Sadly, I was right on all counts.

Tyshon Anderson, eighteen, lived and died in South Chicago, which should not be mistaken for the South Side of Chicago. The South Side is an entire area of the city; South Chicago is its own neighbourhood within that area. It sits thirteen miles south of the Loop – the downtown shopping district – on the city's eastern flank. Bordered by Interstate 90 to the west, Highway 12/90 to the south, the commercial thoroughfare of E. 79th to the north, and Lake Michigan to the east, its proximity to so many transport hubs once made it an ideal location for heavy industry. During the mid-nineteenth century, huge steel and iron works set up there, bringing migrant workers primarily from Poland, Italy and Ireland. In 1911, South Works, which owned U.S. Steel and was based there, employed eleven thousand people. African Americans soon arrived with the Great Migration, along with Latinos from Mexico and the American West.

'Growing up, the mornings here would be busy with people going to work,' one elderly African American who grew up and still lives in South Chicago, but did not want to be named, told me. Her father and uncles had worked in the mill. 'You'd see parents taking their kids to school and saying, "Hurry up, or I'm gonna be late for work." Back then, in the summer, the streets were so clean you could take your shoes off if you were too hot and walk in bare feet.'

Racism transformed the neighbourhood in the fifties and sixties as many of the descendants of European immigrants fled at speed, fearing the arrival of blacks and Latinos. In *The Warmth of Other Suns: The Epic Story of America's Great Migration*, Isabel Wilkerson describes the breathtaking pace and scale of the transformation of neighbouring South Shore after Ida Mae Gladney, originally from Mississippi, bought a house there. 'The whites left so fast Ida Mae didn't get a chance to know any of them or their kids or what they did for a living . . . They didn't stick around long enough to explain.'[11]

In subsequent years, white people would relate their version of that process. 'It happened slowly, and then all of a sudden, boom,' one white homemaker on the South Side told the writer Louis Rosen. 'Everyone gone. Everything changed. Before you know it, this one, that one . . . People didn't want to be the last.'[12]

And what racism did not change, economics did. The decimation of America's manufacturing sector devastated South Chicago. Through the eighties the factories closed. What remains on that site is a post-industrial wilderness – huge concrete barriers, maybe thirty feet high, tower over shrub and bush; railway tracks, which used to ferry steel from the old site, are eroded by time and weather. On a weekday morning the only sounds are the wind and the waves as Lake Michigan slaps the rusting foot of what was once a giant. In its absence, South Chicago became an impoverished residential area wedged between busy roads and the shoreside. Abandoned and derelict homes and shops now pockmark what was once a thriving community. No one in his or her right mind would walk barefoot down these streets any more.

'The neighbourhood has been in a collective depression since the steel mills closed down and left lots of people suddenly unemployed,' explains Olga Bautista, a community organiser who was born and raised in South Chicago. 'The depression manifests itself in the alcoholism, the domestic violence, the drug addictions. There are no mental health clinics here. So that's how you see it.'

This was one of the first areas where the young Barack Obama was taken as a community organiser during the mid-eighties. 'It expressed some of the robust, brutal spirit of Chicago's industrial past, metal beams and concrete rammed together,' he wrote in *Dreams of My Father* after visiting the old Wisconsin Steel Plant. 'Only now it was empty and rust-stained, like an abandoned wreck.'[13]

I'd been reporting in Chicago for several years when I started writing this book, and I knew several community organisers and union activists. But almost no one knew anyone in South Chicago. It was almost as if they felt there was not enough going on down there to organise. 'We're a forgotten people,' says one local campaigner. 'Honestly, I think a lot of people don't even know we're here.'

Today, half of those in the small patch where Tyshon lived earn $30,000 a year or less (roughly two-thirds the national average), and a quarter of the housing units are vacant. And the hollowing out is not yet over. The area lost an eighth of its population between 2005 and 2009, and those who remained saw their median income plummet by 22 per cent.[14]

To the naked eye, this economic trauma is evident but not striking in the few blocks where Tyshon lived and died. Each surrounding block has at least one boarded-up home. East 79th Street, the main drag that marks the border between South Chicago and South Shore, offers standard strip-mall fare for a working-class urban area – a Family Dollar, a beauty parlour, a Dollar General, a laundromat, a pizzeria. The windows on the nearby bodegas are defended with metal grilles.

But the lawns are clipped and the hedges tended, and for every abandoned home there are at least two that, from the outside at least, look comfortable. The census shows that for all the hard times, a sizeable minority here is doing well. One in ten has a bachelor's degree or higher and earns between $75,000 and $100,000 a year.[15] These statistics illustrate the long-standing struggle within what were once solid middle-class communities to resist the decimation of urban black American life and the pathologies and pathos that come with it.

It's a trend Obama witnessed three decades earlier in similar neighbourhoods. 'Despite the deserved sense of accomplishment these men and women felt,' he writes, 'despite the irrefutable evidence of their own progress, our conversations were marked by another, more ominous strain. The boarded-up houses, the decaying storefronts, the ageing church rolls, kids from unknown families who swaggered down the streets – loud congregations of teenage boys, teenage girls feeding potato chips to crying toddlers, the discarded wrappers rumbling down the block – all of it whispered painful truths, told when the progress they'd found was ephemeral rooted in thin soil; that it might not even last their lifetimes.'[16]

The weight of South Chicago's troubles seems to have settled on Tyshon Anderson's eyelids. In most pictures his eyes appear as two narrow slits struggling to make their presence felt as the lids head south in search of slumber. His Facebook pictures show an oval face with a weak chin and a high brow that owes its definition to the dreads cascading from the centre of his scalp and hanging symmetrically to the middle of his neck. They frame a handsome, full-lipped face.

One of his parents was particularly taken with his smile: 'His mouth would twist a little, it was cute,' they told a local reporter.[17] But in the pictures he posted of himself, it is rarely evident; in some he looks pensive, in others wasted (the most likely explanation for those heavy eyelids is that he was often high). 'Even as a little kid he was an old soul,' says his godmother, Regina Gray. For the most part, his Facebook page attests to an unremarkable if somewhat rambunctious teenage existence. In one picture, like Pedro Cortez, he's clutching a bottle of Hennessy in one hand while the other arm is wrapped around a girl. In others, as on Edwin Rajo's page, there are depictions of weed. Elsewhere the occasional kitten and puppy and a range of other girls. If his trousers are in the shot, then the seat is generally halfway down his bottom and his boxers are on full display. His favourite films were *Rambo* and *The Hills Have Eyes*. His favourite TV shows included *Futurama*, *Family Guy* and *Twerkers Exposed*, a soft-porn site of sorts on which mostly barely dressed women take selfies of their sizeable behinds.

Many pictures have him posing without a shirt; he was a slender-built teen with a lean but not particularly well-defined torso of which he was nonetheless clearly proud. On his police mugshots (of which there are quite a selection), he looks quite different. Dreads that are more tousled expose a jawline more defined. His lips have lost their pout; his eyes have clawed back some space from the lids. The stats – five feet eight inches and 145 pounds – indicate that physically, at least, he was an all-American boy: average in every way.

At around 11.05 p.m. on 23 November, on the echoey, rank, first-floor stairway of a four-storey walk-up on East 80th Street, just around the corner from his home, someone walked up to Tyshon, shot him in the head, and left. Whoever called 911 – the Chicago Police Department won't release the recording – found him bleeding on the landing. An ambulance took him on a twenty-five-minute drive to Northwestern

Memorial Hospital. When they picked him up he was in critical condition; by 11.50 p.m. he was pronounced dead.

In the forty-five minutes between Tyshon's getting shot and his dying, a seventeen-year-old boy was shot and injured less than a block away in what might have been a retaliation.

It was less than a year after Sandy Hook, and with the public still sensitised to the ubiquity of such tragedies, there remained a strong civic interest in reporting the victim of every gun death. The *New York Times* still ran its daily 'Gun Report', and Tyshon was on it; *Slate* still ran its Gun-Death Tally, and Tyshon was on that, too. Locally, a website called DNAinfo.com had a mission to report on each homicide, and so the next day a young reporter, Erica Demarest, went to Tyshon's home.

Erica had seen the families of many victims while working on this project, and even three months afterwards, when we met in a coffee shop near my son's school, she recalled Tyshon's family as being one of the more challenging. By the time she'd arrived, relatives had gathered to offer condolences. She spoke briefly with the grandfather, who would not be named. Then a parent arrived and said they would speak to her only with the proviso that neither their name nor gender be revealed – the latter being a stipulation I have never come across in my twenty-one years of reporting. Even then, Erica was in and out of the house within eight minutes – she timed it.

In that time, she learned the following: 'Tyshon was "joyous", "playful" and "a typical teenager". He liked tinkering with electronics, they said, and could often be found watching TV or playing video games with his siblings. [He] had had trouble in school . . . and was looking into alternative education programmes. He was planning to get a state ID this Monday so he could begin applying for jobs.'

'He was trying to get his life straightened out,' his grandfather said.

'He was trying to find an alternative way,' said the parent, who then asked Erica's readers to think twice before inflicting on others the pain they were now feeling. 'You know, it could easily be your family,' said the parent. 'So think about that before you do it to somebody else.' Then Erica was shown the door.

By all accounts, Tyshon had quite a bit of straightening out to do. Police told DNAinfo he was a 'documented gang member' and speculated that the shooting might have been gang-related. The 'parent' confirmed he had been in 'gang trouble in school', and another family member pointed out he was no longer in school.

Sure enough, every now and then Tyshon's Facebook page showcases the brutal alongside the bacchanal. A picture from 14 January 2013 shows at least $400 laid out on a table, about $250 of which is splayed out in a fan with a gun beneath it. The caption reads, 'A days work'. A few weeks earlier, he posted a picture of himself standing in a living room pointing a gun straight at the camera. In many pictures, he's holding both hands out with the thumb reaching in across the palm to touch his ring finger and the rest of his fingers extended in what is most likely a gang sign. His Instagram account went by the name 'Lakesidegangsta'. Just over a year before he died, he stood in a hallway with his left arm held outstretched with his fingers making like a gun while his right hand pointed to the floor with just one finger – like a single barrel. The caption says, 'Get popd'. His Facebook page is littered with RIP messages to fallen friends, shout-outs to others who are in jail, and posters indicating that he was in the Lakeside Gangster Disciples – a nationwide gang. Tyshon was not merely a victim of the media distortions of black pathologies; his actions actually provided the raw material for them.

'Tyshon was not an innocent boy,' says Regina, one of Tyshon's mother's best friends, who says she knew Tyshon 'before he was even thought of'. 'He did burglary, sold drugs, he killed people. He had power in the street. He really did. Especially for such a young kid. He had power. A lot of people were intimidated by him, and they were scared of him. I know he had bodies under his belt.' If

I'd chosen another day, I could well have been reporting on one of Tyshon's victims.

Tributes following his passing blend a sense of loss at his death with a moral ambivalence about his life. Like a soldier slain in combat, expressions of lament are framed with the understanding that such a tragic outcome was, at the very least, an occupational hazard. 'You live by the sword, you die by the sword,' says Regina. 'He lived by the guns and the gangs and the streets, and that's how he died. It was sad to see him laying there at the funeral. I seen him grow up and I loved him and I know he could be a good kid. But there ain't no point in sugarcoating it. He was a bad kid too.'

Many of the messages on his Facebook page took the form of elegies – literally poetic farewells. There's one from his elder sister, Kiyana:

> You're not the devil you just went along with his game.
> But an Angel I still pray to God you became.
> Bad decisions everyone makes,
> But never did I believe for them
> Your life they'd take . . .

And one from his friend Chris:

> It seem like just the other day we was chilling having fun
> Now my Lil Homie gone from another with a gun
> how many more can I take I tell you right now it's none
> the ones who did it I hope they die aint no biting
> my Damn tongue

Gangs are neither new nor racially specific. From the Irish, Polish, Jewish and Puerto Rican gangs of New York to the Mafia, various types of informal gatherings of mostly but not exclusively young men have long been part of Western life. They often connect the social, violent, entrepreneurial and criminal. And although they involve a relatively small minority, it amounts to a significant number of people. According to the National Youth Gang Survey, in 2012 in the United States there were around thirty thousand gangs and over eight hundred thousand gang members[18] – roughly the population of Amsterdam. The terms of membership and rules of engagement differ, as do the perceived benefits, depending on the context. Some people join through fear; others to instil fear in others; some identify just enough to keep below the radar or, like Edwin, associate for the sake of social status. Many aren't really clear why they join; like many teenagers they just blow with the winds that are guiding their friends. Some don't join at all; as was pointed out earlier they are 'gang-related' for the simple reason that in the neighbourhoods where they live gangs are dominant and there's no way to avoid them.

'Joining a gang is free,' says Bautista. 'There are parks around here but they're under-served, under-staffed and under-resourced. They're taking down a lot of the basketball courts. If you don't have money there's very few options to do something thrilling.'

What is new is that in recent years they have become more deadly than ever. According to the National Youth Gang Survey, between 2007 and 2012 gang membership rose 8 per cent, and gang-related homicides leapt 20 per cent.[19] The principal reason why gang activity has become more deadly, it seems, is because of the availability of guns. Studies in Los Angeles County revealed that, between 1979 and 1994, the proportion of gang homicides involving guns increased from 71 per cent to 95 per cent.[20] 'The contrast with the present is striking,' argued sociologist Malcolm Klein after reaching a similar conclusion in Philadelphia and East Los Angeles. 'Firearms are now standard. They are easily purchased or borrowed and are more readily available than in the past.'[21]

But, as brutal as they are, gangs can also offer a sense of community and purpose in a situation where neither seems attainable. 'School failure, unemployment, and family dysfunction tear at the shreds of a young person's self-esteem,' writes Deborah Prothrow-Stith, former Massachusetts Commissioner of Public Health and co-author of *Deadly Consequences: How Violence Is Destroying Our Teenage Population and a Plan to Begin Solving the Problem.*[22] 'Gang membership balms these wounds.' Gangs, she argues, can be places where young men feel they are valued and where a willingness to fight to defend yourself and others compensates for your inability to find a job and mature into more traditional masculine roles.

They become like family, taking under their wing at a young age those who appear vulnerable and giving them a sense of camaraderie and an identity that might otherwise be lacking. 'For many a poor boy the most perceptible difference between the streets and home is that home is danger and squalor with a blanket and a roof,' writes James Baldwin in *The Evidence of Things Not Seen.*[23] Despite several attempts I could not reach Tyshon's mother or anybody else in his house. But according to Regina, however rough the streets were, they offered Tyshon more than his home life ever could:

> Sometimes [his mother] never came out of her room for days . . . And she kept having kids. And the kids had to fend for themselves . . . So they had to get out in the streets. They had to find their own food to steal. They had to do whatever they had to do to survive. So those kids had a rough life.
>
> The older gangbangers, they saw that and they took advantage of that. They made him think that they loved him. They gave him a hundred dollars here and a hundred dollars there. And he thought, 'Oh, these people love me. So I'm gonna follow these people in the street. I'm not gonna listen to her.' So they used him. They knew that kids wouldn't go to jail long. They knew they wouldn't be tried as adults. The streets did that. He turned to the streets because he couldn't go home and call it home. So he was basically a street kid.

*

The key to challenging the fatal consequences of gang culture, Dr Slutkin, from Cure Violence, tells me, lies in treating violent crime like a disease and changing the norms in the worst-affected neighbourhoods to prevent its transmission. 'We need to interrupt the spread, change the script, change the behaviour, and change the norms,' he says.

Cure Violence does a great deal of public education, often in concert with local clergy, to organise communities against gun violence. It also has a team of 'violence interrupters'. These are often ex-offenders and former gang members embedded in the community who try to broker truces or who will go to the emergency room when a victim is hospitalised and persuade family members not to retaliate.

I went out with the interrupters in Englewood, one of the neighbourhoods on Chicago's South Side where gun violence has been most rampant. (They do not operate in South Chicago, where Tyshon lived and died.) It was early in the autumn of 2014 and late in the afternoon, and as we patrolled the streets by car there were signs of life and death. The weather was good and people were out – sitting on the stoop, kids playing basketball, older folks playing cards and having cook-outs. For an area renowned for gun crime, the mood was incredibly relaxed. But, every few blocks, some graffiti or an arrangement of flowers and cards marked the spot where somebody had fallen. And since both of my chaperones had grown up in the area, on many blocks they, too, inevitably had stories about some drama involving a shooting.

Herein lies one of the paradoxes of high-crime areas. The communities are, in many senses, engaged and tight. It is the very nature of life in poor areas such as these that its residents have trouble escaping it. So those who remain know each other well, and over the summer months social life spills out onto the streets. Teens and adults gather on porches and stoops, kids run from house to house, and extended families, connected by endless permutations of baby mamas, baby daddys, and 'uncles' and 'aunts' who have no biological connection (informal family structures familiar to me from my Barbadian family), reach out to each other.

On the other hand, these areas are ripped apart by violence and poverty. Stray bullets aside, the shooters and the shot often know each other. And the boundaries of the community, like most boundaries, are arbitrary, heavily enforced, and inevitably porous. Make friends in school with someone who lives two blocks over, flirt with someone on a different street, or wear the wrong-colour T-shirt on a walk to the store and, like Pedro in San Jose, you could be putting your life on the line.

JC (not his real name), one of the interrupters I was riding with, described the situation that weekend as 'hot'. Nine people had been shot in Englewood the previous afternoon. One of them, Deandre Ellis, twenty-two, was sitting in the 'first chair' of the Suitable Barber and Beauty Salon getting his hair cut when a man dressed all in black came in and sprayed the room with gunfire, killing him and wounding two others.[24]

'I found that this beef going on started behind a female,' JC said. 'These guys went to school together, and once upon a time they were cool together. It's a touchy situation now because there's bodies on the ground.'

So JC and Jamal (not his real name) drive the streets they grew up in, stopping occasionally to talk to family, people they know, and people they were in prison with. As we cruise around, young men look up just long enough to get a measure of the vehicle, in case it means trouble, and then return to their conversations on stoops and corners. The police are also cruising the neighbourhood. At one point we see them line up several young men against a building; the officers make the men place their hands on the wall and spread their legs as they pat them down. Nobody knows where the next shot is coming from or whom it'll be aimed at. But everybody knows it's coming.

'We drive around critical hotspots,' says JC. 'We see someone that's connected to the block who can give us some details about what took place last night, and we put that together with a lot of other information and try and stop things before it starts. We go to talk to these high-risk guys one on one.'

Who's high risk? 'A high-risk guy would be a known weapon carrier who's known for hurting somebody,' he continues. 'A history of violence. Someone just released from prison. Nine times out of ten someone's in war right now.' While we're driving, Jamal gets a call from a woman whose 'baby daddy' got killed the night before.

The transition from prison to civilian life is particularly hard – especially if you've been away for a long time. Keen to reassert their status, ex-cons emerge to find that they have been forgotten. 'A lot of guys come home, and there's no employment out here for 'em,' explains Jamal. 'But if you've been gone for a long time, then the block done change. Brothers live in the past. And they think, "I was the man round here ten years ago. I'm still the man." So he out there showing everybody I'm still that guy. That's where the conflict come in at. People say, "You can't just come here cos we're already established. Your name don't hold no weight no more."'

So how do they intervene in an environment as volatile and dangerous as this? It depends on the situation. Sometimes they can appeal to naked self-interest, pointing out to someone still raging over the death of a family member or gang member what is at stake for them if they act rashly. 'He's on parole,' explains Jamal. 'He just got out. If he's found with a weapon and he goes back, it'll be ten years. And he don't want no more of that.'

Sometimes the roots of the conflict are so deep that the protagonists have forgotten what the fighting was originally about. And sometimes there are people you just can't reach. 'There are brothers out there just wanna shoot,' says JC. 'You can talk to 'em, but that don't mean they're gonna listen.'

In the past, they both agree, there was more structure and discipline to gang life than there is now. They don't even call them gangs any more but 'cliques' (much like Stanley's friends on Beatties Ford in Charlotte) that are loosely affiliated under the old gang labels. 'Basically there ain't no real whole blocks in Englewood no more,' they say, looking out over the vacant lots and boarded-up houses of an economically devastated community. 'Just maybe five or six houses exist on one block. So it's just cliques. They become friends, and when they get older they might do things like smoking and drinking, and that becomes your clique. A lot of the time they name themselves, sometimes after their dead homies. What's your name?' asks Jamal. 'Gary,' I say. 'Say if you passed away and they might call their clique G-boy or Garyworld.'

As we pulled back up to the Cure Violence office, dusk had arrived. 'Now they're going to the liquor store and heading out with their crew to hatch their plans for tonight,' said JC. Four people were shot and injured in Englewood that night. None died.

Tyshon's clique was called Lolo World, after a fallen member who went by the name Lolo. Over the years, Tyshon graduated to a leadership position. His nemesis was Lil Herb, an accomplished rapper from neighbouring South Shore from the NLMB (No Limit Muskegon Boys or Never Leave My Brothers) – a gang found on the East Side.

Lil Herb (who later wanted to be known as G Herbo) was the same age as Tyshon. He hit the big time in 2012 with 'Kill Shit', which he recorded with Lil Bibby, before going on to record with major artists including Nicki Minaj, Chance the Rapper, and Common. In one of his songs, 'Chi-Raq', he celebrates the violence that has blighted his home town.

There is no evidence Lil Herb had anything do with Tyshon's death. But in at least one song, RondoNumbaNine's 'Zeko Pack', which came out six months after Tyshon was killed, he boasts about

Tyshon (who also went by the name Posto) being shot. Tyshon's clique is now called Postogang.

If the streets raised Tyshon, then for much of his teenage life the prison system housed him. He had only just been released from prison that Monday. Little more than six weeks earlier, he'd been arrested for a public-peace violation and for reckless conduct after police saw him in an alley where, they claimed, the Disciples regularly shoot. When they called for him to stop, he ran away, stopping traffic on South Marquette Road, only to be chased down by eight police officers and arrested next to his house. That time he spent only one night in a cell.

On hearing of his death, one of his Facebook friends expressed surprise, because the last time they'd seen each other, they'd been picked up by the police, and she assumed he must have been back in prison. 'Last time i seen u we was together n the back of a cpd [Chicago Police Department] van the crazy part is i was going for talking shit to the police cause they was bout to try to play u they gave me a ticket n took u n i didnt even know u was out so when i got that call i wasnt even thinking of u. Then it hit me . . . u will be missed down here . . . prayers to all feeling hurt behind this . . . when will it end . . . feeling sad . . .'

The pathos in this account is in the assumption that had he been in prison he would still be alive. Herein lies the brutal reality of growing up poor and black in areas such as Chicago's South Side: that two of the most likely outcomes for a black male under the age of twenty-five is prison or death – and maybe, as was the case for Tyshon, both. These aren't options – because no one in his or her right mind would choose them. They are simply the paths most readily available, in the same way that children of privilege approaching their final year of undergraduate study are generally destined either to go on to further study or to start working. True, those young university students might end up unemployed or dropping out, but if they simply float with the tide of their race and class, that's unlikely. From career counselling to peer and parental pressure, both system and circumstance are set up for that transition.

For black youth in low-income neighbourhoods, both system and circumstance are set up for an entirely different trajectory – to escape that fate you have both to swim against the tide and hope for a lucky break. In this sense, as Regina tells it, Tyshon never really stood a chance.

Given the life he lived it's amazing he reached the age of eighteen. A few years earlier, he was shot in the leg on 79th Street. The first day he came out of the hospital, Regina says, he was shot again, just a couple of blocks away from the site of the first shooting. When his mom went to the liquor store, one youth told her they weren't going to stop until they killed him. 'You his mama,' he told her. 'We should kill you too.'

Regina begged her to move. Regina had once lived with Tyshon's family – when she was younger and had a drug problem, and had to leave to straighten herself out. She went first to Indiana, then to Wisconsin, and currently lives in Iowa. She tried to convince Tyshon's mother that she could break the cycle if she left the area and that she could save her children from worse. When his mother refused to move, Regina pleaded with her to let Tyshon come and stay with her, arguing, 'There's so much more to see than Chicago and a liquor store. C'mon now.' But she wouldn't let him go.

We've seen, in previous chapters, how the law of probabilities operates in terms of the criminal justice system, the job market, educational achievement, and so on. What is more difficult to quantify is the psychic load it brings to bear on those who are raised in such environments. 'I think we need to recognise how fatalistic many teenagers, especially inner-city teens, feel about violence – firearms, physical force, injury and death are intimately known to these kids,' writes Prothrow-Stith. 'Many poor, black, inner-city kids are living surrounded by an amount of violence that even those of us who are experts in "intentional injury" find astounding. What you and I read about in the headlines, hundreds of thousands of ordinary kids are living every day, often without protection or guidance of any adult.'[25]

Shortly after Tyshon's killing, a woman who lived in the building where it happened told a photographer for the picture agency Getty Images that 'she was happy that her fourteen-year-old son was locked up because it was safer for him to be incarcerated than to live in the neighbourhood.'[26]

This precariousness pervades everything. In *Gang Leader for a Day: A Rogue Sociologist Takes to the Streets*, a gang leader, JT, explains to author and doctoral student Sudhir Venkatesh why he should always take a less lucrative deal now than the promise of a better one later. 'You always take the sure bet in this game,' he says. 'Nothing can be predicted – not supply, not anything. The nigger who tells you he's going to have product a year from now is lying. He could be in jail or dead. So take your discount now.'[27]

A few years ago, Doriane Miller, the Chicago-based primary-care physician we met in a previous chapter, started noticing a growing number of young patients coming through with physical symptoms for which there was no obvious physical diagnosis. 'They came in with complaints of headache or stomach ache. Things you couldn't quite put your finger on and that didn't seem to be related to any diagnosable physical illness. But they were very sad. And sad in an angry way that you could tell they were very distressed,' she told me. In 2011 she wrote a play about youth violence and depression called *It Shoudda Been Me* after she kept noticing a certain type of tattoo appearing on many of the young people coming to her with psychosomatic illnesses. 'They were not the typical tattoos of fantasy, like naked women, Mom, Dad, or a girlfriend or boyfriend's name,' she says. 'But it'd be a face or a broken heart with the initials of a loved one, RIP, and their year of birth and year of death. And most of those young people were born in the eighties and nineties. The ones that passed away.'

It didn't take long for her to discover, while taking standard medical histories, that many of her patients had either been shot or had a close friend or family member who had been shot. Further probing into how that experience might be related to their ailments was met with stubborn resistance. 'They were showing symptoms of post-traumatic stress disorder. But when I tried to help them tie the pieces between their personal experience around this life-changing event and why they were in the office to see me in primary care, they would say, "This is no big deal, this happens every day, please ask your next question." They wouldn't normally say please. They'd say, "Move on." Because they wouldn't want me to focus on that event . . . I would stop to give them space and time and see if they want to explore it, and they'd say, "No."'

Their refusal to delve into the source of their pain, both the physical one that had brought them to her and the psychological one they were actively denying, was not pigheadedness but a harsh, and arguably misguided, form of self-preservation. For her patients to discuss the effect of gun violence on their lives felt like an exercise in futility. Unconsciously labouring under the guidance of Reinhold Niebuhr's Serenity Prayer (which hung on my own mother's bedroom wall) – 'God, grant me the serenity to accept the things I cannot change, the courage to change the things I can, and the wisdom to know the difference' – they were not being obstinate but, given their limitations as they saw them, wise. Toughing it out was about accepting the things they could not change.

'I was willing to talk about it in the way that I've been trained to do in primary care,' says Dr Miller. 'It's not just about physical health but what people bring to their doctors. Their life experiences. Their life circumstances. All of those things that make up who we are as individuals and can have a tremendous impact on improving health and health outcomes. And so knowledge of those things as a primary-care doctor matters, because that's the way that I was trained. But my patients were not willing to share. Some of them did. But only up to a certain point. They'd say, "What are you going to do about it? Nothing is going to change what's happened." There was also a lack of familiarity with the therapeutic process and being able to get counselling. But there was that sense that this is the way it is in my life and in my community. There is a learned hopelessness around this. And so you suck it up, you man up, and you move on.'

The proximity of so many young people to so many deaths prompts existential questions, even if they are not always articulated in the most sophisticated way. Confronted by their mortality in the full bloom of adolescence, the friends and siblings of those who die are forced to contemplate their own lives and, not unreasonably, to despair, in a similar manner as Camilla, Edwin's friend, had done. 'They think, "What's the point? I don't care. There's nothing you can do about this. Many people I know at the age of twenty-five have passed on in my community, and the same thing might happen to me,"' explains Dr Miller. 'And so in that late-adolescent mind frame in which you tend to do more risk-taking and tend not to think about the consequences of your behaviour on your future, you think, "What the heck, I'm not going to be here anyhow. I might as well live fast, die young, and leave a pretty corpse."'

In Britain during the world wars, people would justify any range of impulsive acts – love affairs, hasty marriages, abandoning family, rash career choices – with the phrase 'There was a war on.' The omnipresence of death and its constant reminder of mortality were not conducive to long-term planning. People lived for the day, never knowing if either they or their loved ones would see sunrise the following morning.

Many of the areas where these young people live, and die, look like war zones – empty lots, half-demolished and boarded-up houses, depleted infrastructure, militarised policing, potholed roads, abandoned churches. But, more importantly, they are experienced as such. People (mostly young men) disappear – either to prison or to the grave – leaving a huge gender imbalance.[28] In Tyshon's census tract 55 per cent of people aged between twenty-one and fifty are female; nationally the divide is even.[29] More than 50 per cent of the black adult male population and 80 per cent of the adult black male workforce have felony records.[30] Times are hard, and the informal economy is rife, meaning there are spivs everywhere making an ostentatious display of their wealth. The distinction between civilians and combatants is blurred; because the entire community has been criminalised, few trust the police any more than they trust the drug dealers. The one major difference is that whereas wars often cement communities as people band together against a 'common enemy', in these areas the enemy is everywhere and, potentially, anyone.

The outward pall that such a calculation – death or incarceration – casts over a neighbourhood is clear: crime tape, bullet holes, police presence, RIP tributes by the roadside, rows of men lined up against walls with legs and arms spread, poverty, decay. But it's obvious only to the few who make the journey there. These areas in cities are like open prisons. Few go in, and precious few make it out. Those who can flee usually do so. Such neighbourhoods loom large in the popular imagination. Everybody in Chicago *knows* about the South Side. But very few who are not from there have been down there (apart from going to Hyde Park).

Moreover, precious few who live the life that Tyshon lived ever come out. 'I bet you most of the kids who live in that neighbourhood have never even been to the Loop, unless maybe if it was a school trip,' says Bautista, the community organiser. The handful that manages to make it out and who have the capacity and space to tell their stories are by definition atypical. Like 'the runner' described by Mario Black, Stanley Taylor's former teacher, they are the ones who got away.

For Tyshon, prison was probably as constant a feature in his teenage years as school. In one letter that Regina has kept, from 2012, he sounds as if he could be having a bad time at camp. After dropping some heavy hints to Regina that he wanted her to send him money, he writes:

> How have you been? I've been alright. Excluding the fact that I'm in the County for doing nothing more than trying to protect my life if them nigga's tried to pull up on me. And the fact that I don't think I'm going to get that probation because they never came to evaluate me for it. I mean I still got a whole month before I go to court but it's not looking too good at this point. I might just have to take that year. I really want the probation because then it won't be on my record. But I'm starting to get tired. Niggas starting to get on my nerves more and more every day. This food is so shitty and they don't give you enough to get full at all. If you have to take a shit you gon be hungry all day so best thing is to hold it. LOL My hair is looking shitty. But hopefully I will be home soon . . . I'm about to get a cool cellie. And I ain't had a fight the whole time. The only thing that keeps me from blanking up is writing these letters. So write me back fool. Lol. Love you and miss you.

But if prison was a constant, an early death felt to Regina like a certainty.

> I hate the fact that he's gone. But I look at it like now I don't have to worry about him being out there killing nobody else or nobody else trying to kill him. It was sad to see him laying there. But I'm just glad it's over, because now every day I have to live is a day when they're not going to kill him. It's a day when he's not going to die. Because we knew it was coming, we just didn't know when. We didn't know it was going to come three days before Thanksgiving. We didn't know it was going to come just when he was trying to get his life together. We knew it was going to come because of the stuff he was

doing. So we tried to prepare ourselves. One day. And so one day, two o'clock in the morning, I get a phone call.

Did he know it was coming? I asked. 'I think he knew it,' she says. 'He knew that a lot of people was after him. He put something on Facebook once that said something like, "If something happen to me who would cry for me?" So I think he knew his time was coming. That's why he wanted to change his life. But it was too late. He'd done hurt too many people. People had got killed because they were walking with Tyshon, and they tried to kill Tyshon and they got the wrong person. It was too late.'

On what would have been Tyshon's twenty-first birthday Bertha Rufus posted on his memorial Facebook wall, 'Happy birthday tyshon its still hard to believe you are gone when your mom had you she was one of the first to have a baby in the student degree so we use to all take turns holding u n church it was like u were all our baby u are loved and truly missed R.I.P nephew.'

His mother, meanwhile, continued to struggle through the bereavement. 'We been talking every day,' says Regina. 'She took it real hard. Real hard. To the point where she was telling me she wanted to die. She said, "Regina, I'm tired and I'm ready to go. But I can't go because I've got three more." She used to be 190 pounds. She's like 130 now.'

By that time, Tyshon's mother had come around to the idea of letting his younger brother stay with Regina. But it was too late. 'He got suspended from school . . . He's thirteen years old. It's the same pattern. And then she want to give them to me. I said, "I can't control him now. You should have given me him when I asked. I bring them to Iowa, and all these white folks gonna be scared of your kids. It's too late for that. You should have given me him then, when I coulda set values and morals. But you didn't." So now she got me sitting there waiting at the phone for another funeral.'

9

Gary Anderson
(aged eighteen)

Newark, New Jersey

24 November, 1.00 a.m. EST

During the Great Migration, when African Americans fled penury and political repression in the South in search of jobs and dignity up north, they often left surreptitiously. If anyone saw them leave, their flight might alert a posse of vigilantes, or even the local sheriff, to prevent their departure. So often they just vanished – if not under cover of darkness then under a shroud of mystery, without explanation or announcement. They took what they could carry and left the rest where it stood, as though they might return at any minute.

'The Delta today is dotted with nearly spectral sharecropper cabins,' writes Nicholas Lemann in *The Promised Land: The Great Black Migration and How It Changed America*. 'Their doors and windows gone, their interior walls lined with newspapers from the 1930s and 1940s that once served as insulation.'[1] Much of Newark today has a similar feeling. Only it wasn't people who led the charge but capital, leaving behind an urban landscape abandoned somewhere between post-industrial and post-apocalyptic. Since the Industrial Revolution, Newark had been one of the nation's manufacturing hubs. 'The trunk you travel with is, nine times out of ten, of Newark manufacture,' wrote the *New York Times* in 1872, around the time of the Newark Industrial Exhibition. 'The hat you wear was made there, the buttons on your coat, the shirt on your back, your brush, the tinware you use in your kitchen, the oil-cloth you walk on, the harness and bit you drive with, all owe to Newark their origin.'[2]

But with automation, suburbanisation of industry, and then neoliberal globalisation, Newark's productive base went into inexorable decline. Those jobs that machines and then computers couldn't do went primarily to the South, to suburbs, or abroad, where land and labour were cheaper, unions were weaker, and regulations more lax.

They were the very same forces that destroyed the South Chicago neighbourhood where Tyshon Anderson was shot. Only in this case they devastated an entire city, as they did cities like Detroit, Buffalo, Pittsburgh, Cleveland and Gary. But, as Brad Tuttle points out in *How Newark Became Newark: The Rise, Fall, and Rebirth of an American City*, Newark was exceptional. 'It stood out for the extraordinary speed, depth, and viciousness of its decline, and for the monumental difficulties the city faced while attempting to dig itself out from the hole.'[3] And when capital fled, jobs and therefore workers were soon to follow. Between 1960 and 1990 Newark lost nearly one-third of its population.[4]

What remains is a hollow vessel of depleted, diminished and decrepit public space where working communities once thrived. Entire housing projects that once provided homes for several thousand people are now bricked up and boarded off. Former factories now house pigeons and growing trees. Abandoned. Derelict. Neglected.

The area in Newark around the Kretchmer complex on Frelinghuysen Avenue, a warren of high-rise affordable-housing apartments not far from the airport, has just such a feel. On a warm day, life pours onto the common lawn area between the complex's towers. Young men and women hang out, teenagers flirt, old folks sit and watch – time rich and financially poor. Opposite sits a McDonald's between scrap-metal yards and mechanics' garages. And, just a short walk away, another whole complex stands uninhabited, windows that once offered a view of the cranes and freight on Newark Bay now stuffed with cinder blocks. This is by far the poorest place where anybody in this book died on 23 November 2013. According to the census, the median income in this tract is just $10,307 – that's less than half of what it was in the next most impoverished area depicted in this book, which was in the part of Houston where Edwin Rajo was shot.

It was here, not long after midnight, that Gary Anderson, eighteen, and his girlfriend went to McDonald's. Gary had been staying at his mother's for the weekend while his father took his youngest brother, Tasheem, to a basketball tournament in Maryland. Gary's father (also named Gary) had had sole custody of Gary Jr since he was five. But in recent years Gary Jr had started to get to know his mother again.

They had bonded, in part, over his hair. Although he'd worn it cropped for most of his life, his mom liked to braid it for him. Gary's braids did not frame his face on each side like Tyshon's did but hung back in light strings over his neck and shoulders, showcasing his high forehead and full-cheeked face. He was a big lad – stocky and tall. His father didn't like the hairstyle but had let it go. 'That was his world with his mother,' he says. 'I keep saying to him, "You need to get to know your mama." So whatever they did they did. I kept telling him I didn't like 'em and didn't want him to have 'em. But it was something between him and his mother, so I just wanted to leave it alone.'

But his dad thinks Gary Jr also liked to go to his mother's because she kept him on a longer leash. At home, his son was always trying to push the boundaries, but Gary Sr laid down the law. Junior had to be home by nine o'clock. 'The problem with him is he always wanted to go to his friend's house because he liked to sit on his friend's porch,' said his dad. 'His friends sit on the porch till, like, eleven, twelve o'clock at night. But I'd tell him, "You've got to be home by nine o'clock. Because I know how it is in the streets." He'd say, "I'm just sitting on the porch." And I'd say, "I don't care. It's late. The streets are not where you're supposed to be." So that was the biggest issue I had with him. He just wanted to sit out on the porch with his friends.'

His mother, however, was less strict. 'They have a complex, and they sit outside or on the balcony. I guess that's what they do,' he says. 'So that's why he liked to go down there. Because he could stay out until ten, eleven o'clock and hang out on the balcony with his mother.'

The McDonald's is just a short walk across the main road from Kretchmer. As Gary walked back to his mother's apartment building at about 1 a.m. on 24 November, three young men jumped out of a car and shot him. Family members say he was trying to protect his girlfriend. 'He tried to shield her,' said his older sister, Linda Bradley. The police conceded this may well have been what happened. 'There were some indications that he may have pushed another person out of the way,' Thomas Fennelly, the Essex County chief assistant prosecutor, told the Newark *Star-Ledger*.[5]

Either way, he fell in a shower of bullets and was rushed to University Hospital, where he was pronounced dead an hour and a half later.

'He don't have a gun. He don't have nothing,' says his dad. 'They say it was a mistaken identity. But he never had a gun on him.'

'Do you wish he had?' I asked.

His father paused. 'No, he still would have got killed.'

Gary's fatal mistake that night was not that he was out late but that he was wearing a red hoodie. His father explains. 'The day before there was a guy who had a red hoodie just like my son who killed somebody up the street. And that was one of their friends he shot. So they came back looking for him the next day, and my son had on a red hoodie. And they shot him.' The feud, some told the local media, was over an escalating turf war connected to the drug trade on Frelinghuysen Avenue.[6]

'This place is like the Wild West,' forty-seven-year-old Hassan Taylor, who was one of Gary's mother's neighbours, told *The Star-Ledger*. 'It's not a bad place to live. It's just that these young people, they've just got this mind-frame that that's the way it is.'[7]

According to Gary Sr, a few days after his son was killed, the boy in the red hoodie for whom the bullet was allegedly intended came up to Gary Jr's mother, hugged her, and apologised. 'You know that was meant for me,' he said. On the night of the shooting, the police would not say whether the bullets that hit Gary had been intended for somebody else. 'I can't confirm that, other than to say the investigation is continuing at this time,' Fennelly told the *Star-Ledger*. 'Whenever we have a crime we always look at whether it's connected to another crime or a pattern.'[8]

Gary Sr says the police think they know who killed his son. But the boy in the red hoodie – currently in jail on a drug charge – won't say because it will implicate him in the other shooting. So six months after Gary's death, the police had not charged anyone. 'They can't arrest him because they have no witness and they have no evidence, so [the suspect] can just say, "I didn't do it." I don't know who it is, and they won't tell me because it's an ongoing investigation. They're hoping that by the time summer gets here somebody's going to get tired and just tell,' explains his father. 'Soon as it gets hot somebody's going to tell, or one of these guns is going to pop up soon. Because they know who they looking for, so they've got people sitting and watching these people until they make a mistake.'

Gary Sr expressed more confidence in the Newark Police Department – or indeed any part of the city's polity – than others I spoke to. Although Chicago has relatively recently taken up the unenviable baton of murder capital of the country, Newark has failed to relinquish its reputation as a violent and dysfunctional city for the best part of forty years. During the seventies, *Newsweek* described it as 'a classic example of urban disaster', the *New York Times Magazine* referred to it as 'a study in the evils, tensions, and frustrations that beset the central cities of America', and *Harper's* branded it 'The Worst American City'. Other cities have vied for this tarnished mantle. DC, New York, New Orleans, and Los Angeles have all been in the running at various times. But what makes Newark particular is that, despite several attempts, there has been no successful makeover since the problems took hold.[9]

Between 1954 and 2006, Newark had just four mayors. Three of them faced indictments on corruption charges either while they were in office or just after they'd left it. A city once known primarily for industry and manufacturing became infamous for decrepitude and kleptocracy. The *Harper's* article pointed out that in a 1975 study of twenty-four major cities, Newark came in last in the percentage of high school graduates, college graduates, percentage of home ownership, acreage of public parks per resident, and amusement and recreation facilities per person. The study concluded, 'The city of Newark stands without serious challenge as the worst of all. Newark is a city that desperately needs help.'[10]

Like Detroit, it soon became referred to not so much as a city but as a failed state – an incorporated entity so crippled with intractable social woes and political pathologies that it was incapable of supporting itself and protecting its citizens. Starbucks wouldn't even set up there until 1999 – the same year that the company expanded into China.

Newark's political leadership effectively conceded its failures. 'Our job is to pick up the garbage, sweep the streets, and provide some measure of police and fire protection, and we can barely do that,' said Kenneth Gibson, the one mayor in that half-century who did not leave office in disgrace (though even he was later indicted for bribery and pleaded guilty to tax evasion).[11]

The problems start with the young. In 1992, more than half the thieves in the city who were caught were under seventeen. And the sense of hopelessness was pervasive: at one stage, Tuttle points out, the city bought 1,750 anti-car-theft devices and raffled them off to residents. That seemed like a better bet than trying to police the city so the cars wouldn't get stolen in the first place.[12] In 2006, 60 per cent of the city's police officers worked only during the daytime. Its gang unit worked 8 a.m. to 4 p.m. Monday to Friday – hardly rush hour for gang activity but a stark improvement on the narcotics unit, which, despite the huge drug problem connected to the gang problem, simply did not exist.[13]

The court system, meanwhile, was a complete calamity. 'Countless people showed up for court dates to discover their names were not listed in the computer,' writes Tuttle. 'Police officers often never received messages requesting them to testify. Prosecutors were always pleasantly surprised when an officer actually appeared in court on the proper day. Well aware that the system was a mess, citizens accused of violations knew that their cases would likely be dismissed so long as they were willing to line up and wait all day to be called by the court.'[14] Newark was the only jurisdiction covered in this book that failed to provide me with an autopsy or incident report for the victim, without a reason for withholding one. Despite my countless attempts to contact the appropriate city staff, they simply did not get back to me.

It was in this system that Gary Sr placed his faith for finding his son's killers. At the time of this writing, no one has been brought to justice.

Beyond mistaken identity, there was nothing Junior ever did that would explain his being attacked in such a manner, Gary Sr said. 'He was never in no trouble. He never got locked up. He never got in no trouble. He got in trouble at school for fighting and things. But that was it. Never had no stolen cars. Never had no guns. Nothing like that. Nothing. Never been in trouble with the police. Never.'

It is a tragic reflection of the state of affairs for low-income black parents that they have to explain why their children did not deserve to be shot, pre-empting the assumption that they are 'unworthy' unless proved otherwise. Taylor, his mother's neighbour, said Gary wasn't like so many of the other kids who caused so much trouble around the complex. He was 'a real nice cat, real respectful', Taylor told the Newark *Star-Ledger*.[15] 'Some days, he would see me struggling and say, "What do you need? I'll go get it for you",' said Taylor, a former supermarket night manager who moved into Anderson's building two years before Gary's death, after one of his legs was amputated.

Gary's two greatest loves were fixing things and dogs. 'He had his little friends around here. They ride bikes, played basketball, and hang out all the time. He played Xbox. First it was PlayStation. And then it was Xbox,' says his dad. 'He had four friends he'd usually play with. That's it. But mostly it was the bikes. They'd ride all the way up to the mountains. That's what he did. He was good with his hands: fixing bikes, fixing computers. He fixed bikes all day. Eight, nine bikes a day and then go through the neighbourhood, riding them around . . . And he loved dogs. That was his thing. Actually he had an application that he filled out for the Humane Society to work there. So they were scheduling him for a blood test. Bikes and dogs, that was his favourite thing.'

But his father says just to live in Newark as a young black man is to tempt fate. 'In Newark you have no choice but to worry about guns. That's the biggest thing. It's crazy. There are kids in the streets just walking around with guns just to have guns.' That's why, he says, he was so strict with Gary. 'He knows there's no way in heck that he's living in my house and is going to walk out the door after ten o'clock without me. I don't even want to walk out my door. Sometime I get off work late and I have to come down at eleven o'clock. I'm walking down the street like this' – and he looks around himself warily – 'because people will just drive up on you and shoot you for no reason. So you have to be mindful of every place and thing that you do.'

The vulnerability such an atmosphere induces among the young was summed up in a poem a freshman student at Central High School wrote a few years before Gary was killed. The teacher wrote *HOPE* on the blackboard and gave the all-boy class a little while to think about the topic before each student penned a verse on it. A student named Tyler wrote:

We hope to live,
Live long enough to have kids
We hope to make it home every day
We hope we're not the next target to get sprayed . . .

We hope never to end up in Newark's dead pool
I hope, you hope, we all hope.[16]

I found Gary's address on whitepages.com by matching the names in his online obituary to a group of names associated with a particular property. It was just around the corner from the church that had performed his funeral service. It seemed like that would be too great a coincidence for it not to be his home, although there was a good chance that, like so many other families who lost children that day, they had since moved. When I got to the address, the house looked derelict from the outside. It sat adjacent to another house, on a desolate block between a bricked-up factory and an empty lot. The curtains were drawn. It seemed as though it had been empty for some time.

The area was run down but it wasn't menacing. While visiting, I struck up a conversation with a woman opposite Gary's house who sat on her front stoop in the sun while studying for her nurse's exam and babysitting her granddaughter. I didn't knock at the house – I'd learned my lesson from Kenneth Mills-Tucker's father that you should not cold call the bereaved. I left an envelope in the mailbox and moved on to the funeral director's to see if they could help me find a family member.

I was sitting with the funeral director when a big fight broke out outside – a family feud caffeinated by grief. While the director went to sort it out, I got a call from Gary Sr. The home I'd seen a few minutes earlier wasn't vacant at all. He'd been in it the whole time. He told me to come straight over.

This was the house Gary Jr had grown up in – a cosy home with a huge flat-screen TV dominating the small living room. Next door was the house in which Gary Sr had grown up and where his mother still lived. His mother – Gary Jr's grandmother – was a regular churchgoer at the St Paul Sounds of Praise church around the corner, where I'd also left a note.

The dilapidated factory building adjacent used to be his grandmother's place of work. It made cosmetics. 'This used to be an OK area,' says Gary Sr. 'You was able to afford different things. Kids were able to do different things. We had some of everything. All kinds of nationalities were in this neighbourhood. White, Chinese, black, Hispanic. There was a factory, so everybody was working around here. So it wasn't so bad. This was the quietest neighbourhood. It was quiet. There was nothing going on.'

Why was he still there? 'I think about moving all the time. I say to my mom, "Let's pack up and move down south." But it's hard because right now I'm working at the Prudential Center [an indoor multipurpose arena that is home to the New Jersey Devils ice hockey team], and the income doesn't come in where I can just pack up and leave. And then there's my mom. She's still next door, and I'm not going to leave her in this crazy neighbourhood by herself.'

That's not to say everything was easy before. There have long been no-go areas around here. 'From here there were only two places you couldn't go,' he explains. 'Avon Avenue and 16th Avenue. Those were the two worst areas. But everything in between was quiet. So you knew that so long as you stayed in this neighbourhood, you were fine. But if you leave to go to Avon there's nothing but gangs. You go to 16th there's nothing but gangs. So you knew not to go into them areas. But stay right here. Go to the park right here, you were fine.'

Gary Sr was just three years old in July 1967 when Newark erupted into a blazing inferno of popular insurrection. Rioting, which extended over several days, pitted the city's black population against its mostly white law enforcement and the National Guard. Police ran amok. 'If you have a gun,' Police Director Dominick Spina announced over the police radio at one stage, 'Whether it's a shoulder weapon or whether it is a handgun, use it.'[17] National Guardsmen came out of tanks to showers of bottles and other missiles thrown by local people.

For six days, the city was ablaze. When the week was out, 26 people (24 blacks and 2 whites) were killed, more than 1,100 were injured, and 1,400 were arrested. There were 350 acts of arson, there was roughly $10 million dollars' worth of damage, and the police used 13,326 rounds of ammunition.[18] In response to the riots here and elsewhere, Lyndon Johnson's federal government produced the Kerner Report. 'Segregation and poverty have created in the racial ghetto a destructive environment totally unknown to most white Americans,' it concluded. 'What white Americans have never fully understood but what the Negro can never forget – is that white society is deeply implicated in the ghetto. White institutions created it, white institutions maintain it, and white society condones it.'[19]

The report sold 2 million copies and was reportedly the best-selling federal report in American history. Gary Sr thinks things have deteriorated since then. Today, he says, the space around his home where a parent might consider their child truly safe has shrunk to the house they live in. 'It's certainly not middle class no more,' he says.

It seems like an obvious but all too rarely acknowledged fact that gun violence, like most crimes, is intricately related to poverty. Since most poor people never shoot anybody and some rich people do, there is nothing automatic about this connection. But if you have a future to invest in, if you can afford lawyers to settle disputes, extracurricular programmes to entertain your children, an expensive private education (or a house in a school zone that ensures a good public education), a private security system, a car to ferry your teenage children through their social lives, money to donate to political campaigns, a community that politicians believe is worth courting, a tax base that can pay for good parks, policing and cultural events – if, in short, you can draw on the full pool of resources available to an American of means, then both the temptation and the threat of gun violence are severely diminished. That does not make you a better person; it simply makes you better equipped to be safe in a country where guns are in plentiful supply.

But, unless you are a trust-fund baby, you don't get any of that without work. And for a particular stratum of American society, the kind of stable work that pays a living wage is hard to find. New technology, free-trade agreements, deregulation, and laissez-faire economic orthodoxy have accelerated and deepened the trend towards less skilled work and more low-paid, low-skilled jobs in ways that couldn't have been imagined back when Gary's grandmother had her job in the factory. Since the seventies, American wages have been stagnant,[20] leaving median male earnings on a par with those of 1964 in real terms.[21] In the seventies, close to two-thirds of prime-age male workers with less than a high-school education worked full time, year round, in eight out of the ten years. During the eighties, that share was down to half.[22] During that decade, William Julius Wilson points out in *When Work Disappears: The World of the New Urban Poor*, the jobs that were lost were in production, transportation and labouring while the new jobs created were in the clerical, sales and service sectors.[23]

This reality has affected most areas of the country and most racial groups. You can see it in the depressed former mining towns of Ohio, Pennsylvania, and Kentucky, former mill towns such as Buffalo, and the auto-parts manufacturers all around the Midwest. But it has affected African Americans more intensely than others for the simple reason that this dramatic shift coincided with their gaining civil rights and moving in ever greater numbers to the very cities and sectors that went on to decline.

'Just as attempts to provide blacks with a greater slice of the labor market pie began in earnest, the pie shrank,' writes Thomas Sugrue in *The Origins of the Urban Crisis: Race and Inequality in Postwar Detroit*. 'Blacks made gains in occupations that became increasingly scarce in postwar decades. The combination of discrimination and profound changes in Detroit's industrial base left a sizeable segment of the black population bereft of hope in the land of Canaan.'[24]

So as the new millennium approached, the secure, decent-paying jobs to which a significant portion of African American men once aspired in a city such as Newark had simply gone. This was particularly devastating for the young. Between 1973 and 1987 the percentage of black men aged twenty to twenty-nine working in manufacturing plummeted from 37 per cent to 20 per cent.[25] As exemplified by the abandoned factory next to Gary's home, nothing but a shell of that former industrial capacity was left. And thanks to segregation – Newark was one of a handful of places that became even more segregated after the civil rights era[26] – these losses devastated entire communities and even whole cities.

One in three of Newark's black residents lives in poverty – black unemployment in the city is more than twice the rate of white unemployment and five times the national average.[27] And with each economic downturn, the impact of these trends – deindustrialisation, segregation, poverty – intensified and became amplified.[28]

What does this have to do with Gary and guns? Well, first, when jobs are scarce, drug dealing becomes one of the few economic sectors available to those with a high-school education or less.

In *Freakonomics: A Rogue Economist Explores the Hidden Side of Everything*, Steven Levitt and Stephen Dubner describe the business model for a drug gang in the nineties, culled from research by then University of Chicago sociology student Sudhir Venkatesh. He spent several years researching one gang on the South Side, the Black Disciples, and was given access to its inner workings. '[The gang worked] an awful lot like most American businesses, actually, though perhaps none more so than McDonald's,' write Levitt and Dubner. 'In fact if you were to hold a McDonald's organizational chart and a Black Disciples org chart side by side, you could hardly tell the difference.'[29]

Within the monthly costs the gang had to cover – this was in the nineties, during the height of the crack epidemic – 2 per cent was spent on weapons and more than 10 per cent on 'mercenary fighters'. If you stayed in the gang for four years, then you could reasonably expect to be arrested 5.9 times, incur non-fatal wounds or injuries 2.4 times, and sustain a 1-in-4 chance of being killed.

These were the kinds of odds that caught up with Tyshon, who died in Chicago just before Gary died in Newark. And in the absence of any concrete intelligence from the police, my guess is they are the same odds that sent Gary's murderers (who were probably not that different from Tyshon's) in pursuit of the boy in a red hoodie, later imprisoned on a drug charge.

Moreover, research by Professor Delbert S. Elliott, founding director of the Center for the Study and Prevention of Violence, in Boulder, Colorado, found a clear correlation between the inability to find work and the propensity towards violent behaviour. Race and class differences related to violent offending are small during adolescence, he discovered, but disparities widen considerably going into adulthood, depending on the availability of work. This occurs for two reasons. First, the absence of employment severely reduces the likelihood that people will get married, which is one of the key routes to more stable, less violent behaviour. Second, growing up in poor, disorganised neighbourhoods inhibits the normal evolution of adolescent development. Young people in such areas, Elliott found, tend to have lower levels of personal competence, self-efficacy, social skills and self-discipline. 'Many are not adequately prepared to enter the labor market even if jobs were available. They are, in some ways, trapped in an extended adolescence and continue to engage in adolescent behavior.'[30]

Gary's adolescent transgressions were unremarkable. His father recalls how the reverend who performed his funeral service once saw him hanging out on the block and asked him what he was up to. Gary smart-mouthed him to the effect that it was none of his business. When the reverend told him he knew Gary's grandmother, Gary said, 'Well, you ain't gonna tell her nothin'', and walked away.

The very next day Gary was on the porch with his grandmother when the reverend pulled up and told the grandmother what had happened. Gary got a slap right there and then, his father told me with a big laugh. 'Since then, he was like, "How you doin', preacher? How you doin', sir?"'

He was thinking of leaving Newark and maybe heading south to start a new life in North Carolina with his older sister. She had been in town just a week before he died and told him he should go with her when she returned. But Gary thought it better to wait until graduation.

He was, his father said, a 'typical teenager'. 'He liked school to a certain extent. You know kids. They like school. But then when the teacher's trying to teach them something they don't want to be bothered. "I don't want to be in school." He passed his classes. He did what he had to do.'

'Typical teenager' in Newark comes with some caveats, which by now are all too familiar. In Gary's room, where his cat Mocha still lurks and his clothes still hang six months after his death, an RIP notice hangs in memory of one of his friends who was shot down.

It was his final year in school, and Gary Jr had initially decided that he had no interest in marking the occasion. 'He didn't want to go to the prom. He didn't want to go to graduation. But as soon as he turned eighteen, he said, "Daddy, I want to go to the prom. I want to go to my graduation. So we need to get my stuff together." He had a little girlfriend. So I said all right. So at the time he was shot, he just talking about going to school and going to graduation.' His father felt that North Carolina might have provided opportunities Gary Jr wouldn't have had in Newark. 'If that's where he's going to go and be successful, I had no problem. I told him that. Because Newark is crazy. Being a young black guy here . . . It's hard,' he said, shaking his head. 'It's hard here, trying to be young.'

10

Gustin Hinnant
(aged eighteen)

Goldsboro, North Carolina
24 November, 3.30 a.m. EST

The twenty-four-hour period in which this book is set ends with a green 1996 Cadillac Sedan Deville rolling to a stop in somebody's yard in the early hours of 24 November on the corner of Walnut and South Audubon in Goldsboro, North Carolina. It's a quiet, verdant street where, in the autumn, leaves are heaped in tiny piles, in a small town that many in North Carolina have not even heard of. When the police spotted the car, while answering another call, its doors were open and its lights were on. The passengers had fled. The driver, eighteen-year-old Gustin Hinnant, was not so lucky. His body lay slumped back between the two front seats, his head hanging where the back-seat passengers' feet might be, dripping blood that collected in a pool on the floor. He'd been felled by a single bullet that had pierced the rear window and hit the back of his head.

Gustin's slender, long face was as dark and smooth as melted chocolate, a gloss finish in a picture that might have been Photoshopped but for the hint of peach fuzz (his autopsy mentions a 'faint beard and mustache present'). Not quite angelic-looking, perhaps, but both youthful and playful. 'In his physique he was a small-statured guy,' says Daina Taylor, a family friend who'd known Gustin (pronounced *Justin*) since he was a small child. 'He was what we'd call light in the butt . . . not meaty. So the only thing he had going for him was that' – she opens and closes her hand as though she were operating a puppet – 'yapping with the hands.'

'He was slim,' says his father, Greg, who raised Gustin by himself for most of his life. 'His body was cut a little from doing weights and push-ups. Muscular, but still no big guy . . . petite.'

Young enough that his favourite movies, according to Facebook, were *Happy Feet* and *Toy Story* and that his favourite hobby at home was to sit in his room quietly and draw pictures. Old enough that just a few days before he died he changed his Facebook cover photo from a graffiti-emblazoned wall to a sprawling array of high-calibre bullets.

Old enough to spend the night with girls. Young enough that they would usually get caught climbing through his window. 'A couple of young women did it,' says Greg, shaking his head. 'And every time they come through I've caught 'em. I tell 'em, "You welcome in my house through my front door any time you want to. But you come in through that window, you ain't welcome in my house. Don't let Gustin talk you into coming through that window."' Too young to respect the considerable leeway he was given by Greg's working hours (his dad was on the night shift at Walmart). 'Listen, bro. I work at night. You know my days off. Don't be hardheaded,' Greg had told him.

'On more than one occasion, his father came home and there were girls in the house,' adds Daina, barely stifling a smile. 'Now if you know that your father gets home at seven a.m., kick them girls out at five or six. Don't defy him fully. Everybody's falling asleep on each other naked and stuff. Check yourself. You want to be a man. This is part of being a man.'

Old enough to be making plans for a proper career, even if there was some discrepancy among those who knew him about what that career would be. According to Greg, he wanted to be a physiotherapist for elite sports players. 'They throw their knee out or something, he wanted to be that guy who would bring them back to the level where they could go back to work,' he explained. But he told Daina he wanted to go to Wake Technical Community College and train to work for a cable company. Hardy, a friend from school, says he wanted to be 'an entrepreneur'.

But Gustin was still too young to let go of his dream of becoming a rapper one day. He spent a lot of time on the computer working on Virtual DJ applications and had started a record label, called Green

Team, with his friends. The one song I heard online, performed with someone called T. Quail, was not bad. Mellow, rhythmic and cut under with some soul. The lyrics are basic. 'Keeps telling niggas to fall in line/You can say that you're better/but we know that that ain't true/all we hear nowadays is disses/that's what rappers do.' Also: 'You see money and you gotta get it/You see money and you gotta spend it.' It's not brilliant. But compared to the other amateur rap that's out there, it's certainly respectable.

Old enough to seek his kicks in forbidden places. For a few months, Gustin had been sneaking out of his bedroom window as soon as Greg left for work and heading to Slocumb Street, which Greg considered a hangout for ne'er-do-wells. Gustin's room was at the back of the house (a roadside cottage opposite an industrial park) that backed up to a wooded area which, of an evening, served as Gustin's escape route. 'He'd go out that window, walk round that fence, and go down that dirt road to where the action's at,' explains Greg.

Too young to realise he was swimming in shark-infested waters and way out of his depth. One of the boys he used to spend time with on Slocumb Street is now in jail for shooting two boys, says Greg, who grew up in the Bronx. 'I said, "Gustin, man, you ain't ready for those boys over there on Slocumb Street, man. You gonna end up getting yourself killed. You ain't growing up like I did. You don't have that killer instinct in you because you don't have to survive like we had to survive. You got a mother and father to buy you stuff."'

Daina, who lives on Slocumb Street, was worried the message wasn't getting through. Raised in Queens, New York, she is, in her own way, a community organiser. As well as running her own company doing residential and commercial janitorial work, she is also director of a charitable organisation that helps ex-convicts avoid reoffending. In the old days people called her 'the book lady'. 'I would ask children what they were interested in and then get books shipped from different publishing companies based on what the child's interest was,' she explains. 'Anything that would make them read. My focus was on the children who didn't know how to read. But Gustin did not need remedial help.' She would also check report cards, and those who got good grades would get a couple of dollars or a trip to McDonald's. Gustin always got a treat.

'I was afraid for him,' she says. 'I know the streets. I grew up in the streets. And Gustin didn't strike me as being street material.' If anything, says Daina, he was 'a little nerdy' – a very bright honour-roll student who liked to play Words with Friends in chemistry class. 'Even when he was hanging out with them boys he kept his grades up,' says Greg. He would have been the first person from his family to graduate from high school. The green Cadillac was originally intended as a graduation present. 'Greg always bragged about his children's accomplishments, especially when it came to the report cards,' says Daina.

There's a reason why car insurers charge higher premiums for young drivers, and why young offenders are – or at least should be – treated with more leniency in the criminal justice system. Adolescence is a stage in life with its own dynamic. Teenagers have the capacity to perform as adults – they can produce children, drive cars, and kill people – without the life experience always to put those abilities to good use. They are more likely to take risks and less likely to understand what those risks entail. They are experimenting not only with substances (alcohol and drugs) but also with relationships (sexual, familial, social) and lifestyles. They are working out what kind of person they want to be, and in that process they are about as likely to make sound judgements as the elderly are to make rash ones.

This is not simply a social and cultural process – a period when young people figure things out and have fun before settling down. It's a physiological one. And its primary driver is not hormonal – though of course hormones have a lot to do with it. At that age our brains are actually changing.

'The brain is a collection of cells that communicate with one another using chemicals called neurotransmitters,' explains Daniel Siegel in *Brainstorm: The Power and Purpose of the Teenage Brain*. 'During adolescence there is an increase in the activity of the neural circuits utilising dopamine, a neurotransmitter central in creating our drive for reward. Starting in early adolescence and peaking midway through, this enhanced dopamine release causes adolescents to gravitate toward thrilling experiences and exhilarating sensations.'[1]

This dopamine rush, explains Siegel, a psychotherapist and clinical professor of psychiatry at UCLA, has three distinct consequences: a tendency towards impulsivity, addiction and hyper-rationality. The last, he explains, can lead to a greater propensity to take risks. '[Hyper-rationality] is how we think in literal, concrete terms. We examine just the facts of a situation and don't see the big picture; we miss the setting or context in which those facts occur. With such literal thinking, as an adolescent, we can place more weight on the calculated benefits of an action than on the potential risks of that action.'[2]

Add to this combustible cocktail a brain that is more prone to novelty seeking, heightened emotional intensity, creative exploration, and peer-group socialising, and you have the recipe for the most volatile, vulnerable, exciting and challenging period of most people's lives. 'While most measurable aspects of our lives are improving during adolescence,' writes Siegel, 'such as physical strength, immune function, resistance to heat and cold, and the speed and agility of how we respond, we are three times more likely to suffer serious injury or death during this time than we were in childhood or than we will be in adulthood. This increase in risk is not "by chance" – scientists believe it comes from the innate changes in how the brain develops during this period.'[3]

Such behaviour is arguably not only natural but necessary. A bid to break through the borders of childhood and strike out on our own as apprentice adults involves facing fears and assessing danger.

Notwithstanding the perils, if we didn't go through this stage then we might be ill equipped to mature at all.

'A similarly lowered risk threshold – indeed, a new pleasure in risk taking – likely propels nearly grown birds out of nests, hyenas out of communal dens, dolphins, elephants, horses, and otters into peer groups, and human teens into malls and college dorms,' write Barbara Natterson-Horowitz and Kathryn Bowers in *Zoobiquity: What Animals Can Teach Us About Health and the Science of Healing*. 'As we've seen, having a brain that makes you feel less afraid enables, perhaps encourages, encounters with threats and competitors that are crucial to your safety and success. The biology of decreased fear, greater interest in novelty, and impulsivity serves a purpose across species. In fact, it could be the only thing more dangerous than taking risks in adolescence is not taking them.'[4]

Greg had another term for all of this. He called it 'hardheaded'. No matter how often he warned Gustin, his son just wouldn't listen. 'I told him, "I'm fifty-seven years old, man. I've been living longer than you, dude. I can tell you what I been through in fifty-something years in ten minutes if you'd listen. You gonna go through the same thing."'

Greg, who thanks to his roguish good looks can still carry off denim jacket and trousers with white sneakers, really did have some stories to tell. 'I used to tell him stuff we used to do. You know, I sold drugs. I gangbanged a little bit. But yo, man. You see me now. I go to work every day. I knew that that life weren't nothing.'

Gustin was Greg's eldest son. He has several children from different 'baby mamas' and is clearly a devoted father – quick to bring out pictures from holidays and home – but he's not exactly a doting one. When I ask him how many children he has, he stumbles. 'I got . . . let me see,' he says, listing them to himself quietly while counting on his fingers. 'I got . . . three girls . . . and four boys.' Then he pauses. Something's amiss. He recites their names to his fingers once more, as though doing his multiplication tables. He forgot one. 'I have five boys and three girls,' he insists. The youngest, whom I saw after day care one day, is just two.

His warnings to Gustin came from bitter experience. About twenty years ago, Greg was shot by some 'random dudes' he hung out with in Goldsboro. 'You don't know these niggas like I know them,' he told Gustin. 'Cos they shot me. I got shot messing with these same cats. Just hangin' in the street with them boys. Gettin' high a little bit, and they tried to rob me. They shot me in both of my legs . . . I had to hide in some bushes. But I got away. I thought they were my friends. But then jealousy set in. We started makin' a little money. They tried to rob me. Then they shot me.'

Pointing first to his left leg and then his right, he says, 'I got a long scar right here. I got a bullet hole in this leg. And a bullet hole back here where they bust my vein open. Shot me in both of my legs. I limped back to my apartment, and my baby's mama called the rescue car for me.'

Gustin would generally dismiss these warnings as the chidings of a fretful old man out of touch with the mood of the moment. 'Oh Dad, you scared, man. You old school. This is our time now. That stuff is old.' (Whenever Greg imitates Gustin as an adolescent, his voice drops half an octave and slows a couple of beats, dragging the syntax through the sentence with all the energy of a teenager hauling himself out of bed.)

Greg separated from Gustin's mother, Melissa, when Gustin was about four. Gustin stayed with his mother for a while before he and his brother, also named Greg, moved back in with their father when they were around seven. But when Gustin reached his early teens, the boys bristled at the boundaries Greg was setting and moved back in with their mother in Raleigh. 'Daddy too hard,' Greg said, mimicking the whiny voice of his boys when they were younger. 'He won't let us do this. He won't let us do that.'

But life didn't end up being too rosy at their mother's either. After a short while, Melissa rang Greg to tell him it wasn't working out. 'She called me up to come and get 'em. I went to get 'em at the roller-skating rink because they were getting ready to talk back to her and stuff,' he explains. Gustin lived with his older sister for a brief period, but that didn't go too well. 'She drove him down here and dropped him off because her boyfriend didn't want him staying with her no more. His sister's boyfriend and Melissa's boyfriend got mad with Gustin and put him out. So she brought him to me.'

Greg took them in but thought moving the boys to Goldsboro at that age was a bad idea. 'I said, "Man, you shouldn't have brought him down here. These little niggas down here don't want nothin'. And they got these guns. And he's gonna get in some mess."'

Goldsboro (population 37,000) sits halfway between Raleigh and the Atlantic coast, but it's off the interstate and on the road to nowhere in particular, with a quaint town centre that is mostly closed by seven o'clock. Wikipedia lists twenty-nine notable people who have come from Goldsboro. Its most famous progeny include Chris Richardson, a contestant on the sixth season of *American Idol*, and Thomas Washington, a First World War admiral and hydrographer with the US Navy.

Being from New York, Greg finds attitudes in Goldsboro limiting and backward. 'This is the dirty South right here,' he says. 'These people round here twenty years behind the time. They still let white people keep them in slavery round here by Uncle Tomming. I say you don't need to Uncle Tom no more. We got a black president. That's over with. We equal with everybody.'

Daina says, 'They didn't care about him because he was black. He didn't come from an affluent family. His mother and father weren't pillars of the community.'

Jasmin, Greg's twenty-eight-year-old girlfriend and mother to his youngest child, agrees. 'They'd get at you about the dumbest stuff here,' says Jasmin, who grew up in California. 'About the colour of your car, your hair longer than theirs, your house smaller than them. It's crazy. And that's just the black people. We ain't even talking about the white people. We don't mess with them.'

Gustin had certainly had it with Goldsboro and planned to move to Raleigh the following Monday to live with his mother, who said she would let him have her apartment while he enrolled in community college. That was the plan, anyway. Greg approved. 'I told him there ain't no jobs around here. The only reason I'm still here is because I'm working at Walmart. If I didn't work at Walmart I'd be working at Raleigh.'

Greg was an involved and engaged father. Every other Saturday, he took the boys to the Golden Touch barbershop. When the tax rebate came every year, he would share the spoils. Daina was impressed by the home-cooked meals he would make. 'I mean from scratch. Like he'd make his own biscuits. Not pop and chips. Who does that?'

'They were like buddies,' says Jasmin. 'They had their ups and downs, but they were like buddies.' Some of those downs were petty. One Thanksgiving, when Gustin could not have been more than thirteen, Greg took the kids to Daina's house in a stinking mood. 'He was flaming,' she says. 'And I was like, "It's Thanksgiving, what's the problem?" And he takes the scarf off Gustin's neck and says, "That's the problem." He had a hickey. The problem was the girl was eighteen, nineteen. Greg was livid.'

Every now and then, Gustin would 'borrow' Greg's cologne or the car without permission or a licence. Over the summer, Greg had promised Gustin some sneakers but hadn't been able to afford them, which Gustin felt was justification for calling him a 'liar' and chastising him for going back on his word. The 'yapping with his hands' would also stoke the embers of whatever strife was in the house. 'He liked talkin' back,' says Greg. 'Normal eighteen-year-old stuff. "Clean up your room." "I ain't gonna clean up no room." Wanting to sleep all day. "You need to cut the grass today." "OK,

I got it." Come back and the grass ain't cut. Stuff like that. Simple stuff. Basic stuff.'

For his part, Gustin seemed to appreciate Greg, even if he felt he spread himself too thin. 'My dad's OK,' he told Daina. 'He's cool. He's just got too many kids. He don't even remember my last birthday.'

But over time, the 'basic stuff' accumulated into more serious conflict. As well as the girls climbing in through the window, there were the boys hanging out at the house. It was bad enough that at times Gustin was running around in the streets, but increasingly he seemed to be bringing the streets home. At one point Greg threatened to deprive Gustin of his privacy completely. 'You don't pay no rent in here, bro, so I might just take the door off those hinges and you be like in the penitentiary. No door. Every time I walk past I can look in your room.'

'I didn't do it,' he told me. 'But I threatened to.'

Greg liked Gustin's best friend, Britt, who went to the same school. Britt's house, says Gustin's friend Hardy, was the 'hangspot' where friends would meet up. But Greg was increasingly worried about other company Gustin was keeping. He would return from work or from one of his baby mamas' houses to find people he didn't know or didn't trust, or both, just lounging about. 'There'd be niggas laying in his room,' he says. 'I'd say, "Who is this?" Every day he's bringing niggas in here and they spendin' nights. I come home and go into his room and there'll be a little boy sleeping over there. I'd be like, "Yo, man. What's this? A motel or something?"'

These were the 'Slocumb Street boys', and Greg knew some were gang members, and he knew he didn't want that for Gustin. 'Every time he brought something in here that looked like it was from a gang, I'd open the door to that woodstove and burn it up. I'd tell him, "Don't bring that mess up in my house, bro."' He knew the signs, and clearly he could see that Gustin was tempted. 'A couple of times he'd buy something red. I'd watch him for a little while and say, "You buying a lot of red every day, boy, so why you doing that? I know you ain't in no gang." If I clean up and I see it, I throw it away.'

Like Toshiba, the mother of Stanley, who'd died almost exactly twenty-four hours earlier not far away in Charlotte, Greg felt that he'd tried everything, including setting clear boundaries and accommodating Gustin's adolescent urges. Like Gary Sr, in Newark, Greg felt that Gustin might have been bristling at the tighter rein that comes with having just a man in the house. 'You have a father who's gonna let you do most of your stuff at the house, so you need to stay at the house. Don't hang in them streets, man, because them boys got mothers who will let them do what they want to do. You got a father who ain't gonna let you do what you want to do, so you have to figure out which way to go. It's a different kind of love. You got rules.'

Greg felt some of those rules were being undermined by Gustin's mother and sister. 'My thing was if he wanted money he had to be working or in school,' says Greg. 'But his mother and sister would spoil him to death. They would keep sending him money through Walmart MoneyGram. But I didn't know. So he's lying home all day like he ain't got no money. And then at night, when I go to work, he jump up and he's gone.'

At times, these tensions got physical. 'I had to junk him up a couple of times,' says Greg. 'He got to thinking he could try me. While he was running his mouth, I just ran up on him and *whoop*. Grabbed him by the neck and told him, "The fight is over, baby." No, no, *no,* it ain't gonna be like that. One time I had to chase him with a baseball bat. He started cussing at me, man, and I said, "Man, I'm the last one you need to be disrespecting because, push comes to shove, I'm the nigga that got your back."'

At one point, earlier in the autumn, Greg kicked him out for two months and Gustin went to stay with Britt and his parents. In October, Daina reached out to Gustin. 'I asked him if he had accepted Christ in his life,' she says. 'The term they use here is *saved.* He said he'd given his life to Christ many years ago. And I said this is a time for you to renew your relationship. Because you need protection. You want to be a man. You're not on the porch any more. You're out there in the street. You're not at home. You're with the big dogs. You need to be covered. And I'm really concerned now.'

She took him to her church one Sunday and introduced him to the men in the congregation and walked away to let them talk. She has no idea what they said. Afterwards, she took him to Applebee's for lunch to discuss his future and encourage him to reconcile with his dad.

She tried to get him to see things from Greg's vantage point. 'You've got to understand he's trying to take care of the household and trying to make sure you have what you need. Sometimes there are disappointments. But that doesn't mean that he's bad . . . When you're responsible for someone else, because you bring them in this world, it doesn't matter how or whatever or what you have, you do the best you can because as a parent you care. And until you're a parent you're not going to get it.'

For his part, Gustin had some sympathy for his father. As Greg remembers it, after staying for about six weeks at Britt's, Gustin approached him. 'Yo, Daddy, man,' he said. 'Shit. I'm tired of sleeping on that mattress.' Greg told him to come on home if he was ready to respect his rules. 'I said, "Look, man, when I come back from work, I don't expect to see five or six niggas waiting in my house sleeping around smoking weed and stuff. I can smell it."

'I used to let Britt stay over here cos I knew Britt was his friend. Britt was his real friend. When he came back I told him, "Now Britt's your real friend. When you got put out he took you in. That's a friend. Where were the rest of them boys at?"'

Gustin consented. 'Some children are a little bit more mature,' says Daina. 'I knew that even if his father had his ways of doing things that I didn't always agree with, there was love there.'

*

Gustin never did graduate. Smart as he was, he wasn't clever enough to stay out of trouble at school, even though he didn't have long to go. In October, he'd been suspended for ten days after he and a friend were found in possession of stolen mobile phones (the details of what they were doing with them and how he got them are sketchy, but no one denies he had them). When the suspension was over his friend went back to school; Gustin did not.

Daina intervened on his behalf to talk with the school administration about getting him back on track. She knew he could apply himself. He'd occasionally worked for her and had done well, with other employees saying he was a sharp lad. But as he approached the point when he should graduate, he was struggling to reach the finish line. Following his suspension he was reluctant to go back to school because he said he'd been bullied by a teacher. He opted for independent study at home instead, but to Daina's immense frustration the school wouldn't cooperate. He needed two or three credits, and he would have finished those classes in January. 'He's right there at the door of graduation,' she told the school administrators. 'He'll be the first in his family to graduate. How are you going to deny him this? At this stage. In this time.' They kept saying, 'We'll get back with you. We'll get back with you.' But by the time they did, it was too late.

So Gustin was out of school and kicking his heels. 'So I cut his allowance short,' says Greg. 'Make him hungry.' He told Gustin, 'I ain't want to give you nothing when you ain't working. Either you go to school or you work. Then you can get anything I get. And I ain't got a lot. But I'll work with you.' When Gustin announced his plans to move to Raleigh on Monday, Greg took this as a positive sign and decided to give him the Cadillac anyway.

'I think where Greg messed up is that he said Gustin had to graduate first before he gave him the car,' says Jasmin. 'And then he just went ahead and gave it to him.'

'I sure did,' admits Greg. 'I went against my word.' He warned Gustin. 'Don't go in the hood with that car . . . It ain't about the fact that you better than nobody. Just cos you're eighteen in a Cadillac, in this town some people gonna hate you for that.'

Daina thought it was a bad idea, period. 'I wasn't happy about the car. He's eighteen years old. What the hell's he doing with a Cadillac?' But the plan had been in the works for some time. Greg had too many kids to fit in the Cadillac and had already arranged to buy a white Suburban from a friend.

Without telling Gustin of his plans, Greg had occasionally let him drive the Cadillac to the barber's or home from school while Greg was with him. Gustin got his driver's licence on Wednesday, 20 November. Greg gave him the keys to the car on Thursday. 'OK,' he told him. 'This is your car. You want it, you gonna have to work on it. I ain't putting no more money into it. I'll keep insurance on it. You have to buy gas.'

The car had been in the garage for a little while and needed some work. Greg was eager for Gustin to figure it out for himself. 'It was leaking a little fluid. I knew what it was. But I wouldn't tell him.' But Gustin was smart. He figured it out for himself, and – as Jaiden's family mourned, as Kenneth planned his last night out as a teenager, and as Tyler and Brandon played video games – Gustin worked on his Cadillac all through Saturday until it was fixed. By the evening it was ready to roll.

'Youth is only being . . . like one of these malenky toys you viddy being sold in the streets,' says Alex, the fifteen-year-old protagonist of Anthony Burgess's *A Clockwork Orange* in the novel's youth-specific language of Nadsat. 'Like little chellovecks made out of tin and with a spring inside and then a winding handle on the outside and you wind it up grrr grrr grrr and off it itties, like walking, O my brothers. But it itties in a straight line and bangs straight into things bang bang and it cannot help what it is doing. Being young is like being like one of these malenky machines.'[5]

The thing is, it very much depends on what kind of path has been laid out for you as to what kind of thing you're going to bang into and how much it will hurt.

For those who are privileged, the long-term consequences of rash moments can be minimal. When former president George W. Bush was questioned repeatedly on the campaign trail about his cocaine use and heavy drinking as a young man, he responded jokingly, 'When I was young and irresponsible, I was young and irresponsible.'[6] There is a wry logic to such an answer, even if Bush hardly exemplifies its most important lesson: there's only so much maturity one can expect from those who are not fully mature.

The Bullingdon Club, an all-male exclusive dining club at the University of Oxford, is notorious for throwing ostentatious banquets at which privileged students get very drunk and then often vandalise the restaurants in which they have eaten before paying for the damage in full. Its members have included British prime minister David Cameron, chancellor of the exchequer George Osborne, and London mayor Boris Johnson – all Tories. 'I don't think an evening would have ended without a restaurant being trashed and being paid for in full, very often in cash,' wrote Johnson's biographer, Andrew Gimson, of the club's activities in the eighties. 'A night in the cells would be regarded as being par for a Buller man and so would debagging anyone who really attracted the irritation of the Buller men.'[7]

Just two months after the day on which this book is set, pop star Justin Bieber was arrested at 4 a.m. for drunk driving and resisting arrest. He was driving at 60 mph in a 30 mph zone while drag racing against Def Jam rapper Khalil Sharieff after a day spent allegedly smoking marijuana, taking antidepressants, and drinking beer. The charges were later lowered to careless driving and resisting arrest after a plea deal in which Bieber agreed to attend twelve hours of anger-management counselling, attend a programme that teaches about the impact of drunken driving on victims, and make a $50,000 donation to the organisation Our Kids. The judge explained his lenient sentence thus: 'Here is someone who is young. His whole life is ahead of him, and he just hopefully will get the message. He will grow up.'[8]

That was a good call. But without an expensive lawyer or powerful parents, few are likely to be treated so leniently. Gustin was, in many ways, a regular teenager. He smoked marijuana, but according to Greg, 'he wasn't no big druggy'; he liked a drink, 'but he wasn't no big drinker'. 'He ain't no angel, now,' says Greg. 'Don't get me wrong. He's the average eighteen-year-old. He do what we do when we were eighteen.' But if you're black and working class, 'average' won't cut it. A minor mishap, even one not of your making, could spell danger.

'I have grandchildren living in the suburbs,' says Daina. 'I don't want to say they're sheltered. But their comings and goings are controlled. There's a lack of resources in this town, and their home is not like Greg's household – with a single father, working at night.' To be caught in even a minor transgression – like marijuana possession – could have major consequences that could leave you ensnared in the criminal justice system in a way that could impact you for the rest of your life and effectively deprive your citizenship rights.

'Once you're labelled a felon,' writes Michelle Alexander in *The New Jim Crow*, 'the old forms of discrimination – employment discrimination, housing discrimination, denial of the right to vote, denial of educational opportunity, denial of food stamps and other public benefits, and exclusion from jury service – are suddenly legal. As a criminal, you have scarcely more rights, and arguably less respect, than a black man living in Alabama at the height of Jim Crow. We have not ended racial caste in America; we have merely redesigned it.'[9]

The law is the law, and those who use cocaine or smash up property know it is illegal. But when the stakes are that high and the odds that skewed, poor people don't have the luxury to learn from their mistakes. For working-class youth, the great American myth of personal reinvention is elusive.[10] For that, you need not only a good lawyer, but the resources for rehab, a new home in a new place away from the entanglements of your past, the chance of a new job, and the chance for new training and education. In the absence of those opportunities, you are less likely to recover from your mistakes than to repeat them.

'You all keep sending me to jail,' said twenty-four-year-old Baltimore gang leader Steven Loney at his sentencing hearing. He'd been convicted of racketeering after bribing prison guards to smuggle marijuana, tobacco and prescription pills into the prison where he was serving time. Loney had a prolific criminal record, including conviction for an assault that involved a shooting. 'Jail is making me worse. You all can't tell that? I ain't been on the streets. I been locked up my whole life . . . They say I've been a substance abuser since I was seventeen. I've been locked up since I was nineteen years old, Your Honour. From nineteen to now, I've been home for a hundred and twenty days. The government never offer me no treatment. They never did nothing. They wonder why I still do stuff. You send me to the same problem. You sent me to Baltimore City Detention Center, where all that's going on. And, obviously, I need help. Ain't nobody can give me a chance to help me.'[11] Loney was sentenced to nine years.

This book is the story of young people most of whom made bad decisions – some were killed, others did the killing. Some did nothing worse than make a poor choice in friends. One needn't excuse a single thing they have done to understand that what distinguishes them from other, more fortunate youth isn't an innate pathology but a brutalising, unforgiving environment. Gustin's friend Hardy is still in school, has a part-time job, and keeps his head down. But although he didn't see Gustin's death coming, he's been surrounded by the possibility of it for what seems like most of his short life. 'I know a couple people who been shot,' he tells me when I meet him at his home one evening after he finished work. 'How many?' I ask. A long heavy pause. 'All my life. Everywhere I go somebody got shot. I know a lot of people who got shot. A lot of people got killed . . . I seen people get shot.' Hardy insists on this with a mixture of resignation and resentment – he knows it's not right, and he knows there's nothing he can do about it. It's his life. He's used to it. It seems as though it's only when he has someone asking questions and has to articulate it that he recognises the weight he's been carrying so silently for so long.

On the evening of 23 November, Greg woke up from his nap in preparation for his night shift to find one of Gustin's friends, one of those 'Slocumb Street boys', 'Lord Henry' (not his real nickname), in the living room. Already Gustin was reneging on the bargain he'd struck on his return to his dad's house and was using the place as a flophouse for unapproved company.

Before Greg could even get himself ready, Gustin and Lord Henry had left. Only this time Gustin didn't need to sneak out and run through the fields at the back. He had the Cadillac that he'd been working on all day. The posse of two soon grew as they picked up a young woman and two other men. Gustin told his brother he was going to 'hang with these dudes one last time' before leaving for Raleigh. What they did for most of the rest of the night is not clear. At some point they went to the Lighthouse, a convenience store and fried chicken outlet that had become a notorious flash point for violent confrontations in the area.

Greg called him around midnight from work. 'Yo, what you doing?' he asked, knowing full well Gustin was already out of the house and, in all likelihood, up to no good. He could hear 'a whole lot of confusion' in the background. Greg tried to talk him straight. 'I thought you was going to Raleigh tomorrow. I didn't give you that car to be riding these niggas around,' he said.

'Ah, Dad, you don't understand, man,' said Gustin. 'It's cool, man.' He was supposed to pick up Hardy that night after their mutual friend TJ got off work. They were going to record a song. But he never called TJ. Just after eight the next morning, as Greg was driving home, he saw police cars on every corner of Ash Street, not too far from his house, but thought nothing of it. He'd tried to call Gustin a few more times in the early hours just to check on him but kept getting his voicemail. He thought little of that either. He went to his baby mama's house to fix some breakfast. When he got home he found a note on the door telling him to dial a number and stay put.

'I thought, "Oh this boy got himself in some trouble."' He called the number. Not long after, he saw two police cars drive up to the house, and at that moment he knew it was one of two things. 'I knew right then, because they don't send two police cars for something small, that either he killed somebody or he get killed.'

They had traced the green Cadillac on the corner of South Audubon and Walnut to Greg. They told him they thought his son had been shot and took him to the hospital. He called Daina from there. He was so distraught that for a little while she couldn't understand what he was saying, and when she did finally figure it out she couldn't believe it. 'Finally he was able to get to a point where I could understand him say, "They killed my son."'

'What are you talking about?' she asked.

'I'm with the detectives,' he said.

'No, they probably loaned the car to somebody else,' she said. 'Not Gustin.'

'I'm at the hospital. They killed my son,' Greg repeated. He was screaming and crying.

'Who's with you?' she asked. When Greg said he was there by himself, she jumped in the car and raced to the hospital. As she came through the door, the detectives were taking him to identify the body. 'Then I just heard him scream from behind the door, and at that point I couldn't deny it. His father's scream confirmed everything.'

The autopsy (which mistakenly categorises Gustin as Native American) describes in detailed technical language what happened when the bullet entered the back of his skull. 'The wound track enters the left occipital tip of the brain and travels medially and upwards, causing extensive damage of the brain, leading to separation into three large pieces: the right hemisphere, the left hemisphere, and the cerebellum, separated at the midbrain.'

In short, a single bullet shattered his skull and split his brain in three. A diagram at the end makes it clearer, showing a jagged line running vertically through the centre of his skull before fanning out horizontally at the top and the bottom – like a capital I.

Four days after Greg had gifted Gustin the Cadillac, it was not headed for Raleigh, as he'd hoped, but being towed back to the house. 'If he'd made it to Monday, he'd a been out of here,' says Greg, wistfully. The car now sits in his garage. He let the air out of the tyres and just left it there – his dream car now inseparable from his worst nightmare. Friends cleaned out the pool of blood on the passenger side but could not erase the memory. A year later, the various veins from the spider's web of shattered glass still spread across the rear window, all coming back to the single bullet hole, the size of an adult thumb, in the top left corner. Greg walks around the vehicle, rubbing the dust off the top with his finger.

Gustin's family and friends knew what had happened to him. But they didn't know why. As Daina helped Greg plan the funeral, they struggled to understand what could have prompted the shooting. 'We were racking our brains to think what the hell would Gustin do to somebody that they would want to take his life,' she says. 'I know some kids who are really wild, that were given over to the street. With them I wasn't surprised. But with Gustin everyone was shocked to be honest.'

'Who did he hurt? We thought maybe it was girls. Somebody's girlfriend. Or maybe he took something or stole something or mouthed off to the wrong person. We knew there was no way he was hated to that degree.'

Then one of Daina's employees approached her with some inside information. The shooters weren't after Gustin. They were after the employee's nephew – Lord Henry, who was found at Wayne Memorial Hospital later the same night Gustin was shot, seeking treatment for minor injuries to his leg. 'They'd been trying to shoot him all week,' explains Greg. 'He get with Gustin, but he don't tell Gustin they been trying to get him. So they see him at the Lighthouse. They see Lord Henry get in the car. So they follow the car. They try to shoot Lord Henry, and they miss him and hit Gustin in the back of the head and killed him.'

Had Gustin been a more seasoned hand at the wheel, the assailants wouldn't have stood a chance, insists Greg, shaking his head at one of the many might-have-beens. 'That car got a Northstar engine. I told his ma, "If he knew how to drive this Cadillac, all he had to do is punch it, and whoever was following him would have been way down the street somewhere. And the policeman would have seen that car flying." But he weren't no experienced driver.'

Lord Henry was a Blood. Gustin's shooter, they think, was a Crip. As small and 'behind' as Goldsboro may be, it had grafted the big-city gang affiliations from Los Angeles onto its reputation as a small Southern outpost. Over the past few decades there has been a proliferation of gang activity in small towns prompted more by popular media, social media and local tensions than by the actual expansion of big-city gangs. Instead of roaming South Central, gang members prowl the less forbidding but nonetheless potentially deadly avenues of Goldsboro, showcasing hardcore urban identities around tree-lined streets named Mulberry, Pineview and Evergreen. Greg insists Gustin was unaffiliated. 'The guys Gustin was hanging around with were Blood dudes. I said, "Dude, why would you hang out with them? You ain't even in a gang. And you hangin' out with them gang niggas." Cos I knew Lord Henry was a Blood. But Gustin wasn't in the gang. That's what I tried to tell the police. I told 'em, "He ain't no gangbanger."' The police weren't convinced. They insisted that Gustin was known by other Bloods as Jersey.

When it comes to how Gustin's memory might be maligned and distorted, this is where Greg draws the line. It's a thin line. But for him it's clearly an important one. 'He may have hung out with those boys. But he weren't no gangbanger. They kept trying to give him a gang name. I told 'em, "You can go in his room, and you can't find nothing that says he ain't no gangbanger." I'd go to court on that,' he says, before clapping his hands to each of the following words. 'He. Wasn't. In. No. Gang.'

Hardy didn't see it coming. 'That came out of nowhere,' he says. 'He weren't in no trouble like that.' He thinks Gustin's vulnerability stemmed not so much from the fact that he identified with one gang as opposed to another but that he identified with people in different 'cliques'. Hardy had warned him that because he was known to go to Eastern Wayne high school, he should stay away from the Slocumb Street boys because they drew from different gang territories. 'I ain't saying this caused him dying,' he points out. 'But once you start hanging with them, it's like you're playing both sides.'

Daina had a similar sense, which may be why she thought he wasn't 'street material'. Smart as he was, he hadn't figured out how the allegiances worked. 'He was friends with the Bloods and the Crips. He was friends with everybody. At the funeral there were black people there, white people there, Hispanic people there. And they were weeping. And that's not the norm in a city funeral. I've been to a lot of funerals of children who have died in the city, and you don't see that.'

Greg insists the police know who did it, but they say they can't do anything because nobody will testify against him. The shooter's been heard bragging about it around town. And one night, while Greg was working at Walmart, the alleged shooter stood right next to him and was selling somebody a mobile phone. 'This dude called his name,' he said. 'I looked at him. But I kept working. I'm from the city. I know how to look at somebody and turn my head. So I looked at him and turned my head and kept on working.'

Greg believes – just as Willie Brightmon did about his son Samuel in Dallas – that because Gustin is black, the police aren't taking his death seriously. 'I haven't heard nothing from them,' Greg says. 'I haven't heard nothing from the police since two months after the funeral. Nobody contact me. Nobody said nothing. They just say it's under investigation. We can't get nobody to testify. They just think it's another black kid. This is the dirty South right here. This is Goldsboro. Like I said, these people round here twenty years behind time.'

Of the ten gun deaths that took place in the twenty-four hours profiled in this book, Gustin's was the fifth in which the police have not yet definitively identified the shooter. (At the time of this writing, the killers of Kenneth, Samuel, Tyshon and Gary have not been called to account.) Of the rest, two of the alleged shooters – Demontre Rice, who shot Stanley, and Balam Gonzalez, who is believed to have shot Pedro – are in prison. Brandon spent ten days in a junior detention facility for accidentally shooting Tyler, and his father, Jerry, spent a year in jail for felony violations and corruption of a minor. Camilla, who accidentally shot Edwin, was not charged with his death. Danny Thornton, who shot Jaiden, was killed in a shoot-out.

According to an analysis by Scripps Howard News Service, of the more than half a million homicides committed between 1980 and 2008, a killer was identified 67 per cent of the time when the victim was black or Hispanic and 78 per cent of the time when the victim was white.[12] The discrepancy, say detectives, is based on the circumstances of the death. When the assailant and the victims are strangers, homicides are much more difficult to solve. That is most likely to be the case in killings relating to gangs or drugs, and African Americans and Latinos are more likely to be killed in circumstances relating to those things, they say.

Whether the police would have solved these shootings if everything else had been equal but the victims had been white is unknowable. Everything else isn't equal. And because the myriad inequalities are known and felt, the families of many of the black victims do not feel that justice has been done precisely because they are black. (It's worth noting that both families whose relatives were killed in 'accidental shootings', the Dunns and the Rajos, don't feel justice has been done either. Those cases had very different outcomes and involved a white and a Latino family.)

They feel their children do not make the news like other children, and therefore little political pressure is brought to bear on the police to step up their investigations. If their child's life was anything less than stellar – preferably an A student, still in school, or on his way to college with no previous convictions or gang associations – then it's almost as if the child was asking for it.

In short, so long as black kids are killing other black kids, it feels to some as though nobody really cares. This is not new. During her ethnographic study of Indianola, Mississippi, in the thirties, anthropologist Hortense Powdermaker concluded, 'The mildness of the courts where offences of Negroes against Negroes are concerned is only part of the whole situation which places the Negro outside the law.'[13]

In many minority neighbourhoods the dial has not shifted greatly. The police treat them as inherently lawless areas, a significant proportion who live in those neighbourhoods feel as if they are living under occupation.[14]

So the desire for better policing is complicated by the fact that African Americans hold in relatively low regard the very people who have the power to protect them more effectively. Combined data from between 2011 and 2014 showed that whereas 59 per cent of white Americans had a great deal or quite a lot of confidence in the police, the figure for African Americans was 37 per cent. At 25 per cent, African Americans were twice as likely to have little or no confidence in the police.[15] 'I fear the police more than the gangs,' one grandmother on the South Side of Chicago told me. 'I don't like the gangs, but the gangbangers still have to live here. The police don't, and they're not here to protect and serve. They think we're beneath them.'

This experience of police harassment – compounded by extensively reported accounts of police shooting or otherwise killing black men – leads many to fear that rather than finding criminals they will just criminalise an entire community. So although a disproportionate number of murders go unsolved, a disproportionate number of innocent young people are also harassed, and those guilty of petty crimes are more likely to be caught and get longer sentences.

'Like the schoolyard bully,' writes Leovy, 'our criminal justice system harasses people on small pretexts but is exposed as a coward before murder. It hauls masses of black men through its machinery but fails to protect them from bodily injury and death. It is at once oppressive and inadequate.'[16]

Daina, too, is disappointed by the police response, but she also feels the black community has to come to grips with the scale and finality of the crisis it is faced with. 'A lot of the men I deal with coming out of the prison system say they won't call the police,' she says. 'They say, "We're not rats." I understand that. I didn't want to be a snitch either. But today it's different because now they're playing with guns for keeps. When I was a kid, the crowd drew in, and whoever had the best set of this' – she puts her fists up – 'won the fight and it was over. Today, we're going to funerals. And I think every parent whose son was murdered at the hands of another kid would prefer to visit their child in jail than to go to the graveyard.' It's an awful set of options, I say.

'Well, he's alive, rather than he's dead,' she says both insistently and matter-of-factly. 'If he's out there doing these things, it's up to you in the community to call the police. Have him locked up. Save his life. So if you leave him out there and he continues to behave that way, the streets are going to take his life. I have told my grandchildren, I have told those who I love dearly, I have told those I know in the community: I don't care about the weed. But if I see you with a gun. You don't have to be pointing it at anybody or shooting anybody. If I see you with a gun, I'm calling the police on you. It's that simple. Because this shouldn't happen. You can't change them, but you can save them. You have to be dedicated enough to recognise that this is one of the hard choices. Labour wasn't easy either.'

Afterword

At 11.15 a.m. on Sunday, 24 November, Cleveland police rushed to the 5500 block of Linton Avenue where they found sixteen-year-old Darnell Jones shot in the neck. Paramedics took him to the Metro Health Medical Center where he later died. There was no profile of who he was or wanted to be; no interviews with his parents. Beyond official records there is no further evidence that he was ever on the planet. And so it goes on. Another twenty-four hours and the first of yet another slew of slain children whose stories will not be told and whose passing will provoke no outrage.

Researching and writing this book has made me want to scream. I've wanted to scream at Edwin and Brandon that guns are not toys; at Jerry either to take the kids or to stay home; at Stanley to quit hanging on the corner; at Gustin to watch who he hangs out with; and at Tyshon's mother to move. I wanted to scream at journalists and police to treat these deaths as though the lives mattered.

But more than it's made me want to scream at anyone in particular it's mostly made me want to just howl at the moon. A long, doleful, piercing cry for a wealthy country that could and should do better for its youth and children – for my children – but appears to have settled, legislatively at least, on a pain threshold that is morally unacceptable.

I want to bay towards the heavens because while kids, like those featured in this book, keep dying, the political class refuses not only to do everything in its power but anything at all to minimise the risks for the kids who will be shot dead today or tomorrow.

As I explained at the outset, this is not a book about gun control. The challenges facing the subjects of this book are more thorny and knotted than that. Poverty and inequality foster desperation;

segregation is a serious barrier to empathy. The more likely you are to be wealthy or white the less likely you are to believe that these children could be your children. Statistically that is true, but the fact remains they are somebody's children and those parents grieve like everybody else.

Better education, youth services, jobs that pay a living wage, mental health services, trauma counselling, a fair criminal justice system – in short more opportunity, less despair – would contribute to a climate where such deaths were less likely.

You can't legislate for common sense and human decency. Neither poverty nor racism puts a gun in anyone's hand, let alone tells them to fire it. But they are a starting point for the conditions of alienation, anomie and ambivalence in which a gun might be used and some gun deaths ignored. People have to take personal responsibility for what they do and live with the consequences. But societies have to take collective responsibility for what they do and live with the consequences too.[1]

As I argued in the Introduction, this is a book about what happens when you don't have gun control. Americans are no more inherently violent than anybody else. What makes its society more deadly is the widespread availability of firearms. Every country has its problems, unique to its own history and culture. But in no other Western society would this book be possible.

To defend this reality by way of the Second Amendment to the Constitution has about the same relevance as seeking to understand the roots of modern terrorism – either to condemn or to condone it – through readings of the Koran. To base an argument on ancient texts is effectively to abdicate your responsibility to understand the present by offloading it onto those who are now dead. It denies not only the possibility of new interpretations and solutions but the necessity for them.

None of the family members I spoke to raised the Second Amendment one way or the other. Almost all believed guns were too readily available; none believed there was anything that could be done about it. Brilliant community groups, often operating on a shoestring, like Mario's in Charlotte, exist across the country and campaign tirelessly against gun violence and for common-sense gun legislation or both. But those who concentrate on protecting 'babes' and 'angels' from felons and gangsters stand little chance of finding roots in the very communities where the problems are most acute. It would appear that, of all the parents who lost children that day, only Nicole, judging by later Facebook postings (including a spoof children's book called *The Gun That Went Around Killing Children All By Itself*), seems to be engaged in some kind of advocacy around the issue. But even she clearly finds the broader conversation about gun control too toxic to engage with. Alongside the portraits of hundreds of children[2] shot dead since Sandy Hook, which also featured Jaiden, she wrote:

> Jaiden was one of the hundreds of children under the age of twelve killed by gun violence in the one year after the Sandy Hook massacre . . .
>
> As the third anniversary approaches for Sandy Hook, there is going to be news coverage, memorials and articles about gun control etc. – I don't want to get into a debate about gun control or violence or mental health problems but what I would like is to ask each of you to take a moment and look at these beautiful gorgeous children and remember them and their families during this holiday season in addition to all those killed at Sandy Hook Elementary.

Otherwise it's as though each death took place in helpless, hopeless isolation: a private, discrete tragedy complete unto itself. The broader context of race and poverty was clear to many. But when I told them of other families that had lost children that day all seemed genuinely shocked that their grief overlapped in real time with that of others. It's as though they had lost a loved one in a war without any clear purpose, end or enemy; a war they could do nothing about; a war they long knew existed but hoped by luck, judgement, discipline and foresight that they might be able to protect their kids from; a war that is generally acknowledged in the abstract but rarely specifically addressed in the concrete. A war that took their children but offered them no allies or community in their grief. A war they knew was taking place elsewhere but experienced alone, as though it were happening only to them – when in fact it was happening to America. Every day.

Acknowledgements

In a book that takes this long and spreads its net this wide there are more people to thank than I can individually acknowledge. Fortunately many are friends; you know who you are and how much your help was appreciated. I particularly want to acknowledge the family members who opened up their hearts, photo albums and memories and trusted me with their stories. Without you there would be no book. Every interviewee who is named in the book gave me their time and insight, for which I'm very grateful.

I specifically need to thank Merope Mills who gave me the idea to write a story on this very premise back in 2007 when she was editor of the *Guardian*'s *Weekend* magazine. The article worked well. But I knew, when researching and reporting at the time, that there was more to this than could fit in a piece for a magazine. But to do it on a larger scale required time and money I didn't have.

The opportunity to pursue it came thanks to my fabulous agent, Jonny Geller, who has advocated for my work for well over a decade, and Frances Coady. When Jonny explained the idea to Frances, then the editor at a new publishing venture, Atavist Books, she understood it immediately. We worked together for over a year. Frances guided the book through its first draft, encouraging me throughout. She knew all the children's first names, the circumstances of their deaths, understood the themes and shaped much of the narrative. Such was her dedication to the project that once Atavist Books closed its doors she carried on working on it. When she transitioned to being an agent she represented me in the US. In the process she has become a good friend, a great champion and a close collaborator. Alessandra Bastagli, of Nation (Perseus) Books in the US, and Laura Hassan, of Guardian Faber Books in the UK, took the book to the finish line with keen but indulgent eyes for details, style and promotion. It has been a real pleasure working with them.

A significant number of people helped with the research on this book, including Micah Utrecht, Benjamin Hattem, Darren Ankrom and Kat Keene Hogue; much thanks to Taya Kitman of the Nation Institute, who agreed to help fund much of this research. But then there are those not mentioned to whom I would like express my gratitude: Jesse Soodalter, Jessica Blatt, Steve Strunsky, Stephanie Lundy, Jessica Smith, Carrie Messenger, Miriam Garcia, Keeanga Yamahtta Taylor, Wendy Posner and Elliott Fineman. Thanks also to Benedick Raikes, Ingrid Jacobson, Taline Voskeritchian, Andrea Levy, Bill Mayblin, Colin Robinson, Mickey Davis and Julie Fain, who read at various stages and encouraged it to maturity. I'm grateful also to Melissa Raymond and Kelley Blewster, who worked with and around my domestic challenges to make sure a contracted production schedule was possible without being overly punishing.

Finally, and primarily, I'd like to thank Tara, for the final read, and Osceola and Zora for putting up with my frequent absences. There wasn't a time, when writing and researching this book, that I wasn't thinking about you.

Notes

Unless otherwise stated, quotations from the families, friends and contacts of the subjects, or from those professionally associated with the circumstances of their deaths, are taken from interviews with the author.

Verbatim transcripts of conversations with the emergency services and 911 dispatchers have been provided by the relevant authorities or are in the public domain.

While every attempt has been made to identify and acknowledge sources and quotations, the author and publishers apologise for any that have been missed inadvertently and would be happy to include acknowledgement in future editions.

Introduction

1 Elisa Fieldstad, 'Deadly storm system moves east, threatens holiday travel', NBC News, http://www.nbcnews.com/news/other/deadly-storm-system-moves-east-threatens-holiday-travel-f2D11650166.

2 John Cornyn, Twitter, https://twitter.com/johncornyn/status/404448260468641792.

3 http://wonder.cdc.gov.

4 Children's Defense Fund, 'Protect Children, Not Guns Overview', 2013, http://www.childrensdefense.org/library/data/state-data-repository/protect-children-not-guns-key-facts-2013.pdf.

5 Adam B. Schiff, 23 November 2013, http://www.nytimes.com/2013/11/23/pageoneplus/.

6 Children's Defense Fund, 'Protect Children, Not Guns Overview', p. 33.

7 http://wonder.cdc.gov/.

8 Nate Silver, 'Black Americans Are Killed at 12 Times the Rate of People in Other Developed Countries', FiveThirtyEight, http://fivethirtyeight.com/datalab/black-americans-are-killed-at-12-times-the-rate-of-people-in-other-developed-countries/.

9 Chris Kyle with William Doyle, *American Gun: A History of the U.S. in Ten Firearms* (New York: HarperCollins, 2013), p. 255.

10 Telephone interview with the author.

11 Amanda Terkel, 'Joe Manchin Ready For Gun Control Action: "Everything Should Be On The Table",' *Huffington Post*, http://www.huffingtonpost.com/2012/12/17/joe-manchin-gun-control_n_2314782.html.

Author's Note

1 'Child Shot by Teenage Brother Dies', CBS Dallas–Fort Worth, 25 November 2015, http://dfw.cbslocal.com/2013/11/25/child-shot-by-teenage-brother-dies/.
2 'Key Gun Violence Statistics', Brady Campaign to Prevent Gun Violence, http://www.bradycampaign.org/key-gun-violence-statistics.

1 Jaiden Dixon

1 Population per census: 38,519. '1990 Census of Population and Housing', U.S. Department of Commerce, 1990, https://www.census.gov/prod/cen1990/cph2/cph-2–37.pdf. 'Grove City, Ohio, Quick Facts', U.S. Department of Commerce, 2015, http://www.census.gov/quickfacts/table/PST045215/3932592.
2 http://boxrec.com/boxer/7409.
3 http://www.10tv.com/content/stories/2013/11/22/grove-city-shooting-schools.html.
4 Douglas Kellner, *Guys and Guns Amok: Domestic Terrorism and School Shootings from the Oklahoma City Bombing to the Virginia Tech Massacre* (Boulder, CO: Paradigm, 2008), p. 14.
5 Ibid.
6 'Grove City, OH Crime and Crime Rate', USA.com, http://www.usa.com/grove-city-oh-crime-and-crime-rate.htm.
7 Lisa Evans, 'Mapping Murder Throughout the World', *Guardian*, 10 October 2011, http://www.theguardian.com/news/datablog/2011/oct/10/world-murder-rate-unodc.
8 http://www.10tv.com/content/stories/2014/07/24/columbus-ohio-shooting-survivor-shares-her-journey-from-pain-to-recovery.html.
9 'Ohio Police Kill Man after Shooting of Woman, Child', *Herald Dispatch*, 22 November 2013, http://www.herald-dispatch.com/news/recent_news/ohio-police-kill-man-after-shooting-of-woman-child/article_cea0d240-975e-533b-92de-b0343e08f52e.html.
10 Associated Press, 'Ohio Boy Shot by Mom's Ex-lover still in Critical Condition', *News-Herald*, 23 November 2013, http://www.news-herald.

com/article/hr/20131123/NEWS/131129642.

11 H. Range Hutson et al., 'Suicide by Cop', *Annals of Emergency Medicine* 32, no. 6 (December 1998): 665–9, http://www.annemergmed.com/article/S0196–0644(98)70064–2/abstract.

12 Harriet Sarnoff Schiff, *The Bereaved Parent* (New York: Crown, 1977), p. 2.

13 Ibid., p. 25.

14 Ibid., p. 23.

15 *Six Feet Under*, Season 1, Episode 9, 'Life's Too Short'; http://www.imdb.com/title/tt0702000/?ref_=ttqt_qt_tt.

2 Kenneth Mills

1 'Three Fountains West', 2011, http://www.threefountainswest.com/.

2 http://www.usboundary.com/Areas/Census%20Tract/Indiana/Marion%20County/Census%20Tract%203103.06/457146#Data – Census Tract 3103.06, Marion County, Indiana; U.S. Census Bureau, 'Explanation of Race and Hispanic Origin Categories', http://www.census.gov/population/estimates/rho.txt.

3 All of Kenneth's tweets quoted in this chapter come from his Twitter page @Nov.26th, https://twitter.com/Ayeee_itsFonzy, Kenneth Mills-Tucker, Twitter posts, September–November 2013.

4 Kyle with Doyle, *American Gun*, p. 259.

5 In Ben Agger and Timothy W. Luke (eds), *Gun Violence and Public Life* (Boulder, CO: Paradigm Publishers, 2014), p. 171.

6 http://www.washingtonpost.com/wp-srv/national/longterm/supcourt/stories/courtguns051095.htm.

7 Samantha Lanchman, 'Wayne LaPierre Warns Fellow Gun Rights Supporters of "Knockout Gamers", "Haters"', *Huffington Post*, http://www.huffingtonpost.com/2014/04/25/wayne-lapierre-nra-_n_5214959.html.

8 Wayne LaPierre, 'CPAC: Wayne LaPierre's Speech', *Daily Caller*, http://dailycaller.com/2014/03/06/cpac-wayne-lapierres-speech/.

9 Aaron Blake, 'Bloomberg Launches New $50 million Gun Control Effort', *Washington Post*, https://www.washingtonpost.com/news/post-politics/wp/2014/04/16/bloomberg-aims-to-spend-50-million-on-gun-control/.

10 http://www.gunviolencearchive.org/reports/mass-shootings/2013.

11 Shannon Van Sant, 'China School Knife Attack Leaves 23 Injured', CBS News, http://www.cbsnews.com/news/china-school-knife-attack-leaves-

23-injured/.

12 'In Memoriam, Emmett Till', *Life* Magazine, October 1955.

13 Michelle Alexander, *The New Jim Crow: Mass Incarceration in the Age of Colorblindness* (New York: The New Press, 2012), p. 71.

14 Ibid.

15 Amos Brown III, 'Black Graduation Rates Fall in State, Many Indy Districts', *Indianapolis Reporter*, http://www.indianapolisrecorder.com/education/article_bbbc4442-81be-11e2-9701-0019bb2963f4.html?TNNoMobile.

16 'Kenneth J. Mills-Tucker', *Indianapolis Star*, http://www.legacy.com/obituaries/indystar/obituary.aspx?pid=168224887.

17 'Keeping Youth Connected', CLASP, http://www.clasp.org/resources-and-publications/files/Indianapolis_Profile.pdf.

18 Tanzina Vega, 'Shooting Spurs Hashtag Effort on Stereotypes', *New York Times*, http://www.nytimes.com/2014/08/13/us/if-they-gunned-me-down-protest-on-twitter.html/.

19 Jessica Durando, 'Users Ask which Photo Media would Use #IfThey-GunnedMeDown', USA Today, http://www.usatoday.com/story/news/nation-now/2014/08/12/if-they-gunned-me-down-hashtag-twitter/13982539/.

20 http://fox59.com/2013/07/21/teen-found-shot-to-death-in-parking-garage-of-jw-marriott/.

21 http://www.indystar.com/picture-gallery/news/2016/04/21/gett-money-gang-members-arrested/83330394/.

22 http://lawdigitalcommons.bc.edu/cgi/viewcontent.cgi?article=1685&context=lsfp.

3 Stanley Taylor

1 Jill Leovy, *Ghettoside: A True Story of Murder in America* (London: The Bodley Head, 2015), p. 29.

2 'Quarterly Homicide Team Report for October–December 2014', District Attorney R. Andrew Murray's office, http://www.charmeckda.com/news/011315_1.pdf.

3 'Turning Point Academy', Charlotte-Mecklenberg Schools, http://schools.cms.k12.nc.us/turningpointAE/Pages/Default.aspx.

4 Chuck McShane, '1993: Charlotte's Deadliest Year', *Charlotte Magazine*, http://www.charlottemagazine.com/Charlotte-Magazine/December-2013/1993-Charlottes-Deadliest-Year/?cparticle=2&siarticle=1.

5 Tim Murphy, 'Black Parents Need to Get It Together, Says Former Tea

Party Congressman Sued Over Child Support', *Mother Jones*, http://www.motherjones.com/mojo/2013/08/joe-walsh-black-parents-need-get-ittogether.

6 Joanna Rothkopf, 'Bill O'Reilly: Black People Should Wear "Don't Get Pregnant at 14" T-Shirts', Salon, http://www.salon.com/2014/12/18/bill_oreilly_black_people_should_wear_dont_get_pregnant_at_14_t_shirts/.

7 'Meet the Press Transcript – November 23, 2014', *Meet the Press*, http://www.nbcnews.com/meet-the-press/meet-press-transcript-november-23–2014-n255256.

8 Leovy, *Ghettoside*, p. xix.

9 'Homicide Trends in the United States, 1980–2008', U.S. Department of Justice, 2011, http://www.bjs.gov/content/pub/pdf/htus8008.pdf.

10 Alexander, *The New Jim Crow*, p. 100.

11 Jamie Fellner, 'Race, Drugs, and Law Enforcement in the United States', Human Rights Watch, https://www.hrw.org/news/2009/06/19/race-drugs-and-law-enforcement-united-states#_ftn51; Ronald H. Weich and Carlos T. Angulo, *Justice on Trial: Racial Disparities in the American Criminal Justice System* (Collingdale, PA: Diane Pub., 2000).

12 'Homicide Rates Among Persons Aged 10–24 Years – United States, 1981–2010', CDC, http://www.cdc.gov/mmwr/preview/mmwrhtml/mm6227a1.htm.

13 http://vizhub.healthdata.org/gbd-compare/; http://www.npr.org/sections/goatsandsoda/2015/12/07/458815891/the-u-s-is-a-world-leader-in-gun-deaths.

14 https://www.washingtonpost.com/news/worldviews/wp/2012/12/14/chart-the-u-s-has-far-more-gun-related-killings-than-any-other-developed-country/.

15 Bill Cosby and Alvin F. Poussaint, *Come On, People: On the Path from Victims to Victors* (Nashville: Thomas Nelson, 2007), pp. 60, 73, 86.

16 Tom Brokaw. *The Greatest Generation* (New York: Random House, 1998), p. 86.

17 'Dr Bill Cosby Speaks', Rutgers University, http://www.rci.rutgers.edu/~schochet/101/Cosby_Speech.htm, p. 87.

18 Ibid., p. 111.

19 Ibid., p. 137.

20 Michael E. Dyson, *Is Bill Cosby Right? Or Has the Black Middle Class Lost Its Mind?* (New York: Basic Civitas Books, 2005), p. x.

21 Ibid., p. 172.

22 North Carolina Department of Justice, 'Crime in North Carolina – 1999 Annual Summary Report of 1999 Uniform Crime Reporting Data', shows

Charlotte-Mecklenburg's crime figures in 1999, http://www.ncdoj.gov/getdoc/448ed7e5-b478-4177-bfde-afd95e5e103e/1999-Crime-Statistics.aspx, when the city had a population of 520,829. Charlotte Police Department 'Year to Date Summary', December 2013, http://charmeck.org/city/charlotte/CMPD/safety/CrimeStat/Documents/CS13Dec-Monthly Summary.pdf shows the figures when the city had a population of 792,862. General downward trajectory of crime from 2002 to 2014 is shown at City-Data.com, 'Crime Rate in Charlotte', NC, http://www.city-data.com/crime/crime-Charlotte-North-Carolina.html.

23 Mecklenburg County Health Department, Epidemiology Program, December 2009, 'Teen Pregnancy Mecklenburg County, 1995–2008', shows the pregancy rate for 15–19-year-olds in Mecklenburg county was 74.4 per 1,000 in 1999, http://charmeck.org/mecklenburg/county/healthdepartment/healthstatistics/documents/teen%20pregnancy%20mecklenburg%20county%201995-2008.pdf. The Adolescent Pregnancy Prevention Campaign of North Carolina, '2013 North Carolina Adolescent Pregnancies Ages 15–19', shows the pregnancy rate for 15–19-year-olds in Mecklenburg County was 33.3 per 1000 in 2013, http://files.www.appcnc.org/data/map/northcarolina/2013_pregnancies_15-19_NC.pdf.

24 Adolescent Pregnancy Prevention Campaign of North Carolina, '2007 NC Resident African American Teen Pregnancies: Ages 15–19' shows the pregnancy rate for African Americans was 84.8, http://files.appcnc.gethifi.com/data/state-statistics/archived-state-statistics/2007_African_American_pregnancies.pdf. The APPC of North Carolina, '2012 North Carolina Adolescent Pregnancies by Race/Ethnicity and County', shows by 2012 the figure was down to 51.8, http://files.www.appcnc.org/data/map/northcarolina/2012_pregnancies_15-19_by_race.pdf.

25 Inter-university Consortium for Political and Social Research, 'Quick Tables: List of Available Quick Tables For the National Survey on Drug Use and Health', 2011, http://www.icpsr.umich.edu/quicktables/quickconfig.do?34481-0001_all.

26 Jo Jones and William D. Mosher, 'Fathers' Involvement With Their Children: United States, 2006–2010', National Health Statistics Reports, December 2013, http://www.cdc.gov/nchs/data/nhsr/nhsr071.pdf.

27 Alexander, *The New Jim Crow*, p. 93.

28 Joseph E. Stiglitz, *The Price of Inequality: How Today's Divided Society Endangers Our Future* (New York: W.W. Norton & Co., 2012), p. 17.

29 'Number of interracial couples in U.S. reaches all-time high', CNN, 2012, http://www.cnn.com/2012/04/25/us/us-census-interracial/.

30 Hope Yen, 'A Census First: Black Voter Turnout Passes Whites', Associated Press, 2013, http://usnews.nbcnews.com/_news/2013/05/08/18131900-a-census-first-black-voter-turnout-passes-whites.

31 Michael A. Fletcher, 'Fifty years after March on Washington, Economic Gap between Blacks, Whites Persists', *Washington Post*, https://www.washingtonpost.com/business/economy/50-years-after-the-march-the-economic-racial-gap-persists/2013/08/27/9081f012-0e66-11e3-8cdd-bcdc09410972_story.html?wprss=rss_business&tid=pp_widget.

32 Ian Millhiser, 'American Schools Are More Segregated Now Than They Were in 1968, and the Supreme Court Doesn't Care', Think Progress, http://thinkprogress.org/justice/2015/08/13/3690012/american-schools-are-more-segregated-now-then-they-were-in-1968-and-the-supreme-court-doesnt-care/.

33 Michael Harrington, *The Other America: Poverty in the United States* (New York: Macmillan, 1962), p. 14.

34 http://www.bostonfed.org/inequality2014/papers/reeves-sawhill.pdf

35 Matt O'Brien, 'Poor Kids Who Do Everything Right Don't Do Better than Rich Kids Who Do Everything Wrong', *Washington Post*, https://www.washingtonpost.com/news/wonk/wp/2014/10/18/poor-kids-who-do-everything-right-dont-do-better-than-rich-kids-who-do-everything-wrong/.

36 Leovy, *Ghettoside*, p. 243.

4 Pedro Cortez

1 Joe Rodriguez, 'San Jose: Teen Slain on Streets Named for Kids' Tales', *San Jose Mercury News*, http://www.mercurynews.com/crime-courts/ci_24593143/murder-fantasy-land-san-joses-44th-homicide-this.

2 Ibid.

3 Ibid.

4 Malcolm W. Klein and Cheryl L. Maxson, *Street Gang Patterns and Policies* (New York: Oxford University Press, 2010), p. 81.

5 Amy Nilson, 'Thanksgiving Marks Violent Crime on San Jose', *Crime Voice*, http://www.crimevoice.com/2013/12/03/thanksgiving-marks-violent-crime-on-san-jose/.

6 Rodriguez, 'San Jose'.

7 Robert Salonga, 'San Jose: Police Seeking Tips in Deadly Weekend Shooting', *San Jose Mercury News*, http://www.mercurynews.com/crime-courts/ci_24607174/san-jose-police-still-seeking-tips-deadly-weekend.

8 Homicide rates, 2013: San Jose, 39 – http://www.sjpd.org/CrimeStats/

crimestats.html; Newark, 40 – http://www.nj.com/essex/index.ssf/2014/11/newark_had_nations_third_highest_murder_rate_in_2013_fbi_says.html; Grove City, 1 murder – https://www.fbi.gov/about-us/cjis/ucr/crime-in-the-u.s/2013/crime-in-the-u.s.-2013/tables/table-8/table-8-state-cuts/table_8_offenses_ known_to_law_enforcement_ohio_by_city_2013.xls.

9 1950: 95,000; 1970: 445,000. 'City of San Jose', Bay Area Census, http://www.bayareacensus.ca.gov/cities/SanJose50.htm.

10 1990: 782,000; 2010: 946,000; 782 x 1.2 = 938. Ibid.

11 'Official Crime Statistics', San Jose Police Department website, table 3 (property crime and violent crime combined), http://www.sjpd.org/CrimeStats/crimestats.html. Compare to national statistics for 2012: 'FBI Releases 2012 Crime Statistics', FBI website, 16 September 2013, https://www.fbi.gov/news/pressrel/press-releases/fbi- releases-2012-crime-statistics. Mike Rosenberg, 'San Jose Crime Rate Surpasses U.S. Average', *San Jose Mercury News*, 16 December 2013, http://www.mercurynews.com/pensions/ci_24737175/ san-jose-crime-rate%20-surpasses-u-s-average-arrests-plummet.

12 Robert Salonga, 'San Jose: Suspects Identified in City's Latest Shooting Deaths', *San Jose Mercury News*, http://www.mercurynews.com/crime-courts/ci_24648168/san-jose-suspects-identified-citys-latest-shooting-deaths.

13 http://www.mercurynews.com/crime-courts/ci_29737765/san-jose-jailed-suspect-2013-killing-now-charged.

5 Tyler Dunn

1 17.3 people per square kilometre in 2010: Wikipedia, 'Sanilac County, Michigan', https://en.wikipedia.org/wiki/Sanilac_County,_Michigan. Compared to Finland, 17.98 per square kilometre in 2014: 'Population Density (People per Sq. Km.) in Finland', Trading Economics, http://www.tradingeconomics.com/finland/population-density-people-per-sq-km-wb-data.html.

2 'Quick Facts, Sanilac County, Michigan', United States Census Bureau, http://www.census.gov/quickfacts/table/RHI105210/26151; https://en.wikipedia.org/wiki/Demographics_of_Norway#Total_population.

3 Michigan Department of Agriculture and Rural Development, 'Michigan Food and Agricultural Systems Profiles', State of Michigan website, http://www.michigan.gov/documents/mda/County_Food_System_Profiles_292923_7.pdf, and https://www.michigan.gov/documents/mda/Regional_Food_System_Profiles_292928_7.pdf.

4 Kate McGill, *The Beginnings of Marlette* (pamphlet).
5 Ibid.
6 George Monbiot, 'Rewilding Our Children', website of George Monbiot, 16 April 2012, http://www.monbiot.com/2012/04/16/2125/.
7 McGill, *The Beginnings.*
8 Justice for Tyler Dunn Facebook page, https://www.facebook.com/Justice-for-Tyler-Dunn-548697351873913/.
9 http://www.wnem.com/story/23881130/2-in-airboat-report-being-targeted-by-duck-hunter.
10 Associated Press, 'Teen Shoots Self in Foot While Hunting in Michigan', *Monroe News*, 29 November 2013, http://www.monroenews.com/article/20131129/NEWS/311299907.
11 'Boy, 12, Accidentally Shot in Hand', *Sanilac County News*, 19 March 2014, http://sanilaccountynews.mihomepaper.com/news/2014-03-19/News/Boy_12_accidentally_shot_in_hand.html.
12 Brad Devereaux, 'Update: Marlette Elementary Student Shot, Killed at Sleepover Identified', *Michigan Live*, 2 December 2013, http://www.mlive.com/news/saginaw/index.ssf/2013/12/sheriff_12-year-old_shot_kille.html.
13 Ibid.
14 G. A. Jackman et al., 'Seeing Is Believing: What Do Boys Do When They Find a Real Gun?', *Pediatrics* 107 (2001): 1247; http://pediatrics.aappublications.org/content/107/6/1247.abstract.
15 Michael Luo and Mike McIntire, 'Children and Guns: The Hidden Toll', *New York Times*, 29 September 2013, http://www.nytimes.com/2013/09/29/us/children-and-guns-the-hidden-toll.html?pagewanted=all.
16 Ibid.
17 'Gun Homicides and Gun Ownership by Country', *Washington Post*, 17 December 2012, http://www.washingtonpost.com/wp-srv/special/nation/gun-homicides-ownership/table/.
18 Linda L. Dahlberg et al., 'Guns in the Home and Risk of a Violent Death in the Home: Findings from a National Study', *American Journal of Epidemiology* 160, no. 10 (2004): 929–36, https://aje.oxfordjournals.org/content/160/10/929.full; Andrew Seamen, 'Gun Access Tied to Greater Suicide, Murder Risk: Study', Reuters, 20 January 2014, http://www.reuters.com/article/us-gun-suicide-idUSBREA0J1G920140120.
19 Michael Luo, 'N.R.A. Stymies Firearms Research, Scientists Say', *New York Times*, 26 January 2011, http://www.nytimes.com/2011/01/26/us/26guns.html?_r=0.
20 Sam Stein, 'The Congressman Who Restricted Gun Violence Research Has Regrets', *Huffington Post*, 6 October 2015, http://www.huffingtonpost.

com/entry/jay-dickey-gun-violence-research-amendment_us_561333d7e-4b022a4ce5f45bf.

21 Ibid.

22 Luo, 'N.R.A.'.

23 Vivek Murthy, Twitter, https://twitter.com/vivek_murthy/status/258393687871074304.

24 http://www.huffingtonpost.com/2014/12/15/surgeon-general-vote_n_6329884.html; http://www.nytimes.com/2014/12/16/us/obamas-nominee-for-surgeon-general-wins-confirmation.html; http://www.thenation.com/article/why-nra-blocking-obamas-surgeon-general-nominee/.

25 Mark A. Schuster et al., 'Firearm Storage Patterns in US Homes with Children', *American Journal of Public Health* 90, no. 4 (2000): 589–94, reprinted on RAND Corporation website, http://www.rand.org/content/dam/rand/pubs/reprints/2005/RAND_RP890.pdf.

26 F. Baxley and M. Miller, 'Parental Misperceptions About Children and Firearms', *Archives of Pediatric and Adolescent Medicine* 160, no. 5 (May 2006): 542–7.

27 Catherine A. Okoro et al., 'Prevalence of Household Firearms and Firearm-Storage Practices in the 50 States and the District of Columbia: Findings from the Behavioral Risk Factor Surveillance System, 2002', *Pediatrics* 116, no. 3 (September 2005); http://pediatrics.aappublications.org/content/116/3/e370.

28 Law Center to Prevent Gun Violence, 'Child Access Prevention Policy Summary', http://smartgunlaws.org/child-access-prevention-policy-summary/.

29 Peter Cummings et al., 'State Gun Safe Storage Laws and Child Mortality Due to Firearms', *Journal of the American Medical Association* 278 (1997): 1084–86.

30 David C. Grossman et al., 'Gun Storage Practices and Risk of Youth Suicide and Unintentional Firearm Injuries', *Journal of the American Medical Association* 293 (2005): 707, 711–13.

31 Everytown for Gun Safety and Moms Demand Action for Gun Sense in America, 'Innocents Lost: A Year of Unintentional Child Gun Deaths', Everytown for Gun Safety website, June 2014, http://everytownresearch.org/documents/2015/04/innocents-lost.pdf, 12.

32 A. L. Kellerman, 'Injuries and Deaths Due to Firearms in the Home' *Journal of Trauma, Injury, Infection and Critical Care* 45, no. 2 (August 1998): 263–7.

33 '"Someone Has to Answer for It": Sheriff Seeks Charges Against Resident

Where Boy Was Killed', *County Press*, 11 December 2013, http://thecountypress.mihomepaper.com/news/2013–12–11/News/Someone_has_to_answer_for_it_Sheriff_seeks_charges.html.

34 Eric Levine, 'Dad, Son Charged in Fatal Shooting', *Sanilac County News*, 19 February 2014, http://sanilaccountynews.mihomepaper.com/news/2014–02–19/Front_Page/Dad_son_charged_in_fatal_shooting.html.

35 Brad Devereaux, 'Michigan Boy, 12, Gets "Intensive" Probation in Shooting Death of 11-Year-Old Friend at Sleepover', http://www.mlive.com/news/saginaw/index.ssf/2014/05/michigan_boy_placed_in_intensi.html.

36 Brad Devereaux, 'Father of 12-Year-Old Michigan Boy Who Killed Friend at Sleepover Gets Year in Jail', *Michigan Live*, 20 June 2014, http://www.mlive.com/news/saginaw/index.ssf/2014/06/father_of_boy_who_fatally_shot.html.

37 http://sanilaccountynews.mihomepaper.com/news/2015-05-27/Front_Page/Father_son_sued_in_fatal_shooting.html.

38 Quoted in Stephen P. Teret and Patti L. Culross, 'Product-Oriented Approaches to Reducing Youth Gun Violence', *The Future of Children* 12, no. 2 (2002): 119–31, quotation on page 123, http://www.kean.edu/~jkeil/Welcome_files/Youth%20Gun.pdf.

39 'The Smith & Wesson Sellout', NRA-ILA, 20 March 2000, https://www.nraila.org/articles/20000320/the-smith-wesson-sellout.

40 Michael S. Rosenwald, '"We Need the iPhone of Guns": Will Smart Guns Transform the Gun Industry?', *Washington Post*, 17 February 2014, https://www.washingtonpost.com/local/we-need-the-iphone-of-guns-will-smart-guns-transform-the-gun-industry/2014/02/17/6ebe76da-8f58-11e3-b227-12a45d109e03_story.html.

41 Dan Roberts et al., 'Tearful Obama Tightens Gun Control and Tells Inactive Congress: "We Can't Wait"', *Guardian*, 5 January 2016, http://www.theguardian.com/us-news/2016/jan/05/obama-gun-control-executive-action-background-checks-licenses-gun-shows-mental-health-funding.

42 Joel Rose, 'A New Jersey Law That's Kept Smart Guns off Shelves Nationwide', NPR, 24 June 2015, http://www.npr.org/sections/alltech-considered/2014/06/24/325178305/a-new-jersey-law-thats-kept-smart-guns-off-shelves-nationwide.

43 Rosenwald, '"We Need the iPhone of Guns"'.

44 Ibid.

45 'Poll Finds Americans Skeptical of So-Called Smart Guns', NRA-ILA, 15 November 2013, https://www.nraila.org/articles/20131115/poll-finds-americans-skeptical-of-so-called-smart-guns.

46 http://www.latimes.com/opinion/opinion-la/la-ol-nra-guns-smartguns-gun-control-20140502-story.html.

47 Michael S. Rosenwald, 'Threats Against Maryland Gun Dealer Raise Doubts About Future of Smart Guns', *Washington Post*, 2 May 2015, https://www.washingtonpost.com/local/threats-against-maryland-gun-dealer-raise-doubts-about-future-of-smart-guns/2014/05/02/8a4f7482-d227–11e3–9e25–188ebe1fa93b_story.html.

48 U.S. General Accounting Office, 'Accidental Shootings: Many Deaths and Injuries Caused by Firearms Could Be Prevented', March 1991, http://www.gao.gov/assets/160/150353.pdf, p. 4.

6 Edwin Rajo

1 Monica Rhor, 'Immigrants from Around the World are Transforming Houston', *Houston Chronicle*, 5 March 2015, http://www.houstonchronicle.com/local/themillion/article/How-diversity-culture-demographics-of-Houston-6117301.php.

2 John Berger, *A Seventh Man: Migrant Workers in Europe* (New York: Viking Press, 1975), p. 68.

3 https://dispositiondisposal.wordpress.com/2013/06/08/from-swingersville-to-the-gulfton-ghetto-a-brief-history/.

4 Ryan Pintado-Vertner, 'The War on Youth', *Colorlines*, 10 December 1999, http://www.colorlines.com/articles/war-youth.

5 Foti Kallergis, Twitter, 24 November 2013, https://twitter.com/heykitty/status/404484915460190208.

6 http://abc7news.com/archive/9339451/.

7 Samuel Brightmon

1 Valerie Boyd, *Wrapped in Rainbows: The Life of Zora Neale Hurston* (New York: Scribner, 2003), p. 65.

2 Quoted in Nancy Gibbs, 'An American Tragedy: The Aftermath of Katrina', *Time*, 4 September 2005, http://time.com/3210311/hurricane-katrina-the-aftermath/.

3 Jens Manuel Krogstad, 'Gun Homicides Steady After Decline in '90s; Suicide Rate Edges Up', Pew Research Center, 21 October 2015, http://www.pewresearch.org/fact-tank/2015/10/21/gun-homicides-steady-after-decline-in-90s-suicide-rate-edges-up/; http://www.childtrends.org/?indicators=teen-homicide-suicide-and-firearm-deaths.

4 Chris Kirk and Dan Kois, 'How Many People Have Been Killed by Guns

Since Newtown?' *Slate*, 16 September 2013, http://www.slate.com/articles/news_and_politics/crime/2012/12/gun_death_tally_every_american_gun_death_since_newtown_sandy_hook_shooting.html.

5 Dan Kois, 'A Year of Gun Deaths', *Slate*, 12 December 2013, http://www.slate.com/articles/news_and_politics/crime/2013/12/newtown_anniversary_what_slate_learned_from_trying_and_failing_to_record.html.

6 Joe Nocera, 'And in Last Week's Gun News', New York Times, 29 January 2013, http://www.nytimes.com/2013/01/29/opinion/nocera-and-in-last-weeks-gun-news.html.

7 http://gawker.com/the-times-killed-its-gun-report-after-the-writer-aske-1592851849.

8 Joe Nocera, 'The Last Gun Report', *New York Times*, 10 June 2014, http://nocera.blogs.nytimes.com/2014/06/10/the-last-gun-report/?_r=0.

9 Melissa Repko, 'Teen Fatally Shot when Walking Down Street in Southeast Dallas', *Dallas Morning News*, 24 November 2013, http://crimeblog.dallasnews.com/2013/11/teen-fatally-shot-when-walking-down-street-in-southeast-dallas.html/.

10 'Dallas Teen Killed by Random Gunfire', Fox 4, fox4news.com.

11 Susan D. Moeller, *Compassion Fatigue* (New York: Routledge, 1999), http://www.savan.nl/data/IntroductiontoCompassion-fatigue_Moeller.pdf.

12 Stanley Cohen, *States of Denial: Knowing About Atrocities and Suffering* (Malden, MA: Blackwell Publishers, 2013), p. 194.

13 Walter Lippmann, *Public Opinion* (New York: Harcourt, Brace & Company, 1922), available to download at http://wps.pearsoncustom.com/wps/media/objects/2429/2487430/pdfs/lippmann.pdf, p. 11.

14 https://www.ssa.gov/oact/cola/central.html.

15 Lars Willnat and David H. Weaver, *The American Journalist in the Digital Age* (Bloomington, IN: School of Journalism, Indiana University, 2014), http://news.indiana.edu/releases/iu/2014/05/2013-american-journalist-key-findings.pdf.

16 http://www.dallasnews.com/news/community-news/dallas/headlines/20100413-Dallas-Morning-News-wins-Pulitzer-for-5971.ece.

17 Jesmyn Ward, *Men We Reaped: A Memoir* (New York: Bloomsbury, 2013), p. 237.

18 Lawrence Wright, *In the New World: Growing Up with America, from the Sixties to the Eighties* (New York: Vintage Books, 1989), pp. 4, 5.

19 'JFK Death Not Associated with Dallas', *Southeast Missourian*, 20 November 1988, https://news.google.com/newspapers?nid=1893&-

dat=19881120&id=1LYfAAAAIBAJ&sjid=S9cEAAAAIBAJ&pg=5675,2700778&hl=en.

20 Molly Ivins, *Molly Ivins Can't Say That, Can She?* (New York: Random House, 1991), p. 37.

21 Douglas S. Massey and Nancy A. Denton, *American Apartheid: Segregation and the Making of the Underclass* (Cambridge, MA: Harvard University Press, 1993), p. 75.

22 Peter Gent, *North Dallas After Forty* (New York: Villard Books, 1989), p. 19.

23 Harvey J. Graff, *The Dallas Myth: The Making and Unmaking of an American City* (Minneapolis: University of Minnesota Press, 2010), p. 127.

24 'Quick Facts, Dallas, Texas', United States Census Bureau, http://www.census.gov/quickfacts/table/PST045215/4819000.

25 Sam Howe Verhovek, 'Dallas Is First Big Texas City to Elect a Black to Be Mayor', *New York Times*, 8 May 1995, http://www.nytimes.com/1995/05/08/us/dallas-is-first-big-texas-city-to-elect-a-black-to-be-mayor.html.

26 Graff, *The Dallas Myth*, p. 169.

27 Jason DeParle et al., 'Older, Suburban and Struggling, "Near Poor" Startle the Census', *New York Times*, 19 November 2011, http://www.nytimes.com/2011/11/19/us/census-measures-those-not-quite-in-poverty-but-struggling.html?_r=0.

28 Hope Yen, '4 in 5 US Adults Face Near-Poverty, No Work for at Least Parts of Their Lives', *Business Insider*, 28 July 2013, http://www.business-insider.com/ap-poll-4-in-5-us-adults-face-near-poverty-no-work-for-at-least-parts-of-their-lives-2013-7.

29 Ibid.

30 Stiglitz, *The Price of Inequality*, p. 10.

31 http://www.usboundary.com/Areas/Census%20Tract/Texas/Dallas%2 County/Census%20Tract%20116.01/493345#Data.

8 Tyshon Anderson

1 https://www.fbi.gov/about-us/cjis/ucr/crime-in-the-u.s/2013/crime-in-the-u.s.-2013/tables/6tabledatadecpdf/table-6; http://www.huffingtonpost.com/2014/11/12/highest-murder-rate-us-cities-2013_n_6145404.html.

2 Gary Younge, 'Gun Violence in Chicago: A Struggle for Answers in Obama's Hometown', *Guardian*, 12 February 2013, http://www.theguardian.com/world/2013/feb/12/barack-obama-gun-violence-chicago.

3 'Crime in the United States 2012', Table 8, Federal Bureau of

Investigation, https://www.fbi.gov/about-us/cjis/ucr/crime-in-the-u.s/2012/crime-in-the-u.s.-2012/tables/8tabledatadecpdf/table-8-state-cuts/table_8_offenses_known_to_law_enforcement_by_illinois_by_city_2012.xls; compared to 'Crime in the United States 2011', Table 8, Federal Bureau of Investigation, https://www.fbi.gov/about-us/cjis/ucr/crime-in-the-u.s/2011/crime-in-the-u.s.-2011/tables/table8statecuts/table_8_offenses_known_to_law_enforcement_illinois_by_city_2011.xls.

4 Matt Pearce, '10 Dead, 43 Wounded in Chicago's Bloody Holiday Weekend', *LA Times*, 29 May 2012, http://articles.latimes.com/2012/may/29/nation/la-na-nn-bloody-chicago-weekend-20120529.

5 'Operation Enduring Freedom, Coalition Military Fatalities by Year', http://icasualties.org/OEF/index.aspx; compared to 'Uniform Crime Reports', Federal Bureau of Investigation, UCR Publications, Crime in the United States https://www.fbi.gov/about-us/cjis/ucr/ucr-publications#Crime.

6 Peter Nickeas, 'Fourth Sibling from Same Chicago Family Killed by Gun Violence', *Chicago Tribune*, 27 January 2013, http://articles.chicagotribune.com/2013–01–27/news/ct-met-ronnie-chambers-dead-20130127_1_gun-violence-gunshot-victims-cabrini-green.

7 Monica Davey, 'In a Soaring Homicide Rate, a Divide in Chicago', *New York Times*, 2 January 2013, http://www.nytimes.com/2013/01/03/us/a-soaring-homicide-rate-a-divide-in-chicago.html?_r=0.

8 Massey and Denton, *American Apartheid*, p. 9.

9 Sean Stillmaker, 'Chicago Still the Most Segregated U.S. City', *Chicagoist*, 31 October 2010, http://chicagoist.com/2010/10/31/chicago_still_the_most_segregated_c.php.

10 Lolly Bowean and Jeremy Gorner, 'Spike in Violence Takes its Toll on Residents in Chicago's Troubled Neighborhoods', http://articles.chicagotribune.com/2012-07-01/news/ct-met-chicago-violence-0701-20120701_1_homicides-last-year-neighborhoods-shootings.

11 Isabel Wilkerson, *The Warmth of Other Suns: The Epic Story of America's Great Migration* (New York: Vintage, 2010), p. 395.

12 Ibid., p. 396.

13 Barack Obama, *Dreams from My Father: A Story of Race and Inheritance* (New York: Three Rivers Press, 2004), p. 249.

14 http://projects.nytimes.com/census/2010/explorer, tract 4603 IL.

15 Ibid.

16 Obama, *Dreams from My Father*, p. 157.

17 Erica Demarest, 'Slain South Chicago Teen Wanted to "Get His Life Straightened Out": Family', https://www.dnainfo.com/chicago/20131124/

south-chicago/slain-south-chicago-teen-wanted-get-his-life-straightened-out-family.

18 'National Youth Gang Survey Analysis', National Gang Center, https://www.nationalgangcenter.gov/Survey-Analysis/Measuring-the-Extent-of-Gang-Problems#estimatednumbergangs.

19 Ibid.

20 H. R. Hutson et al., 'The Epidemic of Gang-Related Homicides in Los Angeles County from 1979 Through 1994', *Journal of the American Medical Association* 274, no. 13 (1995): pp. 1031–6.

21 Malcolm Klein, *The American Street Gang: Its Nature, Prevalence, and Control* (Oxford, Oxford University Press, 1997), p. 81.

22 Deborah Prothrow-Stith with Michaele Weissman, *Deadly Consequences: How Violence Is Destroying Our Teenage Population and a Plan to Begin Solving the Problem* (New York: HarperPerennial, 1993), p. 106.

23 James Baldwin, *The Evidence of Things Not Seen* (New York: Owl Books, 1995), p. 8.

24 http://homicides.suntimes.com/2014/09/27/deandre-ellis-shot-dead-at-west-englewood-barbershop/.

25 Prothrow-Stith with Weissman, *Deadly Consequences*, p. 24.

26 Scott Olsen, 'One Dead, Seven Shot During Violent Weekend in Chicago', Getty Images, 25 November 2013, http://www.gettyimages.com/detail/news-photo/building-resident-signs-a-memorial-to-18-year-old-tyshon-news-photo/451955749.

27 Sudhir A. Venkatesh, *Gang Leader for a Day: A Rogue Sociologist Takes to the Streets* (New York: Penguin Books, 2008), p. 29.

28 Jonathan Tilove, 'Where Have All the Men Gone? Black Gender Gap is Widening', *Seattle Times*, 5 May 2005, http://www.seattletimes.com/nation-world/where-have-all-the-men-gone-black-gender-gap-is-widening.

29 http://www.usboundary.com/Areas/454133#Data.

30 Alexander, *The New Jim Crow*, p. 189.

9 Gary Anderson

1 Nicholas Lemann, *The Promised Land: The Great Black Migration and How It Changed America* (London: PaperMac, 1992), p. 50

2 Quoted in Brad R. Tuttle, *How Newark Became Newark: The Rise, Fall, and Rebirth of an American City* (New Brunswick, NJ: Rutgers University Press, 2011), p. 65.

3 Ibid., p. 8.

4 'New Jersey Resident Population by Municipality: 1930–1990', New Jersey Department of Labor and Workforce Development, http://lwd.dol.state.nj.us/labor/lpa/census/1990/poptrd6.htm.
5 Steve Strunsky, 'Newark Teen Shooting Victim Recalled as "Good Dude" Who Tried to Shield Girlfriend from Gunfire', NJ.com, 24 November 2013, http://www.nj.com/news/index.ssf/2013/11/newark_shooting_victim_recalled_nice.html.
6 Ibid.
7 Ibid.
8 Ibid.
9 All quoted in Tuttle, *How Newark Became Newark*, p. 9.
10 Ibid., p. 208.
11 http://www.nytimes.com/2002/11/01/nyregion/newark-s-ex-mayor-admits-tax-evasion-and-avoids-prison.html.
12 Tuttle, *How Newark Became Newark*, p. 225.
13 Ibid., p. 266.
14 Ibid.
15 Strunsky, 'Newark Teen Shooting Victim Recalled as "Good Dude"'.
16 Dale Russakoff, 'Schooled', *New Yorker*, 14 May 2014, http://www.newyorker.com/magazine/2014/05/19/schooled.
17 Tuttle, *How Newark Became Newark*, p. 162.
18 Kevin J. Mumford, *Newark: A History of Race, Rights, and Riots in America* (New York: New York University Press, 2007), p. 125.
19 Kerner Commission, 'Report of the National Advisory Commission on Civil Disorders', reproduced by the Eisenhower Foundation, http://www.eisenhowerfoundation.org/docs/kerner.pdf.
20 Lawrence Mishel et al., 'Wage Stagnation in Nine Charts', Economic Policy Institute, 6 January 2015, http://www.epi.org/publication/charting-wage-stagnation/.
21 Michael Greenstone and Adam Looney, 'The Uncomfortable Truth About American Wages', *New York Times*, 22 October 2012, http://economix.blogs.nytimes.com/2012/10/22/the-uncomfortable-truth-about-american-wages/?
22 Katie Sanders, '*Time*'s Rana Foroohar Says Median Male Worker Hasn't Seen a Raise in 30 Years', Politifact, 15 January 2014, http://www.politifact.com/punditfact/statements/2014/jan/15/rana-foroohar/times-rana-foroohar-says-median-male-worker-hasnt-/.
23 William J. Wilson, *When Work Disappears: The World of the New Urban Poor* (New York: Vintage, 1997), p. 26.
24 Thomas J. Sugrue, *The Origins of the Urban Crisis: Race and Inequality in Postwar Detroit* (Princeton, NJ: Princeton University Press, 2005), p. 123.

25 Wilson, *When Work Disappears*, p. 31.

26 John R. Logan and Brian J. Stults, 'The Persistence of Segregation in the Metropolis: New Findings from the 2010 Census', US 2010 Project, 24 March 2011, http://www.s4.brown.edu/us2010/Data/Report/report2.pdf.

27 http://patch.com/new-jersey/newarknj/report-newarkers-among-new-jerseys-poorest.

28 Massey and Denton, *American Apartheid*, p. 126.

29 Steven D. Levitt and Stephen J. Dubner, *Freakonomics: A Rogue Economist Explores the Hidden Side of Everything* (New York: HarperCollins, 2005), p. 99.

30 Delbert S. Elliott, 'Youth Violence: An Overview', Center for the Study and Prevention of Violence, 1994, http://www.colorado.edu/cspv/publications/papers/CSPV-008.pdf.

10 Gustin Hinnant

1 Daniel J. Siegel, *Brainstorm: The Power and Purpose of the Teenage Brain* (New York: Jeremy P. Tarcher, 2013), p. 67.

2 Ibid., p. 69.

3 Ibid., p. 108.

4 Barbara Natterson-Horowitz and Kathryn Bowers, *Zoobiquity: What Animals Can Teach Us About Health and the Science of Healing* (New York: Alfred A. Knopf, 2012), p. 285.

5 Anthony Burgess, *A Clockwork Orange* (London: Penguin, 1992), p. 140.

6 'George W. Bush: Out of His Father's Shadow', *BBC News*, 8 November 2000, http://news.bbc.co.uk/2/hi/in_depth/americas/2000/us_elections/profiles/576504.stm.

7 'Cameron Student Photo Is Banned', *BBC News*, 2 March 2007, http://news.bbc.co.uk/2/hi/uk_news/politics/6409757.stm.

8 'Justin Bieber Pleads Guilty to Careless Driving in Deal', *BBC News*, 13 August 2014, http://www.bbc.com/news/world-us-canada-28781437.

9 Alexander, *The New Jim Crow*, p. 2.

10 Alexis De Tocqueville, *Democracy in America* (New York: Harper and Row, 1988), p. 232.

11 Jeffrey Toobin, 'This Is My Jail', *New Yorker*, 14 April 2014, http://www.newyorker.com/magazine/2014/04/14/this-is-my-jail.

12 German Lopez, 'Police Are Much Less Likely to Solve Homicides when the Victims Are Black', *Vox*, 11 June 2015, http://www.vox.com/2015/6/10/8757163/homicide-race.

13 Leovy, *Ghettoside*, p. xviii.

14 Ibid., p. xvii.
15 Frank Newport, 'Gallup Review: Black and White Attitudes Toward Police', Gallup, 20 August 2014, http://www.gallup.com/poll/175088/gallup-review-black-white-attitudes-toward-police.aspx.
16 Leovy, *Ghettoside*, p. xvii.

Afterword

1 http://www.theguardian.com/commentisfree/2014/may/04/gun-control-violence-poverty-segregation-nra.
2 http://www.motherjones.com/politics/2013/12/children-killed-guns-after-newtown-portraits.

Bibliography

Agger, Ben, and Timothy W. Luke, eds. *Gun Violence and Public Life*. Boulder, CO: Paradigm Publishers, 2014.

Alexander, Michelle. *The New Jim Crow: Mass Incarceration in the Age of Colorblindness*. New York: The New Press, 2012.

Baldwin, James. *The Evidence of Things Not Seen*. New York: Owl Books (Tenth Anniversary edn), 1995.

Berger, John, *A Seventh Man: Migrant Workers in Europe*. A Richard Seaver Book. New York: Viking Books, 1975

Bluestone, Barry, and Bennett Harrison. *The Deindustrialization of America: Plant Closings, Community Abandonment, and the Dismantling of Basic Industry*. New York: Basic Books, 1982.

Boyd, Valerie. *Wrapped in Rainbows: The Life of Zora Neale Hurston*. New York: Scribner, 2003.

Braman, Donald. *Doing Time on the Outside: Incarceration and Family Life in Urban America*. Ann Arbor, MI: University of Michigan Press, 2007.

Brokaw, Tom. *The Greatest Generation*. New York: Random House, 1998.

Burgess, Anthony. *A Clockwork Orange*. London: Penguin, 1992.

Cohen, Stanley. *States of Denial: Knowing About Atrocities and Suffering*. Malden, MA: Blackwell Publishers, 2013.

Coles, Roberta L. *The Best Kept Secret: Single Black Fathers*. Lanham, MD: Rowman and Littlefield, 2010.

Cosby, Bill, and Alvin F. Poussaint. *Come On, People: On the Path from Victims to Victors*. Nashville, TN: Thomas Nelson, 2007.

De Tocqueville, Alexis. *Democracy in America*. New York: Harper and Row (Harper Perennial Edition), 1988.

Dyson, Michael E. *Is Bill Cosby Right? Or Has the Black Middle Class Lost Its Mind?* New York: Basic Civitas Books, 2005.

Feldman, Richard. *Ricochet: Confessions of a Gun Lobbyist*. Hoboken, NJ: John Wiley and Sons, 2008.

Gent, Peter. *North Dallas After Forty*. New York: Villard Books, 1989.

Graff, Harvey J. *The Dallas Myth: The Making and Unmaking of an American City*. Minneapolis, MN: University of Minnesota Press, 2008.

Harrington, Michael. *The Other America: Poverty in the United States*. New York: Scribner, 2012.

Ivens, Molly. *Molly Ivins Can't Say That, Can She?* New York: Random House, 1991.

Kellner, Douglas. *Guys and Guns Amok: Domestic Terrorism and School Shootings from the Oklahoma City Bombing to the Virginia Tech Massacre.* Boulder, CO: Paradigm Publishers, 2008.

Klein, Malcolm. *The American Street Gang: Its Nature, Prevalence, and Control.* Oxford: Oxford University Press, 1997.

Klein, Malcolm W., and Cheryl L. Maxson. *Street Gang Patterns and Policies.* New York: Oxford University Press, 2010.

Kopkind, Andrew. *The Thirty Years' Wars: Dispatches and Diversions of a Radical Journalist, 1965–1994*. New York: Verso, 1995.

Kyle, Chris, with William Doyle. *American Gun: A History of the U.S. in Ten Firearms*. New York: HarperCollins, 2013.

Lemann, Nicholas. *The Promised Land: The Great Black Migration and How It Changed America*. London: PaperMac, 1992.

Leovy, Jill. *Ghettoside: Investigating a Homicide Epidemic*. London: The Bodley Head, 2015.

Lepore, Jill. *The Whites of Their Eyes: The Tea Party's Revolution and the Battle over American History*. Princeton, NJ: Princeton University Press, 2010.

Levitt, Steven D., and Stephen J. Dubner. *Freakonomics: A Rogue Economist Explores the Hidden Side of Everything*. New York: HarperCollins, 2005.

Lindqvist, Sven. *'Exterminate All the Brutes': One Man's Odyssey into the Heart of Darkness and the Origins of European Genocide*. New York: The New Press, 1997.

Lippmann, Walter. *Public Opinion*. New York: Harcourt, Brace and Company, 1922.

Massey, Douglas S., and Nancy A. Denton. *American Apartheid: Segregation and the Making of the Underclass*. Cambridge, MA: Harvard University Press, 1993.

Moeller, Susan D. *Compassion Fatigue*. New York: Routledge, 1999.

Mumford, Kevin. *Newark: A History of Race, Rights, and Riots in America*. New York: New York University Press, 2007.

Natterson-Horowitz, Barbara, and Kathryn Bowers. *Zoobiquity: What Animals Can Teach Us About Health and the Science of Healing*. New York: Alfred A. Knopf, 2012.

Obama, Barack. *Dreams from My Father: A Story of Race and Inheritance*. New York: Three Rivers Press, 2004.

Prothrow-Stith, Deborah, with Michaele Weissman. *Deadly Consequences: How Violence Is Destroying Our Teenage Population and a Plan to Begin Solving the Problem*. New York: HarperPerennial, 1993.

Schiff, Harriet Sarnoff. *The Bereaved Parent*. New York: Penguin Books, 1978.

Siegel, Daniel J. *Brainstorm: The Power and Purpose of the Teenage Brain*. New York: Jeremy P. Tarcher, 2013.

Stevens, John Paul. *Six Amendments: How and Why We Should Change the Constitution*. New York: Little, Brown, 2014.

Stiglitz, Joseph E. *The Price of Inequality: How Today's Divided Society Endangers Our Future*. London: Allen Lane, 2012; New York: W.W. Norton & Co., 2012.

Sugrue, Thomas J. *The Origins of the Urban Crisis: Race and Inequality in Postwar Detroit*. Princeton, NJ: Princeton University Press, 2014.

Tuttle, Brad R., *How Newark Became Newark: The Rise, Fall, and Rebirth of an American City*. New Brunswick, NJ: Rutgers University Press, 2011.

Venkatesh, Sudhir A. *Gang Leader for a Day: A Rogue Sociologist Takes to the Streets*. New York: Penguin Books, 2008.

Waldman, Michael. *The Second Amendment: A Biography*. New York: Simon and Schuster, 2014.

Ward, Jesmyn. *Men We Reaped: A Memoir*. New York: Bloomsbury, 2013.

Weich, Ronald H., and Carlos T. Angulo. *Justice on Trial: Racial Disparities in the American Criminal Justice System*. Collingdale, PA: Diane Publishing Company, 2000.

Wilkerson, Isabel. *The Warmth of Other Suns: The Epic Story of America's Great Migration*. New York: Vintage Books, 2010.

Willnat, Lars, and David H. Weaver, *The American Journalist in the Digital Age*. Bloomington, IN: School of Journalism, Indiana University, 2014.

Wilson, William Julius. *When Work Disappears: The World of the New Urban Poor*. New York: Vintage Books, 1997.

Wright, Lawrence. *In the New World: Growing Up with America, from the Sixties to the Eighties*. New York: Vintage Books, 1989.